NEW YORK, HARPER & BROTHERS.

WESLEY,

AND METHODISM.

BY ISAAC TAYLOR.

NEW YORK:
HARPER & BROTHERS, PUBLISHERS,
FRANKLIN SQUARE.
1855.

PREFACE.

The Methodism of the last century, even when considered apart from its consequences, must always be thought worthy of the most serious regard. But, in fact, that great religious movement has, immediately or remotely, so given an impulse to Christian feeling and profession, on all sides, that it has come to present itself as the starting-point of our modern religious history. The field-preaching of Wesley and Whitefield, in 1739, was the event whence the religious epoch, now current, must date its commencement. Back to the events of that time must we look, necessarily, as often as we seek to trace to its source what is most characteristic of the present time.

Yet this is not all, for the Methodism of the past age points forward to the next-coming development of the powers of the Gospel; and it is especially as thus involving what may be called a predictive meaning, that the reader's attention is now invited to the subject.

It is also with a view to the future—that is to say, in relation to those changes, a silent preparation for which is now in progress, that I venture upon the task of reviewing, as announced on the last page of this volume, the course and the principles of the Nonconformists of the past age. Assuredly it is with no thought of setting in a disadvantageous light the good and great men who ranged themselves on *that* side of the Protestant movement of the times, that I enter upon such a service.

Should this task be completed, one that must be accounted still more venturous and difficult, would present itself as next in order; if, indeed, it should be permitted me to complete a plan which should embody those views that seem to give coherence to the past history of Christianity, considered as a preparation for its destined universality.

Stanford Rivers,
November, 1851.

CONTENTS.

NOTICE

RELATIVE TO THE PORTRAIT OF WESLEY

The engraving which accompanies this volume has been executed, with much care, from an outline in the Author's possession; and which has been attributed to Worlidge, whose imitations of Rembrandt are well known to amateurs. That artist died, however, long before Wesley had attained the age which the sketch represents. Whoever was the artist, the outline exhibits a practiced hand and eye, and is full of character: it was said to have been taken from the side gallery at the Foundery, while Wesley was preaching. This, at least, is the tradition which accompanied it when it came, many years ago, into the Author's hand.

METHODISM,

AS

RELATED TO THE PRESENT TIME.

A FORTY OR FIFTY YEARS has been the term, more or less clearly defined, within which each of those revolutions that mark the history of the human mind has had its rise, has passed its climax, and has gone forward, commingled with other moral forces, and having its own abated.

Some reasons that are quite obvious, and some that are occult, and perhaps not cognizable by science, might be assigned in explanation of a fact which obtrudes itself as we follow the luminous track of those outbursts of light and warmth which take place in the lapse of centuries. It might seem enough to say, that, as every such time of renovation and movement takes its rise in the bosoms of two or three individual men, and as these, for the most part, occupy nearly the same level as to age, a term of forty or fifty years gives the extreme limits of the personal energy and influence of any such band of men; and never hitherto has any new impulse, or any strenuous moral movement, been taken up and carried forward, by the sons and successors of its originators, in the same mind, or with the same, or with nearly the same singleness of purpose. Great men do not repeat themselves in their immediate followers; or if the mantle of an Elijah has in some rare instances rested upon an Elisha, yet never, hitherto, has the spirit and power of a company of distinguished persons come upon, or remained with, those who have stood up to represent them before the world.

Methodism, it is true, survives among us, and may long so survive, in its broad array, and its ample frontage; but the Methodism with which, in these pages, we shall have to do, went to its place in the history of Christianity when its originators stepped off from the scene of their labors. An interval of full sixty years since the recession of the men who breathed their souls into it, is enough to put us in a vantage position for bringing this great movement under review. No disparagement to that body of eminently useful men who now, in their stations, farm the spiritual inheritance bequeathed to them by their fathers is intended, when we affirm that their own peculiar relationship to those men—the fathers and founders of their communion, appears, to the eye of an impartial bystander, to be made up more of what is technical, or conventional, than of what is substantial, in a purely religious sense.

We assume then that we, at this time, stand far enough off from the Methodism of the last century to enable us to contemplate it with advantage. But another question here presents itself at the threshold of our subject; and it relates to the qualifications, for their part, of those whom a writer may suppose that he is challenging to sit with him in judgment upon the men and the system which are so to be reviewed.

This second question involves more than may at first appear; and it implicates, not merely the dispositions of the writer, and of his reader, individually, but the religious characteristics also, and the tendencies of the times we live in.

Without some self-scrutiny a writer should not engage in a task such as this; nor, without some self-recollection, should an individual reader take his place beside the writer; nor, without some looking to itself, should the Christian body of one age allow itself to pass judgment upon that of another age. We must not forget that there is action and reaction among moral, as well as among mechanical forces; nor that every judgment we pronounce has a reciprocal sense; and that, whether or not it truly bears upon the one party, it bears upon the other with infallible precision.

It might seem superfluous formally to advance so obvious a truth as this—that, as often as we cite another to our tribunal, the sentence we utter has a double import, and may be read off *first* as touching the party so cited, and in which application it may be an equitable decision, or quite otherwise; but that when regarded in its reflex sense, no such judgment can be fallacious; and it carries with it a fearful certainty, just in proportion as it has been deliberately formed, and has received the full consent of mind and heart. The metallic reflector which the astronomer presents to the celestial field may image the bright objects before it truly or falsely, clearly or dimly; but infallibly it gives notice of any flaws that mar its own surface, and tells of its own variations from an exact parabolic figure.

A writer calls before him men such as those were who originated Methodism; and then, with philosophic ease and a feeling of irresponsibility, he deals with his worthies, and sets upon them their price and value—mind and heart, motive, purpose, and intellectual power, and his reader assents, perhaps, and consents, and nods approval while the arraigned are thus disposed of at the bar. But in which of its bearings does this process of judgment convey most meaning? Undoubtedly in its reflex bearing; for, read in this reverberative sense, every word tells; nor could eternal justice itself ask for evidence more conclusive than that is which is comprised in the deliberately pronounced opinion which individually we frame, or which we assent to, when other men are brought up before us for judgment. We decide, in each instance, according to our own dispositions, our principles, and our moral condition.

But what is thus true individually, must be true also, and in a more comprehensive sense, when a set of men, or a certain marked revolution in the moral world, comes on, as it always does in its course, to receive, in various modes of expression, the judgment of the times next ensuing. When the vessel, with the wind in its sails, loosens from its moorings, it is not easy for those on deck to resist the belief, at first, that the quay, and its lighthouse, and the ranges of docks, and the ships at anchor, have all taken to themselves wings and are flitting away. Yet we oth erwise think the moment when our own ship meets the swell of the open sea. A similar involuntary feeling, not so soon corrected, attaches to most minds as often as the persons, the events, and the moral and political condition of other periods are brought in review before them. *We* are at rest, *we* are stationary, having established ourselves immovably upon a certain terra firma of steadfast opinions, usages, and modes of thinking. An infatuation of this sort infests all minds, more or less, but in some—from constitutional arrogance, and from the induration of early prejudices—the feeling is far too strong to be in any way broken up or disturbed. Such persons hold a sort of Ptolemaic idea of the moral and intellectual world; and, in their view, sun, moon, planets, stars, are all whirling around the spot on which they stand.

It is not under the influence of any such illusion as this that we now propose to look back upon Methodism and its authors. Are not we ourselves, that is to say, the Christian community of this passing moment, afloat upon the eddying Euphrates of time? Is our standing any thing better than a foot's breadth upon a raft which is whirling itself onward, as borne on the heaving bosom of "many waters?" If we speak thus it is in relation to those specialities of opinion, of practice, and of feeling, which will present themselves as the points of contrast between ourselves and the bygone Methodism. And is it certain that every thing in respect of which we may find ourselves to differ from that scheme of things, is a difference in our own favor? The reader will not ask the writer to do his best for holding him safe in any such conclusion. Rather we go into Methodism ingenuously and modestly, wishing, while in that strange region, fairly to measure it, and ourselves also with it; perhaps to gather thence some sharp lesson of humiliation.

The Methodism of the 18th century has, we say, ceased to have any extant representative among us. None are there now who, with an entire congeniality of feeling, can interpret to us its phrases, or can warmly and forcibly speak of it, and plead for it, as a reality with which they are themselves conversant. We must be content then to understand it in our own sense, as well as we may.

A vast interval, as if it had been of a thousand years, divides us, of this present time, from the obsolete religious condition of our ecclesiastical progenitors of the last century. The extent of the revolutions that have come in to constitute this interval, is not to be grasped without an effort of thought. Methodism itself has had a great share in bringing about these revolutions; and itself too has undergone transmutations greater, perhaps, than those that have affected other communions.

The vastness of that religious and moral interval which seventy or eighty years have given room for, between ourselves and our religious predecessors, severally, to whatever communion we may belong, will become visible, or it will make itself felt by us, if we choose to take notice of it in the course of that review of the Methodistic movement which we have now in prospect; and the reader is here invited to give attention to those indications which will meet him of the fact—that every religious community among us has distanced its place as abreast of the Methodism of the last century by many leagues, of which they have taken little or no reckoning. The reader, to whatever body he may belong, will be advertised of the fact of this unconscious movement in different modes.

During these sixty, or seventy, or eighty years that have slipped by, the absolute number of persons in England, or the *proportion* of such persons, has vastly increased, whose range of view, in matters of religion, has been so much widened that, in disregard of sectarian restrictions, and even holding in abeyance some notions which they have not discarded, they are more than coldly willing to think and speak of Wesley and of Whitefield as great and good men, and to admit their claim to stand prominent among the benefactors of their country, and the worthies of all time. Concomitant with the increase of this class of liberally-feeling religious persons, upon whose assent and consent a writer may safely rely, there is a proportionate decrease of the number of those who would tolerate, or approve of that style of frigid levity,—half banter, half admiration, and whole infidelity—which, only thirty years ago, passed as the appropriate mode in which a candid and philosophic writer should deal with Methodism.

At this moment then—and the change indicates an immeasurable advance and improvement—there is a large class of religious persons, or more strictly speaking, there are several such classes, who would demand, in a writer upon Methodism, far more of serious purpose, and more of sympathy with what is great and good, and more depth of thought—in a word, more of *reality*—than would have been required only thirty years ago. Wesley, Whitefield, and their companions seem, therefore, so far to have gained upon us of late; and so it is that a writer may now speak of these worthies cordially, and yet not incur the risk of being called "Methodist."

And then, during the lapse of this same period, the religious body has so much come into the habit of refining upon its own principles, and it has so far drawn itself in from all extremes, and it has become so nicely observant of proprieties, and is so abhorrent of excesses, and it is so discreet, that when, with truthfulness and impartiality, the unpleasing characteristics of Methodism (at its rise) are noted, and when the errors fallen into by its founders, the irregularities which were sanctioned by them, and the illusions of which they were the victims, are, with temper and precision specified, a writer may be sure that his readers (very few excepted) are going with him, and will be prompt to give a verdict on the same side, upon every count of the indictment. The refinements and the religious tact and taste of this time, make the task a very easy one, of marking for disapproval and rejection whatever in the early Methodism may seem to be obnoxious to criticism.

But just at this point the modern religious reader's unhesitating approval is likely to receive a decisive check. He would, indeed, resent it if Wesley and Whitefield were treated flippantly; or if a want of sympathy were shown with what is noble in their conduct and character. On the other hand, he allows their faults and errors to be temperately specified; but when this has been done—a writer who would fain look at Methodism as it appears from an elevated position, whence the entire course of Christian history comes also within the range of sight, and who, in the spirit of serious belief, endeavors to separate the accidents of the system from those things which were its substance—such a writer will know that he must not expect to find his reader prepared to go forward with him as cordially as before. This same period—this sixty years—which has made us so much more liberal, and in a sense, more serious too, than were our fathers, and in which refinement and discretion have done so much for us, has touched—not our creeds indeed, so as to remove any one article from them; but it has touched the depths of our convictions as to the whole, and as to several points of our belief. There is little, perhaps, in the cycle of our predecessors' confession of faith which, if challenged to relinquish it, we should consent to see erased. But, whether we be distinctly conscious of the fact or not, there has come to stand over against each article of that belief a counterbalance—an influence of abatement, an unadjusted surmise, an adverse feeling, neither assented to, nor dismissed, but which holds the mind in perpetual suspense. The creed of this time is—let us say—word for word, the creed of sixty years ago; but if such a simile might be allowed, these *items* of our "Confession" *now* fill one side of a balance sheet, on the other side of which there stands a heavy charge which has not yet been ascertained or agreed to.

If this alleged state of the case be resented—as it will, by some—it will be tacitly assented to by the more thoughtful and ingenuous reader. Such persons will often be saying to themselves in reviewing the early Methodism, and in listening to its wakening voice, "I do not deny that there is truth here; but, as to myself, I have little or no sympathy with it; on the contrary, I draw back from it." This feeling, this honest acknowledgment, measures as it indicates, the width of that space which intervenes between ourselves and that which was of the very substance of Methodism: it may indicate also the difference between our outward conventional selves, and the "inner man."

In anticipation of meeting, in his reader, a reserved and hesitating accordance as to much with which we shall have to do, the writer would at once plant a firm foot on the ground he intends to occupy.

In attempting to treat a subject such as the one before us, a choice must necessarily be made among the three assumptions following:

1st, It may be said that Christianity being true in the sense of this or that Church, Methodism ought to be rejected as a spurious development of it; and that its founders should be solemnly denounced as schismatics and enthusiasts.

Or, *secondly*, that neither Christianity nor Methodism being true in its own sense; but both true in the much abated sense of the recent spiritualizing philosophy, therefore while both alike may claim some kindly regard, neither of them is entitled to any submission.

Or, *thirdly*, that Christianity being true, without abatement, in its own sense, Methodism, as a genuine development of its principal elements, must be religiously regarded as such; while yet it may be open to exceptions on many grounds, as the product of minds more good and fervent, than always well-ordered.

This last supposition is then our ground; and in assuming it, while we use the liberty it allows, we yield without fear to the consequences it draws with it, be they what they may.

These consequences are momentous; for we can not allow Methodism to have been a genuine development of the principal elements of Christianity, without admitting it to take a prominent place in that providential system which embraces all time, and which, from age to age, has, with increasing clearness, been unfolding itself, and becoming cognizable by the human mind. So far as Methodism truly held forth Christianity, it was a signal holding of it forth; for a more marked utterance of the Gospel has occurred only once before in the lapse of eighteen centuries; and that, at the Reformation, was not less disparaged than this is by a large admixture of the errors and inconsistencies of its movers or adherents.

Christianity, given to the world at once in the ministry and writings of the Apostles, has, from the first moment to this, held its onward course under a system of administration inscrutable indeed as a whole, or as to its reasons and yet not entirely occult. On the contrary, at moments, Heaven's economy has seemed to receive a bright beam, as through a dense cloud, making conspicuous, if not the *motives* of the divine government, yet the fact. The Reformation is held by Protestants to have been such a manifestation of the providence of God in restoring the Gospel, and in proclaiming it anew among the nations; and thus the events of the sixteenth century brought out to view that which is always *real*, whether visible or not—namely, a divine interposition—maintaining truth in the world, and giving it a fresh expansion from time to time. In perfect analogy with the events of the Reformation were those which attended the rise and progress of Methodism.

What may be the relative value or importance of these

two courses of events is not a question we are now concerned with; and it may easily be allowed that the former surpassed the latter in importance; but that the one, as well as the other, was a marked development of the scheme which is moving forward toward the subjugation of the human family to the Gospel, is here confidently maintained.

In making good this position, it will be well, and especially for the purpose of setting ourselves clear of all entanglements as to the personal merits or demerits of the men who were the prime movers or originators of Methodism, to gain as distinct an idea as we can of each of them, as to those qualities, intellectual and moral, which make the individuality of each. Such an idea must of course, be gathered from the incidents of his life; which, however, it is not our purpose here to repeat; for these have been often and well recounted, and it may be presumed that they are familiarly known by almost every reader. If, in the exercise of due discrimination, we succeed in placing Wesley, Whitefield, and others in their true position, we shall be free to consider what, in its substance, Methodism was; and next to entertain an inquiry as to the diffused influence of this movement upon other communions, and to ask also what probably may be the ulterior product of it as related to the Christianity of the times next ensuing.

This sort of continuity is necessarily implied when it is affirmed that Methodism, as did the Reformation, formed a signal epoch in religious history; for every event, or course of events, that may deserve to be so spoken of, must stand related to the *future* as well as to the *past*. Methodism, the coherent dependence of which upon the Reformation may be traced, will, no doubt, be seen also to reappear among those greater religious movements which are destined next to agitate the social system. An attempt to predict distinctly those future movements ought to be reprehended as presumptuous: nevertheless, it may be warrantable to pursue an analogy thus far: that is to say, while considering the relationship of Methodism to the Reformation, to consider *also*, what it is to which Methodism may have been the proper preliminary, or to what order of events, yet future, it may seem to point.

Hitherto the intervals have been long between one remarkable religious era and the next. At present the belief is strong and general, whether resting upon any sufficient grounds or not, that such intervening periods will be cut short, and that all things are now hastening to reach their final results.

THE FOUNDERS OF METHODISM.

THE TWO WESLEYS.

The band of men who had already attracted the eye of the world in the year 1740, and who, most of them, finished their labors some time before the close of the century, were connected together, partly by the ties of natural affection, or of Christian love, partly by voluntary compact and subordination, as members of a religious association, and partly by no stricter tie than that of a discordant accordance in promoting, separately, the same great purposes. Methodism did not appear before the world as if it had issued from a conclave; for although it came to be ruled mainly (but never wholly) by one master spirit, it was not devised, plotted, modeled, touched, and retouched by its two or three protectors, who, when thus they had set their hands to its code, prudently hushed their individual opinions, and presented a front of unanimity to the world. This was true of Jesuitism; but it was not true of Methodism.

Methodism rose as great rivers do, from several springs of nearly equal volume; and it spread and strengthened itself as much by its contrarieties as by its agreements; and eventually the great ends of this movement were secured by a doctrinal antagonism that was not then, and and has not since been adjusted. As a matter of mere convenience, and to avoid circumlocution, we speak of Wesley and his colleagues as one; but, in truth, they were not one; and their individuality, and their independent concurrence, and their opposed proceedings, are facts essentially attaching to the history of this course of events. We must bring them, therefore, into view singly in their distinct personality; and this, as we have said, is best done before the great features of Methodism *as a whole* come to be considered.

But with what order of men is it that we have now to do? Let it be confessed that this company does not include one mind of that amplitude and grandeur, the contemplation of which, as a natural object—a sample of humanity—excites a pleasurable awe, and swells the bosom with a vague ambition, or with a noble emulation. Not one of the founders of Methodism can claim to stand on any such high level; nor was one of them gifted with the philosophic faculty—the abstractive and analytic power. More than one was a shrewd and exact logician, but none a master of the higher reason. Not one was erudite in more than an ordinary degree; not one was an accomplished scholar; yet while several were fairly learned, few were illiterate, and none showed themselves to be imbued with the fanaticism of ignorance.

Powers of popular oratory were among them such as to set them far out of the reach of rivalry with any of their contemporaries, in the pulpit. Not one was a great writer; but several of them knew how to hold the ear of men with an absolute mastery. As to administrative tact and skill in government, the world has given them (or their chief) more praise than they or he deserved, while baffled in its own perplexed endeavor to solve the problem of Methodism, in ignorance of the main cause of its spread and permanence. Apart from the gratuitous supposition of a profound craft, as the intellectual distinction of Wesley, "what intelligible account shall we be able to give of Methodism?" No credible account can be given of it by aid of any such supposition, nor until the presence of causes has been recognized, of which the philosophy of such persons knows nothing.

The persons claiming to be named as the founders of Methodism, or as principally concerned in its rise and spread, are—John and Charles Wesley, Whitefield, Fletcher, Coke, and Lady Huntingdon. Of the lay preachers, that is to say, those who were Wesley's helpers and instruments, several were men gifted in an extraordinary manner; nor can their memoirs be looked into by a generous and Christianly-minded reader without emotion or benefit. But these men do not appear individually, or *singly*, to have left their own impression upon Methodism; and here, while a place is saved for *a very few* exceptions, it may be affirmed that it is not given to men of no early discipline, or who have not, before attaining middle life, made good their want of education by extraordinary efforts, to exert much influence extending beyond their immediate sphere, or which can last a year after the moment of their death. It is the prerogative of the educated class to extend themselves, by the products of their minds, over space and time.

Dissimilar as they were, as men, it is yet not easy to speak of John and Charles Wesley separately; for the influences affecting in common the early course of the brothers, though affecting them very diversely, can be properly spoken of only as constituting one order of things.

The rectory at Epworth might be brought forward as an instance in abatement of much that has lately been said of the "state of religion and the Church" in the early part of the last century;—just as Luther's home contradicts the exaggerations in which some Reformation-champions have indulged themselves. That rectory was not a solitary instance; it was a *sample*, if not of many, of more than a few, clerical homes; and besides, it furnished indirect evidence concerning another main element of the religious condition of England at that time, and which is too little regarded. The characteristics and the excellences of the antecedent and contemporary nonconformity, were there extant—in an occult manner, perhaps, and yet really. Some of the very choicest samples of the firm, consistent, English Christian character have been the product of the non-conforming or puritanical soul, blended with the better-ordered and more broadly-based Christian temperament of the Episcopal Church. Need we name Leighton, Tillotson, Butler, Secker, as instances? While, on the other hand, the brightest adornments of nonconformity have been men who, having been bred in that Church, were thrust out of it.

Wesley, the father, had renounced nonconformity, and had cordially surrendered himself to the guidance and control of the Church: he had put off the dissident, so far as he could, or as far as he was conscious of it; but he could not lay down that in nonconformity which belonged to the inner man. A stern moral force, and a religious individuality, went with him into the Church, nor left him as he entered it; and it showed itself as an inherited quality in his sons. It must not be regarded as a refinement, when it is affirmed that the special characteristics of religious communities—that is to say, those properties that visibly mark such bodies—do go down to the second, third, and fourth generation, in the instance of families that have walked forth from the inclosure within which they were born and bred. Family peculiarities may have disappeared—the *physical* type, perhaps, has been lost; and yet a note of the *religious* pedigree survives, and reappears in grandchildren, sons and daughters. The Wesleys—John and Charles, if not Samuel—inherited from both father and mother, qualities most serviceable for their after work, which their father, if not mother, would have disallowed and rooted out from their bosoms. So it is that Heaven takes care of the original temper of its tools.

Mind is from the mother: such we conclude to be a law of nature, on the evidence of very many bright instances. The Wesleys had the advantage of this law; and their mother, a woman of extraordinary intelligence and force of mind, of correct judgment, and vivid apprehension of truth, conferred also upon her sons whatever advantage they might derive from her composite excellence as a zealous churchwoman—yet rich in a dowry of nonconforming virtues. The Wesleyan organization of an after period, which gave life, consistency, and permanence to Methodism, may we not trace it up to its spring head, in the conforming nonconformity which the brothers had imbibed with their mother's milk?—a bold following out of a conscientious belief, still governed by the love of order, and an abhorrence of anarchy, and of individual willfulness. The Wesleys' mother was the mother of Methodism in a religious and moral sense; for, her courage, her submissiveness to authority, the high tone of her mind, its independence, and its self-control, the warmth of her devotional feelings, and the practical direction given to them, came up, and were visibly repeated in the character and conduct of her sons.

When Mrs. Wesley, writing to her husband concerning the irregular services she had carried on during his absence, in the rectory kitchen, for the benefit of her poor neighbors, said—"Do not advise, but command me to desist,"—she was bringing to its place a corner stone of the future Methodism. In this emphatic expression of a deep compound feeling, a powerful conscientious impulse, and a fixed principle of submission to rightful authority, there was condensed the very law of her son's course as the founder and legislator of a sect. This equipoise of forces which, if they act apart, and when not thus balanced, have brought to nothing so many hopeful movements, gave that consistency to Methodism, to which it owes its permanence. If the Wesleys had started on their way—let us suppose it—fired with the same evangelic zeal, but impelled also by the modern political fanaticism, which assails every *authority* as a strong-hold of Satan, that zeal would quickly have given place in their own bosoms to a turbulent rancor, and in the time that followed toward the close of Wesley's course, every Wesleyan congregation throughout England would have been a club, fraternizing with those of France.

The belief of being destined to the achievement of a great work has probably sprung up, at an early age, in the mind of every man whose destiny this has actually been. Doubtless, also, a vague feeling of this sort has heaved the bosom of many an aspiring boy, who, in fact, never makes himself known to fame—some, because they were wanting in the inborn quality for any such work; and some from the want of opportunity. There are, however, grounds for believing that a call has been heard in the still moments of every youth's eager onward course, who in manhood has led other minds. It was so with John Wesley, if not with Charles, and his rescue, as by miracle, from the fire at the rectory, gave point to such a feeling, which fixed itself in his motto, "Is not this a brand plucked from the burning?"

Wesley's instinct of belief, which was a prominent characteristic of his mind, met no counteractive force in its structure, which was not at all of the philosophic cast. He *reasoned*, more than he thought: this, however, is a too significant fact not to claim distinct consideration hereafter. The often-told story of "Jeffery's" tricks, and antics at the Epworth parsonage, need not in this place be repeated; but they must be alluded to in passing, for this strange episode in his early history took effect upon Wesley in a decisive manner. Might we say that it so laid open his faculty of belief, as that a "right of way" for the supernatural was opened through his mind, and to the end of his life there was nothing so marvelous that it could not freely pass, where "Jeffery" had passed before it.

In thus speaking, we are far from intending to make light of so well-attested and remarkable a story as that of the long-continued noises and jostlings of the Epworth imp. There is no need, in an instance like this, to feel as if the alternative were either to reject a mass of well sustained and copious evidence; or, if it be admitted, then to talk of "Divine interpositions" or "miracles," and so to make ourselves liable to the indeterminate question, "What purpose, worthy of God, can be subserved by these, or similar occurrences?" The mistake is, when such occurrences are not of a kind that can be rejected as tricks or fictions, immediately to attribute to them a religious meaning, or to see in them the hand of Heaven.

Why should any such hypothesis be resorted to?—we do not so think in parallel instances. Once in a century, or not so often, on a summer's evening, a stray Arabian locust—a genuine son of the desert—tempest-borne, we know not how, has alighted in Hyde Park, or elsewhere. This rare occurrence, and which it is so difficult to explain, is indeed out of the course of nature; but it is not supernatural; certainly it is not a *religious* event. Nor, to judge of them by their apparent characteristics, are many other inexplicable occurrences, similar to the Epworth rectory noises and disturbances, to be thought of as touching any religious question. In truth, there is nothing in these facts of a *celestial* complexion; nor are they grave enough to be reputed *infernal.* We can incur no risk of committing sacrilege when we deal with occult folk, such as "Jeffery," huffingly and disrespectfully. Almost, while intent upon these quaint performances, one seems to catch a glimpse of a creature—half-intelligent, or idiotic, whose pranks are like those of one that, using a brief opportunity given it by chance, is going to the extent of its tether in freaks of bootless mischief.

Why may not this be thought? Around us, as most believe, are beings of a high order, whether good or evil, and yet not cognizable by the senses of man. But the analogies of the visible world favor the supposition that, besides these there are orders, or species, of all grades, and some, perhaps, not more intelligent than apes or than pigs. That these species have no liberty, ordinarily, to infringe upon the solid world is manifest; nevertheless, chances, or mischances, may, in long cycles of time, throw some (like the Arabian locust) over his boundary, and give him an hour's leave to disport himself among things palpable.

In Wesley's mind all instances went on to their utmost limits, and with him the preternatural was equivalent always to the supernatural; nor does he seem to have noted the distinction between what is supernatural and what is miraculous; and thus every thing not ostensibly natural, he was prone to interpret in a sense wholly religious. This credulity did not sensibly impair a mind so high-toned and vigorous as his; but, beside that it gave the world an occasion against him, and lowered his influence out of the pale of his own communion, it set a premium within it upon marvels, and tended to throw confusion upon the popular notion of religious faith. Besides, in minds of a relaxed temperament, credulity is a leakage through which all belief, sooner or later, oozes out and is lost. But we shall see presently in what way Methodism at length shook off this ill-adjunct, which had sprung from the infirmity of its founder.

It is characteristic of the man, that Wesley's self-possession, his ardor in study, and the powerful instinct of order within him, so operated to render him unconscious of outward ills, that he could look back upon his boyish days at Christchurch, not merely without horror, but with delight! If, as a general truth, it be good for a man "to bear the yoke in his youth," indispensable is this severe condition in the training of those who are born to command. Wesley learned, as a boy, to suffer wrongfully with a cheerful patience, and to conform himself to cruel despotisms without acquiring either the slave's temper, or the despot's. If an ill consequence resulted from the severities of his school course, it appeared long afterward, in those misunderstandings of human nature which he embodied in the code of the Kingswood school: he seems to have imagined that little boys, as a species, are much like what, as he remembered, John Wesley was at twelve and thirteen, a prodigy of energy, assiduity, and unconquerable patience.

Oxford at once brought out the robustness of Wesley's intellectual structure. To speak of that ability which enabled him, with ease, to make himself master of any subject to which he directed his attention, is saying little;

for the same may be affirmed of hundreds of men of whom the world hears nothing after they have won for themselves their academic status. Wesley was thus almost intuitively master of all arts—or of all but the highest, to which the predominance of secondary faculties bars the way. Many facts characteristic of himself, and of the system he gave to the world, are explicable on this ground of that energy of the intuitive reason which precludes the philosophical faculty. Yet this intellectual characteristic in Wesley is not to be spoken of with regret, if we are thinking of the work he was to accomplish; for it is certain that while the power which was his characteristic fits a man to lead and command others, the philosophic faculty —its opposite—shows itself to be a peremptory disqualification in any one who would sway the multitude. The mass of men follow, or think they follow, the well-forged chains of reasoning which logicians deal in; and they delight to find themselves ferried over a stream they could never have forded, and safely landed upon some irrefragable conclusion. The very populace like to be reasoned with, and to be forcibly driven in upon a definite doctrine; but no graces of illustration, no powers of oratory, ever avail to induce the crowd to think, or to tread the bottom of a subject.

Yet in speaking of Wesley as a master of technical logic, we must screen him at once from the imputation of ever having played the part of a scholastic sophist, or wordy wrangler. The high tone of his mind, and the thorough seriousness which belonged to him, and his reverence for truth, and, afterward, his religious awe, forbade him to engage as gladiator in any disputation. Such an imputation he resented warmly. Many indeed were the sophisms (logically compacted) which he himself bowed to, but never did he defend one, the fallacy of which he secretly discerned.

Writers who, of late, have spoken of Wesley's want of the philosophic faculty—a topic easy to enlarge upon and illustrate—have, as if by way of compensation, allowed him the praise of being an accomplished logician. And so perhaps he was, or seemed to be, while dealing, from the moderator's chair, with scholastic sophisms. But it is inaccurate, or unphilosophical to make the logical faculty —that is to say, an expertness in technical reasoning—the intellectual contrary of the philosophic faculty. In that order of mind to which Wesley belonged, it is the irresistible force, or one might say, the galvanic instantaneousness of the intuitions, which forbids and excludes the exercise of the abstractive and analytic power. With him the grasp of what he thought to be a truth, was so sudden, and so spasmodically firm, as ordinarily to preclude two mental processes to which minds of a higher order never fail to submit whatever offers itself for acceptance as a verbal proposition or conclusion:—namely, *first*, a ridding the terms, so far as may be possible, of the ambiguities that infest language; and *secondly*, the looking through the medium—the verbal proposition, into the very midst of the things so presented. Wesley's habits as a logician stood him in some stead as to the first of these processes; but he scarcely seems to have been capable of that equipoise of the mind which the second demands.

At the time when Wesley was acting as moderator in the disputations at Lincoln College, there was no philosophy abroad in the world—there was no *thinking* that was not atheistical in its tone and tendency, and the whole energy of his moral nature would have drawn him off from any commerce with it, even if the structure of his mind had allowed him to tread at all on that path. But while thus officiating in a scholastic chair, that preparation was in progress which, in due time, was to issue in the peremptory and categorical style which became the marked characteristic of the Wesleyan ministrations. The fervor of Methodism, carrying upon its surface, as it did, so well defined a character of dialectic precision, might suggest the idea of a sharply-struck medallion, retaining its nicest features while molten and incandescent. In this feature we find what was to constitute a main distinction between the Wesleyan and the Whitefieldite Methodism; and it is curious to note the fact, that while, as we shall see, the former exhibited at its commencement ostensible extravagances and distortions which in a much less degree attached to the latter, it was Wesley's community that crystalized itself in geometric figure; while Whitefield's followers passed into an organized condition very slowly and very imperfectly. Wesley's Methodism excelled in external order; Whitefield's in a deep and more true harmony. But what we have just now to do with is, that training in verbal precision, which was to give life and form, both to the theology of Wesley, and to his institutions.

EARLY STAGES OF WESLEY'S RELIGIOUS COURSE.

At Oxford, Wesley's religious feelings went through a two-fold transmutation, which, however, brought him very little way forward toward the position whence he was to exercise his ministry. At each step of his progress he had yielded, after some resistance, to a force partly logical, and partly suasive; and his so yielding might, by a bystander, have been anticipated as certain to ensue. Nevertheless, his conversion, taking place as it did in this manner, by successive *vanquishments*, gave to his own religious opinions, and so afterward to Methodism, a marked character of abruptness and antagonism.

The conversion of several of his companions was less, or not at all, interrupted by distinct *epochs:* and therefore, while it was less logical, it was of a more even color, and the doctrinal system adopted had in it more of harmony, and less of paradox. *Wesleyan* Methodism, so far as it was the product of its founder's mind, and the representative of his individual experience, and the symbolic record of his personal religious history, came forth—a cramped Christianity; nevertheless, it had a recommendation, most important in whatever is to control the mass of the people—that of being sharply chiseled on every side: it was shaped and bounded with intelligible definitions. Thus it was, that those extravagances which attended its early progress, subsided and went off in no permanent ill consequence, for every thing, after a while, collapsed within the limits of rules, and of decisions of "Conference."

We have said that at Oxford Wesley passed through two stages of his religious course. The *first* was that which brought him over from the unbroken hilarity of his natural temper, to a fixed seriousness, and a determination to frame his course of life under the sovereign control of religious reasons and motives. The *second* stage was not passed through until he, although to much the firmer temper of the two, and although the master mind, had come under a spiritual influence of a deeper sort, namely, that of his brother Charles, and his praying companions. Charles Wesley's soul had more in it of *altitude* (profundity and elevation) than John's, and it is always seen that force and energy give way to, and receive their form from, depth and intensity of feeling; one might say, in like manner, as the bony structure of the animal frame takes its shape from the softer parts and the fluids. Let the Wesleyan hymn-book be examined, and the relation between the minds of John and Charles Wesley will become apparent, nor will it seem strange that the maker of the best of those hymns should have governed the robust spirit of the founder of Methodism.

Wesley misunderstood the first religious book that much engaged his attention—the *De Imitatione*. He read it as if it had been intended to represent the Christian life under its ordinary conditions; and so it was that his good sense, and his untamed youthful feelings, prompted him to resent that abnegation of human nature which the writer throughout supposes. Wesley, probably, had then made little acquaintance with the mediæval monastic and ascetic system; otherwise he would have perceived that the *De Imitatione* looks no further than the cell, and that the abstraction, the elevation, the purity of intention, and the reserve which it speaks of and recommends, are scarcely imitable in the open world; or are so only in a very limited sense. The breadth, the richness, and the power of Jeremy Taylor, at once vanquished Wesley's mind, and under this guidance he became, without reserve or abatement, the religious man. How far this solemnity, fervor, or intensity of soul came short of the amplitude and liberty of evangelical piety, can not be precisely determined; but that it did fall far short of that standard is certain; at least, he himself thought so, for it was not until long after this time that he fixed the date of what he termed his "conversion."

But using, as we must, the liberty to speak of Wesley, as from broader ground than that of his own views, we must first reject his condemnation of himself, as "not a regenerate man" at this period; for if not, then many of those whose names adorn Church history, during a full thousand years, were not Christians; and moreover, if we compare him as a Christian, at a period later than the date he assigns to his conversion, with some who, since the Reformation, have shone as lights in the world, we must think that he, less clearly than many, apprehended the height and depth, the length and breadth, of the Christian scheme. If he had been less argumentative, and less categorical, and more meditative, he would have set Wesleyan Methodism upon a broader theological basis. We ask leave, then, to speak of John Wesley at Oxford, as a Christian man, notwithstanding his own protestations to the contrary; and the very same liberty we use in thinking of the matured Wesleyan theology as an immature Christianity. Wesley's first impressions at Oxford had made him a man not of this world; his second placed him in open antagonism to the levity, the indifference, and the impiety which on all sides surrounded him; and if this impiety had been less extreme, the reaction from it would have been less vehement and decisive. In fact, this reaction, of which so many instances present themselves in religious history, went on, as in analogous cases it usually does, beyond the stage of a stern protest against abounding evils, and it passed into what is so little thought of by fervently religious persons—religious egotism.

Wesley's state of mind, and his habits at Oxford, included much intensity of feeling, brought to a focus-spot upon his individual welfare. It would be harsh and inaccurate to designate this introverted feeling as *selfishness:* or if we were to do so, an appeal might fairly be made to the self-denying labors and charities of Wesley, and of others who may come under the same description. But there may be much egotism, where there is also much self-denial for the good of others. That which disperses this species of concentration, and which gives full play to a genuine benevolence, is a better understanding of the Gospel than Wesley had at this time, or until long afterward, attained.

And yet we might say that Wesley's ascetic notions and practices, and the dangerous extent to which he went in fasting, were less indicative of his imperfect apprehension of Christianity, than was the pertinacious opposition he made to his father's proposal, that he should take steps for being appointed as his successor at Epworth. In fact, his earnest piety had brought out, and given force to that self-determining energy which was to qualify him for his function as founder and ruler of a society; but at this time it showed itself in an immovable resolution to think only of his own (supposed) spiritual welfare; and in defending himself in this position, he stretched sophistry to the utmost, evading, by shallow pleas, at once the import of his ordination vow, a clear call to extensive usefulness, and (if such considerations might be listened to) the duty of a son toward his parents. While we mark the overruling hand which had otherwise disposed Wesley's lot, his own part on this occasion—that is to say, in clinging to his college life when a populous parish was before him—shows clearly enough that a willfulness still held its mastery in his mind, which years of severe discipline were needed to dispel; yet this state of his mind was nothing more than a stage in his progress; it was not a mood in which a nature so noble (Christian principles apart) could have remained stationary. Christian principles, with a discipline efficient for its purpose, did at length thoroughly set him free from the bondage of every restrictive or self-regarding motive, and thenceforward as large and warm a philanthropy as a human bosom has ever admitted ruled him supremely.

WESLEY'S EARLY RELIGIOUS CONNECTIONS

Except so far as it formed part of the discipline we have just spoken of, Wesley's adventure in Georgia claims little notice in relation to our immediate purpose. His voyages to and fro, and the months of his stay in the colony, were indeed incidentally important in bringing him within the circle of the Moravian influence. It was in that circle that the new and strange idea first met him of a Christianity more elevated and excellent than his own. One or two of the Moravian ministers were—and he felt it—far-advanced in knowledge and experience beyond his own rate of attainment. At Oxford he had found himself stepping forward always in front of those around him. But on board the ship in which he crossed the Atlantic, and afterward in the colony, he met with men who, without assuming a tone of arrogance toward him, spoke to him as to a novice, and who, in the power of truth, brought his conscience to a stand by questions which, while he admitted the pertinence of them, he could not answer with any satisfaction to himself. Thus it was that he returned to England in a state of spiritual discomfort and destitution. He had been stripped of that overweening religiousness upon which, as its basis, his asetic egotism had hitherto rested. He rejoined his friends in a mood to ask and receive guidance, rather than to afford it.

At a later time, and when his judgment in spiritual

matters had ripened, he became the censor of the Moravian community:—he rebuked it, and in the end, broke connection with the body, from which, however, he borrowed certain rudiments of Methodistic organization; but the spirit of the two communities was widely—we might say essentially—different, and the two have subserved purposes wholly dissimilar. Within the Moravian circle the prevailing force is centripetal; within the Wesleyan it is centrifugal. The Church of the Brethren has conserved within its small inclosures an idea of what was imagined to be pristine Christianity; and it has moored itself, here and there, in sheltered nooks of the world, amid the wide waters of general impiety or formality; but no such tranquil witness-bearing to primitive principles could have satisfied Wesley's evangelical zeal; and the Methodism which he framed was an invasive encampment upon the field of the world: it never was in *his* view or purpose a CHURCH: its original principles and practices were *exclusive* of those to which Moravianism attached the highest importance. This is an instance, and such present themselves on all sides, in which some accidental and unsubstantial analogy, or some merely apparent resemblance, has been hastily taken up by writers, and repeated one after another;—"Methodism—it is our protestant Jesuitism;"—or, "it is our English Moravianism." Nothing, in such comparisons, agrees with the facts, if these be correctly thought of.

Wesley's was a mind in the history of which no gradual transition-periods—no seasons during which the understanding and the moral sentiments should, in equipoised conjunction, work their way onward from one position to another—could have place. Each change was either a leap from a precipice, or a being thrown with violence from one standing place to another; and the very next moment after he had regained his feet, or even before he could do so, he turned upon those whose company he had thus left, and assailed them with eager, yet never with bitter upbraidings. Such are the characteristics, not of a mind of the highest order, which passes from one condition to another harmoniously, as to all its faculties; but of a spirit of energy, destined to command the multitude.

Thus it was that Wesley, whose spiritual confidence had received a death-wound from the hand of the Moravian brethren, turned so sharply upon his former master—William Law; and although confessing himself to be yet only treading the threshold of Christian faith, he sternly rebukes his teacher, as a blind leader of the blind. With Law's moonlight Gospel we have not now to do; but his modest and pertinent reply to this rude assault proves at least, that this spurned teacher had much the advantage over the recusant disciple, on the ground of humility and patience.

The elastic force of his mind prevented his imbibing from other minds any more of a foreign influence than he might, at the moment, be in a state to assimilate. Thus it was that, in his visit to Herrnhut—too short for any purposes of intelligent inquiry, as to the principles and practices of the society—he took up from Moravianism that which he then most needed, namely, a clearer apprehension of the first principle of the Christian life; or, to speak technically, he learned the doctrine of Justification through Faith. It does not appear that hitherto his notions on that subject had acquired any coherence, or had produced the fruits of peace in his own soul. Just so much aid as he then required, and which the Moravian brethren were qualified to afford, he received from them. That his mind did not undergo more transmutation than this, may be accounted for by the shortness of his stay among these people, and by that restlessness which prevented his seeing or understanding what was beneath the surface. It is probable, too, that his very limited knowledge of the German language stood much in his way. With the Moravian ministers, or with some of them, he conversed in Latin; but such conversations, in which a deliberate and formally theological style would prevail, could not convey to him what he might have gathered from an unfettered and promiscuous colloquial intercourse with the Herrnhut community. From Georgia, Wesley had returned—we might say—dilapidated; from Germany he returned edified; or at least, his Christian sentiments thenceforward rested upon a better foundation, and which was afterward to be built upon: as to the superstructure of a settled faith and peace, it did not yet appear. Unity of purpose, singleness of intention, was in the highest sense his characteristic; but *simplicity*, in a genuine sense that is to say, ONENESS of the mind and soul, leading to repose, could not have been his distinction. Several of his friends, who were far his inferiors as teachers, or leaders, or as rulers, stood in advance of him, as to the homogeneousness of their religious sentiments. On this ground his brother Charles was always his superior; and Whitefield immeasurably so.

THE FIRST METHODISTIC PREACHING.

WESLEY, at Whitefield's invitation, and following the example he had set, commenced his public ministry as a field-preacher, in 1739. This was a course utterly repugnant to his most cherished notions of Church order, as well as to every instinct of his nature; yet it was by field-preaching, and in no other possible way, that England could be roused from its spiritual slumber, or Methodism spread over the country, and rooted where it spread. The men who commenced and achieved this arduous service, and they were scholars and gentlemen, displayed a courage far surpassing that which carries the soldier through the hail-storm of the battle field. Ten thousand might more easily be found who would confront a battery, than two who, with the sensitiveness of education about them, could mount a table by the roadside, give out a psalm, and gather a mob.

In looking down upon this field-preaching it is easy to make out a list of inferior motives which might prompt to such a course, and which, although singly they must be reckoned wholly inadequate for the purpose, yet when heaped together, and when piled up in the periods of a swelling paragraph, may seem enough to resolve the difficulty presented by such a line of conduct, begun and persevered in. Let those who so reason, and who so write, themselves make an experiment for effecting great things, on a difficult ground, at the impulse of an accumulation of motives singly insufficient for the purpose. Such reasoners can know little of human nature; and they must be ignorant of the laws which take effect upon it, when its utmost energies are put in strenuous movement. It is a mistake to imagine that the sum of small motives can ever constitute, or be equivalent to, a great motive; on the contrary, such an accumulation produces, not concentration, but distraction, vacillation, and infirmity of purpose. Arduous achievements demand powerful motives: this, indeed, is something like a truism; but let it be added that powerful motives are simple in their structure, and they love to have the whole man to themselves.

As a point of philosophy, nothing is gained by the frigid flippancy of attaching to the names of men who have achieved arduous conquests in a long course of persevering activity, the designation—"Enthusiasts;" for how does this phrase help us forward? Not at all. Unless a serviceable word is to lose its significancy, and therefore, to drop out of its place in the dictionary, this term must be held to convey the idea of that which is spurious, unreal, and which, as compared with the reality it counterfeits, is inefficient, nugatory, and inconstant. The word Enthusiasm, undoubtedly, is one of a class of terms which has no meaning apart from its correlative. When therefore, men whose very aspect, and whose whole course of life, indicates that there is in them the highest rate of constitutional energy and courage, pass before us, and we see them achieving great things, and bearing up, undis mayed, amid discouragements, perils, and reproaches—when (to condescend to the cant of a philosophic style) all the "*phenomena*" show the presence of motives that must be true *in* human nature, and true *toward* human nature, and toward the moral system—when, with facts such as these in view, we think the word enthusiast appropriate, as applied to the principal actors, we either write English miserably, or we think confusedly, or we ourselves—and this is the most likely supposition—are staggering in front of facts which no sympathy in our own bosoms enables us to comprehend.

Perplexities of this sort which so much embarrass a certain class of writers whose good-nature would impel them to deal kindly with useful "madmen," and who would fain be thought masters of philosophic equanimity, are much enhanced by the occurrence of those excesses, or of those inexplicable agitations which have so often run alongside of great religious movements. "May we not," say they, "fairly call those men Enthusiasts who, whatever their virtues may have been, stand before us implicated in disorders that are frightful to think of?" So it may appear; yet leave must be taken to apply a stricter analysis to the facts.

It is a circumstance worthy to be noted that although Whitefield's oratory was of a far more moving sort than that of Wesley, bodily agitations and outwardly expressed agonies were less frequently excited in his audiences than in those of his friend. In fact, it was seldom except when Whitefield followed immediately upon Wesley's track, that any of these disturbances took place, beyond such as might arise from the copious weeping of a large proportion of the congregated thousands that listened to him. When they did occur in his presence, Whitefield stood in doubt as to the source to which they should be attributed. He could see in them no indubitable indications of the hand of God. He looked for such fruits of his preaching as are of a less questionable kind. It may be thought, and with some reason, that it was Wesley's too ready acceptance of these supposed proofs of the presence of God, that tended to produce, and to aggravate them. But this natural explication of the difference is not sufficient. The tone and quality of the popular addresses of the two preachers has also to be taken into the account; for while Wesley—in his earlier years especially—made a vehement appeal to the instantaneous impressions of his hearers, thus throwing inward upon the imagination and the nervous system the whole amount of emotion which he had raised, Whitefield worked upon the human mind in a manner that is more in harmony with its laws; that is to say, he roused genuine feelings to a high pitch by vividly presenting to the mind the proper external objects of such feelings, and by sustaining the *outward* tendency of these feelings toward their true objects. Those paroxysms of feeling which agitate the body, take place in consequence of some sudden introverted action and shock produced among them.

There is, however, something further, calling for inquiry on this ground, and the problem may be looked at quite fearlessly; for the danger, if there be any, lurks among mistaken apprehensions of danger.

There is nothing that should tempt one to recount them, in the extant narrations of those appalling scenes that were of frequent occurrence when Wesley preached. They became, however, less and less frequent in the progress of Methodism, and he himself less inclined to regard them with favor. But while these disorders were at their height, they resembled, in some of their features, the demoniacal possessions mentioned in the Gospel history. The bodily agitations were perhaps as extreme in the one class of instances as in the other; nevertheless there is no real analogy between the two. The demoniacs (clearly distinguishable from lunatics) were *found* in this state by Christ where he went preaching:—they did not *become such* while listening to him. In no one instance is it said that frenzy seized upon any among the thousands who pressed around him, eager to catch his words. In no one instance, recorded in the Gospels or Acts, did demoniacal possession, or any bodily agitations resembling it, come on as the initial stage of conversion. Some, indeed, out of whom demons had been cast, gratefully accepted so great a deliverance with a devout consciousness of whence it came; and afterward they followed their Divine Benefactor;—and so did the leper, the blind, the lame, when "healed." But there was no recognized dependency, no sequency of a spiritual renovation, as the issue of demoniacal possession;—far from it: and yet, when this apparent analogy has been dismissed as unreal, there remains not another word in the writings of the New Testament (or only one, and that not pertinent—1 Cor. xiv. 25) which should compel us to pay the least regard to the Wesleyan agitations, as if they implicated, in any way, Christianity itself: they are to be looked at as facts sundered from all real relationship to those truths with which they stand in this temporary and accidental juxtaposition.

Thus far, then, all is secure; Christianity is in no way entangled in questions concerning the occult cause, or causes, of the still unexplained phenomena that attended the Wesleyan preaching. Even Methodism itself stands clear of this difficulty; for it held on its course, and wrought its beneficial effects, after these disorders had subsided, or where they did not occur. Yet, in some degree, our opinion of Wesley himself does take a color from this source, inasmuch as he failed to extricate himself entirely from the difficulties thence arising; and so it was that he left many of his thoughtful and more sober-minded followers painfully struggling with a very serious doubt—a "temptation," as they would call it, when—with these bodily agonies taking place in their presence, they knew not whether they should attribute what they saw to the finger of God, or charge it, as a work of confusion, upon the "father of lies."

In the present state of what, by indulgence, may be called intellectual or psychological science (no such science being, in fact, in existence) some room may be found for suppositions which a few years ago would have been scouted as chimerical; for there is now observable among intelligent persons an unwillingness to believe too little, as, years ago, there was a nervous dread of believing too much. The progress of the physical sciences has tended to bring about this change, by its often recurrent and startling discoveries. "What is there," we are tempted to ask, "that may not turn out to be true?" In the same direction minds, not the credulous only, but the incredulous, have been led on toward an enlarged belief on that ground where psychological empirics have encamped themselves; and where they wait until a true philosophy shall drive them off, with its regular inclosures. In a word, it is now felt, more than heretofore, that human nature occupies a position bordering upon a world, or a region, unknown and unexplored, but with which it has certain obscure relationships, and which, hitherto, have been little regarded.

This tacit and general recognition of an unknown neighboring system, may be held to bear in some manner upon our present subject. That which we *need* in relation to inexplicable occurrences, such as those that are now in view, is *first*, to be relieved from the necessity, real or imagined, of either doing violence to the established laws of evidence, or of resorting to a flippant skepticism, as the only means of dismissing a troublesome narration of alleged facts. We next need an alternative supposition, serving to preserve the deep realities of spiritual religion from all implication with what is merely physical or incidental. Now for securing both these ends, nothing more is requisite than that we keep in view certain *negative* principles, such as these:—*First*, That, as the laws of sentient life are at present almost wholly unknown—this ignorance having of late glared upon us in an unwonted manner—there is *reason* in the modesty which gives a hearing to the most extraordinary recitals, in suspended faith, as to the causes of what has occurred.

Such and such demonstrations of occult powers in human nature are to be recorded, and are to be thought of, until materials more abundant shall have been accumulated which may render them explicable.

Another negative principle may undoubtedly be held, and may safely be resorted to, when facts that are thus inexplicable claim to be listened to. It is this—That no analogy of the visible universe contradicts the supposition, which several such analogies suggest, namely, of the vicinity of orders of being, infringing, on rare occasions, yet with violence when they do, upon the human system, and which are fenced off from it by the ordinary conditions of their existence. Be it so, that we thus live in a more crowded and busy neighborhood than we have been used to suppose, or than we know how to include in a census: no belief of this sort will, in a sound mind, any way disturb its notions of moral principles, or will make other than it is our prime relationship to the Divine government. To entertain such a belief, or to reject it as gratuitous, is a point of perfect indifference, religiously. Nothing, on this ground, is deeply important, except our well observing always the distinction between what is physical, and what is moral and spiritual.

In the present instance the writer would not expend half a page upon the endeavor to recommend, as better than a mere conjecture, any hypothesis he might be inclined to admit in explication of the Methodistic bodily paroxysms. Let us make our way into Mr. Berridge's church at Everton. It is as when the juniors of a hive have been driven forth in June, and are clustering around their queen upon a willow bough; so is this church packed and piled with human beings:—pews, aisles, ledges, pulpit stairs, pulpit rails, and sounding board! The vicar one thinks must be crushed and stifled, as he pants for breath at the core of this dense living mass. Faintings and fits will no doubt occur; and as the preacher, in solemn tones, touches upon themes which are felt by all, or most present, to be real, and of immeasurable moment, it is only natural that the feelings of such a crowd, thus wrought upon by means of statements and representations admitted to be true, should burst over the limits of customary restraint, and that sighing and weeping aloud—especially after the first reserves of diffidence have given way—should become general, and that the heavings of compunction should, each moment, reach a higher and a higher pitch. Thus far nothing presents itself in this scene which is not readily explicable. Those objects of thought which, if they were duly dwelt upon, might well shake the stoutest heart, and which, if vividly presented and profoundly believed, might agitate the dullest congregation, are now exerting their unabated force—not upon a *congregation*, in the ordinary sense of the word, but upon a living condensation of souls and bodies.

We ought not peremptorily to say within what limits, under circumstances such as these, bodily agitations, which may easily be accounted for, would be confined; but, in some instances, they pass quite beyond any limits which it might seem possible to allow as proper to them. Robust men, hale and insensitive, fall in an instant, as if thunderstruck, upon the ground, where they roll, plunge, stamp, kick, and howl, as if molten brass had been poured into their stomachs! The face is swollen and livid, or it glows with crimson! This access of mortal agonies lasts, perhaps, some hours, and is then, and in a moment, succeeded by a calm or ecstatic joy. The *permanent* result is, in some cases, good and happy; in other cases, the contrary: these instances, moreover, are always intermingled with cases of mere folly and fraud.

Now, in contemplating this scene of confusion, after we have set off from it the utmost amount of what is fairly attributable to known causes, there will remain more than a little to which such causes afford no admissible explication. How, then, are we to dispose of them? Perhaps not at all to our satisfaction; except so far as this, that they serve to render so much the more unambiguous the distinction between themselves, and those genuine affections which the apostolic writers describe and exemplify. Among the inspired writers let those of them who were uneducated be brought forward as witnesses in support of this conclusion—that the most vivid affections of which our nature is capable, when directed toward objects purely spiritual, may take their hold of the human heart, and may fill it—apart from any bodily demonstrations or agonies. Christianity when proclaimed, in its substance, severs itself easily from whatever is not moral and spiritual in the results of preaching such as that of the Methodists. Christianity rescues *its own* out of these tumultuous assemblages; and then, content with its indisputable triumphs, it leaves the ambiguous residuum in the hands of scoffers, or of philosophers, to be dealt with as they please, or can.

WESLEY'S SEPARATION FROM WHITEFIELD.

THE harmony of sacred truth, when at length it shall bless the world, will not be seen arising from the bosom of a tempest-tossed Church. The Reformation yielded no such fruit, and with less reason could it have been looked for as likely to spring from among the excitements of Methodism. Wesley and Whitefield were destined to bear testimony, independently of each other, to great but dislocated principles. Each seized his doctrine, and well maintained it, so long as he dealt with it in its form as a positive truth: but each failed, and Wesley the most glaringly, when he used this doctrine as a weapon wherewith to demolish that of his friend and antagonist. Neither of them had the leisure, or the furniture, or the grasp of mind, that might have brought them to an understanding as theologians; and Wesley, by the structure of his mind, wanted that equipoise of the faculties which the bringing about such an agreement would demand.

The rupture between them was inevitable; and, on

the whole, it has had a beneficial result. Neither Wesley's theology, walled up as it was to heaven, nor Whitefield's, unwalled and open to the tread of the unclean and the lawless, could have stood, or been tolerable by itself.

In times of coolness and indifference Arminians and Calvinists find it easy to be cheaply wise, and may agree to hold their differences in abeyance: they pass the time of their hybernation peacefully enough in adjoining dens. But it can not be so with men who, in solemn earnestness, believe their belief, and who are called out to utter their convictions in terms decisive, and intelligible to the multitude. Wesley and Whitefield loved each other; but it was not desirable, indeed it was not possible, that they should continue to address, in turn, the same congregations; for such congregations would have been kept in the pitiable condition of a ship, thrown on its beam ends, larboard and starboard, by hurricanes driving alternately east and west.

Whitefield, not indeed as a theologian, but by the genuineness and simplicity of his Christian instincts, and by the more entire harmony of his religious affections, had advanced beyond his friend's position, and had gained a wider and more elevated ground. As well attempt to stitch his arms down to his sides while preaching, as to shackle him with logic when, with uplifted hands and a true heart, he made known to the thousands around him the "unsearchable riches of Christ." Evils and abuses, he knew not what or how many, might come to claim affinity with his ample Gospel; nevertheless, he must preach it, at all risks.

Wesley foresaw these evils; and, indeed, they had already met him on his ministerial course, in their most revolting forms; but he was frightened beyond the occasion, and in his terror he lost sight of truths which seemed so beset with abuses. Besides, in adhering to his habit of reasoning, rather than of thinking, and by the irresistible affinity of his mind with categorical positions, Wesley had caught hold of the paradox of "Perfection," which, in the form in which at first he announced and defined it, must meet its contradiction in the depth of every ingenuous bosom. The somewhat harsh pertinacity with which he maintained this article, combining it with the assertion of a consciously instantaneous passing from death unto life, made it necessary that he should stand alone as the teacher and chief of a community that was willing to receive law from his lips. It was not likely that he should find a *thoughtful* colleague, who would move on by his side, while he so rigidly insisted upon a doctrine which assimilates itself in no mind that is not more or less sophisticated. There are mysteries which rightly ordered minds accept, knowing well that the subjects embraced in them are beyond the grasp and range of the human faculties. Transubstantiation is a mystery which contradicts only our senses; and these perhaps may fail us; but the doctrine of perfection, as at first taught by Wesley, contradicts that with which every man has the most intimate and infallible acquaintance, namely, his individual consciousness: it is a mystery lodged on the very pathway between a man's mind and heart.

Yet the difference concerning the "Election of Grace" necessitated, in a still more peremptory manner, the separation of the two friends. It was not Whitefield's fault that, in giving expression to his belief concerning the sovereignty of Him from whom every good gift comes, he should employ the only terms and phrases in which this belief had, by divines and controvertists, been conveyed. This phraseology need not have been rejected because it was anthropomorphic—for the language of theology can in no way be relieved from this disadvantange; or it need not, if its anthropomorphism had not been made to sustain a superstructure of crude sophism, and of crazy metaphysics. Calvinism is quarreled with, by serious persons, not because it is not scriptural and philosophical; but because it has been conveyed in a medium that has been rendered insufferable by the bad uses to which it has been applied. Yet Whitefield, taking up, by the necessity of the case, the Genevan dialect, sweetened it by passing it through the warm charities of his own loving heart. We must not then blame him when, in speaking of things heavenly, he uses a language which is not heavenly, but which yet he utters in tones of evangelic charity. He was no philosopher that he might have framed for himself a less exceptionable style; he was not a theologian, not a proficient in biblical interpretation, so as that he might have brought these truths into a nearer relationship to the very style of the Inspired Writers. He spoke of the "Election of Grace" in the only manner that to him was practicable. May it be hoped that the Whitefield of the coming age will have at his command a language—not theological, not metaphysical, not encrusted with logic;—but new-born from the hearts of men who will utter truth before they have learned to define it in controversy!

But then, in all fairness, if so much indulgence as this is granted to Whitefield, while he preaches the Gospel—Calvinistically, as much, also, should be accorded to Wesley, while he protests, against what he thought the Antinomian abuse of it, in the ill-compacted dialect of Arminianism. He may claim such an indulgence with the more reason because, impelled as he was by a stern regard to the great principles of Christian purity—which he saw to be endangered—so to protest, he was not *thinker*, not philosopher enough to perceive that his protest, though quite good and solid as related to Antinomian enormities, was only a film, or an evasion, as it stood related to Calvinistic truths. Every thing for which a Calvinist—not of fanatical temper—would contend, is embraced within the compass of Wesley's own preaching language, and might indubitably be thence inferred.

Wesley rejected, in terms, the "Election of Grace," on account of its alliance—inseparable as he supposed, with Reprobation; but in so doing he fought a wordy phantom; and while thus engaged he lost sight of the *reality*

—the unsolved and insoluble mystery of the spiritual condition of the human family. No Calvinist insisted with more force or point than he did upon the *facts* of this awful condition; and no one availed himself in more solemn terms of the incentives thence arising, for urging men to repentance. He went forth among the impenitent million as he ought to go;—not as if, in slender tortuous tones, he would beg a hearing, that he might excuse, evade, or unriddle the mystery of the wide-spread ruin; but as the Apostles went—assuming, without doubt or abatement, its reality, and then laboring to rescue men, one by one, from its fatal bearing upon their immortal destiny. No effective assault has ever been made upon the consciences of men, whether educated or uneducated, on any other ground than this. The unmitigated *fact* which Reprobation assumes, Wesley also assumed. The exact difference between himself and the Reprobationists was this—that they put an anthropomorphic and unwarrantable interpretation upon the fact, and an interpretation which was sure to be blasphemously rendered by fanatics. He, with a genuine zeal for the honor of God, spreads over it a thin sophism, also anthropomorphic.

Fiery arrows they were, indeed, which his sinewy arm aimed at the hearts of men from the pulpit; yet each arrow was fledged, if not with Reprobation, with that which is not much rather to be chosen than itself. Wesley's preaching, so far as it was effective for dispersing the infatuations of the human mind, although it was clear of Calvinistic fanaticism and bad taste, carried with it, in the view of thoughtful men, the undiminished load of its difficulties. Lighten this load at all, and Methodism could not have spread, and would not have been.

And yet there was nothing disingenuous in Wesley's conduct in this behalf; for, verily he believed that that ill-judged burst of rhetoric, in which he himself borders so near upon blasphemy, and apostrophizes "the Devil," was as sound in theology, as, in fact, it was shallow and unseemly. In this, and in many other similar instances, we easily save his reputation, as a thoroughly honest disputant, by alleging his entire want of the deep reflective or analytic faculty. Almost a particle of that power of mind which looks through wordy propositions and examines the substance beneath, would have sufficed for enabling him to embrace that rudiment of the Christian system which the Seventeenth of the articles he had subscribed so wisely embodies. On *this* ground, if he could have taken it, Wesley might have repelled Antinomianism more successfully than he did; and might have placed the Wesleyan theology also on a broader and less precarious basis. This was not to be; for the time was not come, nor is yet come, when the harmony of truth can exist otherwise than as an abstraction painfully disentangled from antagonist dogmas.

LAY PREACHING, AND THE LAY PREACHERS.

Rid at length of his friend, and standing clear, as he believed, of all implication with Calvinistic election and reprobation, and yet, as a preacher, strong, as well in the truths which he misunderstood, as in those which he proclaimed, Wesley took his position upon the field of the world—the friend of man, the enemy of nothing but sin. On this ground he has a claim to be regarded with reverent affection and admiration, which is as valid as that of any of the worthies to whom a place has been assigned among the benefactors of mankind. The very inconsistencies that mark his progress (when properly considered) do but enhance his demand upon our sympathies. If, indeed, as heartless writers have affirmed, he had been nothing better than an ambitious plotter—the builder of a house in which he should rule and be worshiped—no such inconsistencies would ever have come to the surface, or would for a moment have made him halt on his path. Unquestionably it was from the want of a plot at the beginning, and from the lack of ambition as he went on, that he found himself compelled to yield, once and again, to the instances of some who seem to have been deficient in neither.

As a field-preacher, the courage, the self-possession, the temper, and the tact (and the same praise is due to his brother) which he displayed, places Wesley in a position inferior to none with whom it would be reasonable to compare him. After setting off from the account his constitutional intrepidity, his moral courage was that which is characteristic of a perfect benevolence, and which, in the height of danger, thinks only of the rescue of its objects. When encountering the ruffianism of mobs and of magistrates, he showed a firmness as well as a guileless skill, which, if the martyr's praise might admit of such an adjunct, was graced with the dignity and courtesy of the gentleman. In looking at the two brothers, while they are thus quietly bearing themselves in the midst of a furious rabble, a wish is generated, that they had been used to read their Bibles always in as calm a mood as that in which they pushed their way among wolves and tigers.

In making their assault upon the obtuse moral sense of men, the first Methodists enjoyed, and they well knew how to use it, an advantage of position which perhaps has not been duly considered. Wesley's own style of pulpit oratory was, in a remarkable degree, logically direct and conclusive: each blow was a blow straightforward, and was such as could scarcely be parried or resisted. And so it would have been under any circumstances; but he, as a preacher, stood in relation to the human mind, close home upon the conscience; whereas others have had to make their way thither through a strong defense of inveterate error. The preachers of the Gospel, in the apostolic age, were thus disadvantageously placed, for they had to dispel several forms of *misbelief*, before they could assail unbelief, and they seldom found men in what might be called the rudimental condition of impenitence and impiety. As to the Jewish conscience, it could be reached only through a coating of national pride, and of Rabbinical evasions; so it was that in the synagogue, the evangelist was challenged to prove, from the Scriptures, that "Jesus was the Christ;" for, until this was done, he could get no hearing for that which was to move the conscience. And on the other hand, in proclaiming the Gospel among the Gentiles, a bulwark of monstrous polytheism stood across the preacher's path. The host of divinities was to be driven from the ground, before men could at all be reasoned with as immortal and responsible beings. And thus, too, it was with the Reformation preachers, for they were led and indeed forced, to address men, not primarily, as "dead in sins," but incidentally as blinded by superstition.

With a happy simplicity of purpose, Wesley, and so Whitefield and others, would know nothing in addressing the multitude but that which is equally true of all men, always, and every where:—he spoke of and to them as the "servants of Satan," amenable to Eternal Justice yet embraced in the purposes of God's mercy through Christ. Well indeed it was that these preachers held themselves wholly clear, as they did, of the fatal error of making it a preliminary to their own ministrations to assail, and to endeavor to overthrow, the ecclesiastical system under which the people of England had lapsed into heathenism —or a state scarcely to be distinguished from it.

It was in following the better leading of this right view of human nature, and in thinking of men, not as the victims of a wrong guidance, but as the dupes of Satan, that these preachers lodged their arrow at once in the conscience of the impenitent. "I hold you fast as a rebel against God." In this challenge there was no flattery; but self-love finds much aliment in the argument that is to end in showing that another—a former guide—has been the cause of whatever is blameworthy in the disciple.

The same simple intention, and the same vigorous grasp of the true purpose of his mission, carried Wesley well over the rough ground of his own ecclesiastical prejudices. These prejudices, if they had been permanently adhered to, as would have happened with a mind of less energy, must wholly have prevented his fulfilling his ministry; or, if, on the other hand, they had been abandoned without a struggle, there might have been room to impute to him an unscrupulous ambition. The occasions on which his deep-rooted predilections gave way, and the mode in which this change was brought about, it is edifying to consider; for the man who could never have occupied a subordinate position, or even move forward with an acknowledged equal by his side, is seen listening in mid-life, to his aged mother, and yielding himself to her influence. This worthy mother of such a son had, at an advanced age, fallen in with Methodistic principles. She had not, however, surrendered her independence of mind; and she gave her son now, as she had done at the commencement of his religious course, the benefit of her perspicuous judgment. Wesleyan lay preaching may be traced up to that word—well weighed before it was uttered by this "mother in Israel,"—"John, this lay preacher is as truly called of God to preach, as you are." The Sunday morning when in compliance with his mother's request and opinion, he sat listening to Thomas Maxwell, showed that truth, or what he thought truth, held a sovereign power over him. He had hastened to London in very ill-mood, intending to silence this man; but in hearing him exercise the gifts of nature and of grace, he bowed to the manifested will of Him from whom "every good and perfect gift comes." The lay preacher was therefore encouraged; and lay preaching, without which there could have been no Methodism, received his sanction, and was put in course of operation.

In any instance, to "forbid" the "gifted" is to take upon ourselves a very serious responsibility; and if we venture so to do merely on the ground of ecclesiastical principles, we should have made ourselves quite sure *first*, that these principles are (at least in their rudiments) warrantable on evidence of Scripture; and then, that they stand confirmed by a sufficiently wide induction of precedents, as applicable to the case in hand.

Christianity is indeed conserved by Church order; but surely it does not exist for the sake of it. This, however, has shown itself to be the feeling of heartless and mindless men in every age. "Order first," say they; "and Christianity next." The conduct and the language of men of this stamp seems to mean nothing less than this: That the salvation of the human family entire would be dearly purchased at the cost of any inroad upon Church usages. It is manifest that in neglect or contempt of order, Christianity could not have been handed down from age to age; but unless, once and again, order had given way to a higher necessity, the Gospel must, by this time, have lain deep buried beneath the corrupt accumulations of eighteen hundred years. How, think we, would it have been held in its brightness and purity by those who, idolizing ancient rules and modes, become petrified around the altar where they kneel? It is to minds of a very different mould that the commission is given to restore what has fallen, and to build again the waste places, and to re-create order by means of an hour of confusion. Yet is it a fact worthy of all regard—That, when Heaven sends its own chosen men to bring about needed reformations, at the cost of a momentary anarchy, it does not give any such commission as this to those who, by temper, are anarchists. The anarchist is not to be trusted in any good work, for, as he acknowledges no rule but that of his own capricious arrogance, it is not he who will bring home fruit for the general good.

The Wesleys furnish a notable illustration of this principle. Great innovators, indeed, they were; but *anarchists* they were not. Themselves bred within a strict ecclesiastical inclosure, and firm in their attachment to its principles and practices, and far from indifferent to the prerogatives which personally they thence derived, and by temper also abhorrent of schism, and inclined to defer to authority, they were doubly and trebly guarded against the temptation to violate rules and usages at the impulse of mere self-will or caprice. Nevertheless these were the men who, in fact, and before they had advanced far on their path, found themselves compelled with their own hands, to snap asunder, as well the staff "beauty," as the staff "bands;"* and they rent, not a Church they denounced, but the very Church they sincerely loved and fondly clung to. And how wide is the rent which was then made; for the Methodistic schism—which, however, did not commence with the Wesleys' own irregular ministrations, but with the sending forth of lay preachers—has not merely drawn off certain classes of the community from the Episcopal Church, but, by the new life it diffused on all sides of itself, it has preserved from extinction and has re-animated the languishing nonconformity of the last century, which, just at the time of the Methodistic revival, was rapidly in course to be found nowhere but in books.

Charles Wesley would have been stopped on his course while struggling with his abhorrence of that only means of carrying forward the work they had commenced—lay preaching. But John could be stopped by no interior reluctance, as by no external obstacle or opposition, when once the work he was born to achieve stood out clearly developed before him. At this time it did so stand developed in his view; and while he, of all men, was the most self-determining in relation to whatever came under his entire control, none was more docile than he, or more quick to adapt himself to new circumstances, when called upon by his religious convictions, or by his practical good sense, to relinquish his cherished opinions. Besides, men of his order of mind are seen more readily to give way to the course of events,

* Zech. xi. 7.

than otners do, because, while they do so, they inwardly rely upon that inexhaustible store of expedients, and of ready skill, which will enable them, though driven from their path for a time, to return to it anon. So great was the disparity, on every ground, between himself and his irregular coadjutors, of which disparity he and they were fully conscious, that he doubted not he should be able to avail himself always of the zeal and ability he had called to his service, precisely so far as he thought good, and then effectively to curb its excesses. This anticipation was grounded, too much, upon a confidence in his own powers; and it included too little thought of those powers that were about to be developed under his hand. Nature (if we may use a profane term) is more rich and various in her bestowments than those are apt to imagine who feel that the crowd around them are much their inferiors. Such master minds are startled when the highly gifted step suddenly upon their path.

But we need not ask whether Wesley could, by any means, have dispensed with lay preaching; or whether he might better have controlled it than he did, or, whether he ought altogether to have denied himself the use of this perilous engine. Who is so earth-prone in eye as not to see that Christianity (and especially as consigned to the care of the Anglo-Saxon race—God's now "chosen people") then failing in its influence, and as it might seem, likely to be discarded, was to be granted afresh to the world, and to be brought back upon its own potent rudiments. The great principle of the apostolic ministry and writings, was anew to be proclaimed, as with a loud voice, "in the midst of heaven." Let ecclesiastics plant their chairs upon the rim of the rising waters, and thence prohibit the tide of salvation for the world; or let the wise and "moderate" show us by what means, even if Protestant bishops had been as supple and crafty as are popes and cardinals, Wesley and his lay preachers might have been enticed into Church inclosures, and there beguiled till they had forgotten their fervor.

If no other obstacle had stood in the way of a coalescence with the Church, the inçongruous articles of Wesley's creed, and to which he so pertinaciously adhered, as of prime importance, must have forbidden it, even if the rulers of the Church had condescended to consider a project of the kind. None, in the Church, could have thought themselves warranted in propounding those concessions upon which Wesley would have insisted. But at this time it was not a consentaneous, but an antagonistic impulse that was needed; and lay preaching was the very force which this urgent occasion demanded.

It is not disingenuousness merely, but obtuseness of perception as to human character, that has led certain writers to insinuate that Wesley's professed repugnance to lay preaching was feigned. Inconsistent in its expression it might be, and was; but genuine, if there be any thing at all trustworthy in human nature. Manifestly the course which he and his brother had been pursuing, in forming religious societies, could not reach any useful issue otherwise than by calling forth a new species of ministrations. This new ministry was his own work; and yet he quailed in the presence of it; and like the Demiurge of Gnosticism, he dared not look at the creature he had unadvisedly evoked from chaos. Not as yet had he learned the import of those words, within which so much of the Christian history is summarily comprehended—"No man putteth new wine into old bottles; but new wine must be put into new bottles." So has it been from the days of "Peter, James, and John;" and so—may we not be sure?—will it be at the time, yet future, of refreshment and "restitution of all things."

Dispassionately looked at, Wesleyan Methodism did not so much violate, as it rendered an homage to the principle of Church order; for if it broke in upon things constituted, with a violence that threatened to overthrow whatever might obstruct its course, it presently afterward emerged from its own confusion, and stood forth as a finished pattern of organization, and an eminent example of the prevalence and supremacy of RULES. Wesleyan Methodism, such as it continued to be while its founder lived, was not (like the Romish orders) an organization of the few who were to act upon the many, but an enrollment of the few along with the many: Methodism, in a word, was LAW—written upon the "fleshly tables" of thousands, and thousands again, of heretofore lawless hearts.

The enlightened adherents of ecclesiastical institutions might well persuade themselves, therefore, to see in Methodism—not, as they are wont, a horrible Vandalism; but the most emphatic recognition that has ever been made of the very core of Church principles, namely, that Christianity can not subsist, does not develop its genuine powers (longer than for a moment) apart from an ecclesiastical organization; and this seems to mean nothing less than a well-compacted hierarchical system. This surely is the *true* inference which should be drawn from the facts before us; but the more obvious meaning of Methodism is chosen by minds of a certain class. If it had been Wesley's fortune to be trampled to death by a brutal mob, quite early in his course, and while yet guiltless of schism, he might have been allowed to stand in a fair place among martyrs; but when he is seen with his lay preachers clinging to his presbyter's gown, nothing can be done but leave him, and them, to sink together into the deeps of ecclesiastical perdition.

Several of the first lay preachers were men of very extraordinary natural powers, as well as of deep and genuine religious feeling. Some had made acquisitions as biblical scholars; yet generally, the irreparable want of education among them, and their ignorance, often, of the Bible they were to expound, threw them upon their *own*, and their *only* resource: that is to say, upon a single-minded and fervent consciousness of the reality, power, and excellence of the Gospel, thought of in its first principles. They were men, some of them, whose power over the people, as preachers, was little less than that of their educated masters: nevertheless, their range of subjects was limited, and they were confined, by a necessity thence resulting, to the straight and strait path of elementary teaching. This confinement, however, does not imply meagreness of thought, or a dull iteration of things, uttered in the same phrases ten thousand times. True indeed it is, that when a genuine fervor declines, and when ignorance collapses into vulgarity—that is to say into itself—then the ministrations of uneducated men become insufferable. But this was not the case with the foremost of Wesley's lay assistants. The "powers of the world to come," and the brightness and efficacy of the Gospel, gave them their inspiration. So it was that, while Wesley and his three or four educated colleagues held to the few and great principles of the Gospel by the intentness of their minds, and the fervent simplicity of their zeal, and while the lay preachers, by the paucity of their ideas, and the slenderness of their knowledge, kept to the same narrow path, the *result* toward the people was to prevent the vast disparity between the two classes of teachers from becoming painfully apparent. This is seen, by contrast, every where in communions from which evangelical fervor has departed; for there, all the vast difference between one preacher and another, in natural ability and in furniture, is fully felt, and is accurately measured by practiced hearers. Yet let but the energies of heavenly truth return to such bodies, and these disparities would become less conspicuous, or would almost cease to be regarded.

A hundred times it has been said, by those who would fain show their liberality in getting up an apology for lay preaching, that it is the lay preacher's employment of a dialect colloquially understood by the mass of the people, and at the same time the low level of his ideas, that fit him for his office as their instructor. But, in fact, men of the highest culture make themselves thoroughly intelligible to the rudest minds, if only they have a soul and purpose thereto adapted; and they find they can do this without vitiating their style by any admixture of colloquial vulgarities. It is *concentration*, and not a low familiarity; it is the elementary grandeur of first truths that forcefully opens a way into the human heart, whether cultured or rude. Whether it be the bearer and winner of academic honors, or the recently-washen mason or shoemaker—the preacher who feels with power and *freshness* such truths, and who brings to bear upon the utterance of them some natural gifts, is always listened to by the mass of men;—for the hearer feels that the preacher is dealing out what he imparts, as if from an unexhausted treasure. He never seems to have nearly uttered all his mind, or emptied his heart. Cultured congregations, it is true, must be addressed by cultured preachers, who are qualified to entertain a sophisticated religious taste with what is discursive. But with the multitude, all is well so long as the preacher, whether bred in the college or the shop, utters with feeling, and in a concentrated style, that which is acknowledged to be of primary importance.

The great effects produced in the early years of Methodism, by some, even of the less gifted of the lay preachers, has not been understood by those who, in attempting to account for the fact, have themselves been wanting in sympathy with those primary truths. Wesley in one set of phrases, and Whitefield in another, spoke, sometimes with a startling conciseness, sometimes with an overwhelming copiousness—of heaven, of hell, of eternity, of the power, and justice, and mercy of God, of an ample redemption, of an immediate release from guilt and danger, and of a present fruition of the Divine favor. The style and manner of these preachers seemed like a clearing of the clouds from the heavens, so that the sun in his strength might shine upon the dead earth. And so the lay preachers, taking up the same style, and fraught with the same powers, became at once terse from intensity of feeling, and copious from the fullness of their subject. This copiousness filled and overflowed the channel of their individual minds. Ignorance or narrowness of faculty were lost and overpowered;—neither speaker nor hearer knew what was the small measure of the earthen vessel whence flowed the rich nourishment of the soul. To the lay preacher, while thus ministering from out of his penury, the words, in an accommodated sense, might have been addressed—"I know thy poverty—but thou art rich."

Notwithstanding that many who at first offered themselves to the service sickened of it under its severe conditions, and went back, yet in most places Wesley found it not difficult to supply his societies with teachers; and here there presents itself a principle of Christian statistics which deserves some notice. Whatever might be alleged as to the meagre teaching of the local preachers, the greater number of the itinerant preachers were men fairly qualified for the service for which Wesley had accepted their aid. If not fastidious in his taste, he did not indiscriminately, or in a slovenly manner, avail himself of such help. He looked to his men—he heard them—proved them—held them awhile on probation; and not in any large proportion of instances was he shown to have too hastily admitted any to Wesleyan "orders."

It may be inferred, then, from this instance, that a religious body, within which there is vitality, will ordinarily supply itself with an adequate proportion of ministers. And it may be taken as a rule that the supply will come from what may be considered as the *mean level* of the society, as to rank and knowledge. So it appears to have been in the Wesleyan body, and the instance, when assumed as a ground of reasoning, embraces a very wide surface, and includes great varieties of circumstance.

A crowding toward the sacred office is not a fact of frequent occurrence; but a lack of candidates, or, what is nearly of the same import, the derivation of its ministers, in any communion, from a rank below the *mean level* of the people, is an ominous symptom and should engage the most serious attention of those who undertake to think and care for the body.

But if the instance of Wesleyan Methodism is taken to establish the general rule—that a religious community, when it is in a healthy condition, will supply itself with ministers, it gives negative evidence also in confirmation of another rule, which this body has too little regarded, namely—That although such a body may supply itself with preachers, it is not without a CHURCH that pastors are to be reared. And here we are not thinking so much of a hierarchy; and of a settled scheme of government, as of that more broadly-based economy, and of that more deep-seated organization, which should bring the Christian system, entire, to bear upon Christian homes. Here has been (and we must return to so important a subject) the main point of defectiveness in Wesleyan Methodism; and it sprang unavoidably from Wesley's reluctance to break away from the Episcopal Church;—it was an association of Converts: he would not call it, and did not make it, a Church. The Nonconformists, to some extent, had fallen into the same fault, which is that of protesting sects generally. Methodism regarded its converts *individually*—it knew them not, or knew them imperfectly, in their home relationships. The head of a family—husband, father, and master—was, in its view, a convert only, or chiefly; he was not recognized as the hierarch of home. Unless a Christian body becomes vital throughout its mass, *in a domestic sense*, it will neither be conscious of its want of pastors, nor will it furnish such from its own bosom. An itinerating ministry, useful as it is in certain respects, and well adapted to the wants of a recently-evangelized people, must be regarded as indicative of a crude Christian condition:—it is a practice that belongs to a transition state of things—a state which is not to be remedied by a more careful training of itinerating ministers; but in no other way than by a far-reaching renovation of the social mass;—in a word, by carrying Christianity, in its silent energies, from the chapel to the house. Wesley at length permitted his preachers to administer the sacraments, and therefore to baptize infants. But where there is no CHURCH—where children are not thought of as "members of Christ," and where they come under no discipline as such, the rite of baptism administered in infancy, is a five minutes' operation—profitless, perplexing, unintelligible, and out of harmony, as well with the Christian scheme, as with the system under which it takes place. An incongruity, not perceived by the parties, but yet serious, was it when these preachers, whose function was only convert making, welcomed infants into a society from which they were instantly afterward thrust out; or thenceforward forgotten by it, until they were of age to listen to sermons.

LAY PREACHING; AND A POINT OF COMPARISON SUGGESTED BETWEEN METHODISM AND ROMANISM.

THOSE who are in any degree conversant with religious history will be apt to think that a religious system promulgated and maintained to so great an extent by a body of fervently-minded but uneducated men, could not fail to generate within itself various forms of error, and that it would go more and more astray every year of its continuance. In looking into the "Memoirs," the "Journals," the "Experiences," of some of Wesley's lay preachers, the sober reader is perplexed, if not scandalized, by what he there finds, and he becomes painfully perplexed while —fearing lest he should compromise sacred truths—he resents and rejects so much of that with which they are there mixed. After reading some of these personal histories one may think it inevitable that, when so much heat has cooled down, extravagance will pass into enormity; and that what has begun wildly, will finish worse. Such has actually been the course of things in a few instances; nevertheless, no such gradual vitiation of its doctrine and of its practices has broadly marked the history of Wesleyan Methodism. On the contrary, like a liquor of good body, it has well passed through its season of fermentation, and has become brighter and clearer than at first, and better flavored. Yet even the most favorably disposed of by-standers might have been warranted in predicting a different course of things, when it was seen in how perilous a manner Wesley himself cherished and fomented, as well among preachers as people, tendencies which it should have been his part to repress. Not seldom it was he, rather than they, that set reason at defiance, and forgot sobriety.

But the issue, so much more favorable as it is than might have been anticipated, doubtless has its cause; and this cause becomes manifest when, in the exercise of a cool discrimination, we institute a comparison (once so unfairly drawn) between the "enthusiasm of Methodists and Papists." Let a point or two of such a comparison be considered. The contrast in each particular (however many might be adduced) would be found to turn upon one and the same ground of essential dissimilarity. Methodism, amid all its early wanderings, still kept its hold of that Gospel, which Romanism had never possessed, or had deeply perverted. Principal truths, proclaimed distinctly, and held always in a prominent place, exhibit a repellant force; they clear the atmosphere, and disinfect all things around them. Those irregularities and excesses of opinion and behavior which usually attend religious excitements, and which have their rise in human nature, do not perpetuate themselves, and do not tend toward a worse issue, until the system under which they have appeared has itself lost its vitality. Thus it has been with Romanism, and it is easy to put the finger upon the instances. It is not Romanism, or any other system of belief; but it is our human nature that is to be blamed for its tendency, under powerful excitements, to germinate a wild and bitter growth of enthusiastic and fanatical extravagance. But while under one system of belief this produce blossoms only for a day, and then withers and disappears, under another it gets possession of the soil, and overshadows every thing. A religious system may be such as that, beneath its influence, every weed of the human heart finds what it seeks; enthusiasm, wherever it touches, inflames, and fanaticism secretes poison, as a gangrene. But let the instances, or one or two such, be noted.

At the time when Bishop Lavington's book appeared—"The Enthusiasm of Methodists and Papists Compared," many features of the Wesleyan polity were of a kind that might seem to warrant the institution of this comparison; and they were such as would bear out the author's professed intention—to disparage the one, by linking it to the other. But a century almost has elapsed since that comparison was drawn; and in this course of time, while Romanism has retained, unaltered, each of its characteristics, Methodism has passed its season of effervescence, and has taken to itself a form, matured and defined, in which its *tendencies*, whatever they may be, have become fully developed; nor can we, unless by our own fault, misapprehend them. What, then, would be the issue of an equitably conducted comparison of Methodism and Romanism, as they now stand before us, both perfectly known, at this time, or, indeed, at any time subsequent to the decease of the Founder?

We take, then, that which has ever been a marked feature of all the religious fervors which Romanism has cherished and recognized—namely, ascetic extravagances This same feature attached also to Methodism, in its early stages, in a very decisive manner. We have here before us, therefore, a well-defined and prominent instance, characteristic alike of the two systems.

Wesley's constitutional tone, and the nerve and iron of his frame—mind and body, as well as his early training and his adopted opinions, all favored the growth of the ascetic temper, and impelled him to give way to that which is the constant leaning of severe and deep-felt religious fervor. The rigid abstinences and mortifications of his initial course had nearly cost him his life: and although the sharp lesson of prudence which he then learned, together with his native good sense, taught him to moderate these voluntary severities, he was, to the end, in feeling and opinion, the ascetic, and, under favoring circumstances, he would, no doubt, have indulged himself largely in these tastes. But in fact the hard conditions of itinerancy came in the place of fasts and scourges; for those may well think their shoulders excused from the discipline of the flagellum, who are used so freely as he did, to expose their bosoms to the brutality of mobs.

Many, perhaps most, of the lay preachers, either spontaneously, or in following the example of their master, trod the same rugged path, at first; and some of them carried to the most extreme point the experiment of what the body may endure, and yet survive, so long as the agonies of the soul are always keeping ahead of the miseries of the flesh. Often did the lay preacher, after a day of toil in the line of his business, as mason, baker, shoemaker, spend half the night in fervent devotional exercises, and, at five in the morning, come fasting to take his place in the pulpit, so utterly spent as that he was fain to prop his trembling frame by clinging to the rail, or throwing his weight upon the desk.

In these instances—and they were varied in every way—the unavoidable burden of toil, pain, and privation, incident to the preacher's course of life, was made to press cruelly both upon mind and body, by ascetic practices—not less extreme than those which have been so much boasted of by or on the behalf of the canonized of the Romish Calendar. Such was Methodism—such was *its* "enthusiasm" at its commencement. But have these errors gone on increasing to more extravagance; or have they rooted themselves in the system? It is far otherwise, and the reason why they have not done so is obvious; it is not that human nature does not always, and every where, favor the growth of religious extravagance, but because this tendency has met its proper counter-action.

To take the instance of the lay preacher whom we have just spoken of—fainting under a self-imposed burden; and let it be asked, what is the doctrine which, when excitement has come to his aid, he is passionately enforcing? It is that very doctrine which Rome has never understood, and in presence of which asceticism, whether murky or fanatical, disappears. This error need not be formally rebuked;—it was not rebuked, but rather invited, by Wesley and his preachers; yet, spite of the favor shown it, room was not found for it; austerities withered in their own lifelessness; and the phantom—righteousness by starvation—met its end in the most suitable mode, by atrophy, that is to say, by lack of doctrinal nourishment. The pardon of sin—free, full, immediate—a redemption obtained for man, and, by a sovereign act, granted to him without money and without price—children's privileges in the household of faith—these announcements, these first principles, giving life to the desponding spirit, and imparting the energy of hope to the moral nature, would not fail to supersede asceticism, or to disenchant it. The fascination of these frivolous severities is gone when once the heart has freely admitted the Gospel in its grandeur and simplicity. Methodism, then, or rather the Christianity it embodied, absorbed the errors incident to a season of extraordinary religious agitation. In this respect, if in no other, Methodism, since Bishop Lavington's time, has come right.

But how has it been with Romanism? There can be no need to swell a paragraph with many instances in contrast, where the broad facts are within every one's familiar knowledge.

The ancient asceticism sprang naturally, and without blame, out of those influences which bore upon the Church in the third century, and afterward. On various grounds the *early* solitary and ascetic life claims a respectful regard; but a very few years elapsed before a simple and blameless species of enthusiasm started off at a rapid pace, and continued advancing on the road of extravagance and fanaticism, in a manner that is revolting to think of. The athletes of one generation were quite eclipsed by their ambitious successors of the next: what had seemed much in one age, seemed little in the following: there was a constant progression, on this ground. Inartificial and mild austerities gave way to systematized enormities; and the spontaneous privations of an earlier time were brought under the iron tyranny of rules in a later time. The innocent and picturesque romance of the herb-eating recluse, in his cavern or sepulchre, was despised by the Christian fakir who, a few years afterward, took his place. So it was, whether in hermitages or in convents, that *a something more* was looked for from those who professed "Perfection." Fifty Pater-nosters in the twenty-four hours gave way to three hundred; three days' total abstinence from food, to ten days or a fortnight; a leathern girdle, to a spiked iron band. Frenzy drove out folly, and fraud took up the game when frenzy had spent itself, and could go no further. Summarily stated, is not this the history of asceticism as originated in the East long before the rise of Romanism, and as adopted, and carried forward, and canonized by it, and as it is now lauded and imitated by the Romish Church?

The reason of the progress and permanence of this tendency of human nature within that Church can not be misapprehended. Even if the Gospel had not, at a very early time, been dimmed and nearly lost, this same exuberance would, no doubt, have been developed; but the supervening, so early, of "another Gospel"—that is to say, of a Christianity interpreted according to the leaning of the human heart toward formalism and self-dependence, not only left asceticism unchecked, but gave it a direct encouragement. That doctrinal system which, as afterward defined and matured, is what we mean when we speak of the theology of Romanism, allotted a place to this species of enthusiasm, and fixed it immovably in that place. Sin, expiated by austerities, and merits won and laid up in store by courses of voluntary torture—these notions and these practices became indispensable parts of that one scheme of salvation which Rome propounded to the Western nations. On this ground of comparison, therefore, the "enthusiasm of Methodists" is seen in decisive contrast to the "enthusiasm of Papists."

There is, however, one other very significant point of comparison between the two systems, which claims to be regarded; and it deserves the more attention because a century ago the Methodistic enthusiasm seemed to fall little short of the Romish on this ground.

What we have in view is the encouragement given, at first, by Wesleyan Methodism, as also by Romanism, to whatever touches upon the supernatural and the miraculous. Wesley's most prominent infirmity was his wonder-loving credulity;—from the beginning to the end of his course this weakness ruled him. Few were the instances in which he exercised a due discrimination in listening to tales involving what was miraculous, or out of the order of nature. It is, in fact, mortifying to contemplate an instance like this, of a powerful mind bending like a straw in the wind before every whiff of the supernatural. It was only in the course of things that, with a leader thus minded, those who followed, and they being for the most part the uneducated, should be relators of wonders, and should eagerly listen to whatever brought with it this ever-coveted species of excitement. The personal histories of the Methodistic worthies, their autobiographies and obituaries, are rendered distasteful by the too copious admixture of incidents which try the faith of a cool-tempered reader. In truth, some of these narratives are much in the style of those "Lives of the Saints," which none but good Catholics should be allowed to look into.

And yet, notwithstanding the decisive start which was thus given to the supernatural at the commencement of Methodism, it presently fell back from its foremost position in the system, and came to be less and less sought after every year. At the present time, and so it has been for a long while past, no more encouragement is given to this morbid appetite by the regular Wesleyan ministers than is done by any other body of instructed religious teachers. Miracles are neither looked for, nor are they desired, in that communion. A Wesleyan superintendent would, in most cases, be forward to sift to the bran any wonderment story that he might find to be agitating his circuit; and the spread of a popular delusion within the body, involving an alleged miracle, would be regarded by Wesleyan principals only in the light of an ill-omened occurrence. Let the attempt be made to persuade the lower classes of that communion that a certain bust of Wesley may be seen, now and then, to wink, weep, and grin! Would such an attempt be authorized by "Conference?" and yet, a hundred years ago, "the enthusiasm of Methodists" might have been thought to be rapidly advancing toward such a stage of credulity as this; but this tendency has entirely ceased to show itself.

How is it with the analogous enthusiasm of Romanists? A hundred years ago the Church of Rome professed, as it always has done, the command of miraculous powers, and vaunted the healing efficacy of its holy relics. But was this a lingering remains only of the superstition and trickery of the dark ages? The enthusiasm of Methodists and Papists once ran abreast on this road: are the two abreast at this time? Intelligent Romanists can not complain of unfair treatment when notorious facts are adverted to, and which show that, notwithstanding the enlightenment of the times, the mass of the people in Roman Catholic countries have so been trained by their religious teachers, as that an eager and mindless credulity, if at all it be less now than it was a century ago, has received its check, not from the lips of the priest, imparting a sounder instruction, but from the spread of a licentious atheism, and contempt of all religion. Yet this is but one side of the facts that bear upon our immediate purpose; for, not only are the people, where not mad with atheism, as credulous as ever, but the chiefs of the Roman Catholic polity—popes, cardinals, and bishops, have not shown any shame (scarcely common discretion) while laboring to meet the popular folly, and to supply it with aliment. Is it not so? Whatever accident throws in the way of the clergy which may be made to serve as the nucleus of a wonderment agitation, has been eagerly caught at, and made the most of. Let it be acknowledged that any unusual fact, not easily accounted for, and over the circumstances of which the Church could hold control, would be welcomed by cardinals, bishops, priests —yes, and by educated laymen and nobles—as a providential favor of inestimable price! How can this be doubted when, by such authorities, at this moment, the nauseating and stale frauds of the darkest times are set a-going among the people as authentic wonders!

If, then, at this time a balance were to be struck, on this ground of comparison also, namely, the enthusiasm of credulity and of popular infatuation, as between Methodism and Romanism, the odds would be great. Nor are the reasons of the difference obscure, for they spring manifestly from the moral and theological qualities of the two systems.

Untutored minds, or any within which impressions and emotions are little controlled by reason, when powerfully wrought upon by religious excitements, become incapable of discrimination as to the objects that move them. Such minds, while thus agitated, are scarcely conscious of the difference between *sensuous imaginative* impressions, and such as are moral and spiritual. The imagination, the sensuous faculties, the moral sense, the spiritual consciousness, have all received an impulse together, and these continue for some time in a state of disorderly and commingled agitation. Hence it is that, in seasons of religious quickening among the uneducated classes, illusions, delusions, and rude excesses abound; and on this ground it is that self-government, wisdom, and tact are so much called for in those to whose zeal such movements, instrumentally, owe their origin.

Yet these disorders reach their end safely, and at an early time, if only the religious system—the scheme of doctrine wherewith they are connected—contains within itself the true principles of moral and spiritual renovation. Bring to bear upon minds religiously excited the proper objects of genuine moral and spiritual feeling, and there will take place, silently, yet speedily, what might be called a spontaneous process of discrimination—a separation of incongruous elements, and a disappearance, entire or partial, of the grosser matters, while the purer gain ascendency.

Visions, trances, semi-miracles, lose their value and become vapid inanities, where great truths hold their place. Let the human heart, quickened in its relationship to the spiritual world, meet, or come in presence of, its true objects; and it embraces them, assimilates itself with them; and then, whatsoever is spurious or unreal, loses its hold. When within the bosom the "day dawns," and "the day-star arises in the heart;" when (still we screen ourselves in scriptural terms) "Christ is formed in the heart;" when the soul becomes conscious that it has been made "partaker of the Divine nature," then, and as this illumination increases more and more "unto the perfect day," shadows disappear, the gliding forms of superstition melt away, the fatuous glare of a sensuous fancy loses its charm, and the soul rejoices in its tranquil consciousness of living under the light and warmth of heaven. This is the history of the early disappearance of spurious miracles within every communion that has held to the Gospel.

But the Romish Church has not retained any such knowledge of first truths; or it has covered them with perversions. Therefore it is that, after stretching charity and candor to the utmost, we must still, in speaking of this system, plainly call it "The Romish *superstition*:" therefore it is that we can not withhold from it the designation "idolatrous:" therefore it is that whatever has the most revolted reason, and whatever has combined absurdity, frivolity, and profanity, has found within it a shelter, and a market too. It is not possible otherwise than thus to speak of Romanism, such as we find it even now, wherever it has been undisturbed by correcting influences from without.

Romanism has at no period of its history dispelled the terrors of superstition from the minds of men, or allayed the grim forebodings of an evil conscience: how should it do so, with its purgatory, and its promise of release thence at a price which legatees may refuse to pay? It has not, on the other hand, chastised the wantonness of luxurious and debauched imaginations: how should it do so, in presence of its gaudy array of divinities—male and female? Yet it is not Romanism, but it is our common human nature that, ever and anew, and with inexhaustible fecundity, generates, on the one hand, the creatures of superstition, and on the other those of spiritual voluptuousness. But Romanism, in having retained no one main principle of Christianity in its simple integrity, is not seen to exert, among these spurious creations, any corrective or repellant force. It has never righted itself where once it has gone wrong; it has cut off from itself no excrescence that has appeared upon its surface. Enthusiasm and fanaticism are its own moods. Delusion has settled down upon it as the thick atmosphere of its climate.

WESLEY AS FOUNDER OF AN INSTITUTE.

The ingredients, the spirit, and the tendencies of Methodism, as an Institute, will claim to be considered apart from our immediate purpose, which relates only to Wesley's personal qualities and character.

It was under the guidance of the broadest principle, as well as at the impulse of the most expansive charity, that he had gone forth upon the field of the world as an evangelist preaching repentance. On the broadest principle also it was that he laid the foundation of the institution which was destined to conserve the fruits of his preaching; and if, on such a foundation as this, he had raised a superstructure more free than it was from admixtures of perishable matter—if he had somewhat better understood human nature, and had on some points less misunderstood Christianity, this INSTITUTE, which was so ably administered for forty years by himself, could scarcely have failed to secure for itself a paramount position in England, and it might have planted itself territorially upon the ruins of a then dilapidated and almost deserted Church. This was not to be.

If the Episcopal Church—and many of its enlightened adherents have not hesitated to acknowledge this—owes to Methodism, in great part, the modern revival of its energies, so (may we not say it?) does it owe to Wesley's misapprehensions of certain principles, its own survivance through that critical period, in which there was not enough of life or force left in it to make head against what Methodism might have been, if Wesley's compass of mind, as a legislator, had been of as ample dimensions as his heart. This INSTITUTE was not, and *is* not, a CHURCH, nor did he himself so designate it: the "Society" was the product of that peculiar view which he was led to take of human nature, and of the social system, from his position as an EVANGELIST, or preacher of repentance. The Wesleyan Societies were constituted for the one purpose of gathering and of retaining converts, and they had little adaptation to the purpose of Christianizing the social mass, otherwise than by vehement assaults upon the consciences of those who could by any means be got together to hear sermons.

The Wesleyan Institute grew out of the work of conversion; and it comprehended little that would not press itself, as urgently needed, upon the notice of the itinerant evangelist, who, in revisiting the scene of his first successes, would not wish to find all that he had done scattered and lost. For securing these temporary ends, and for retaining its conquests, and for spreading them over the enemy's territory by incessant sallies, as from evangelic forts, and for perpetuating the same machinery of aggression, the Wesleyan Institute has shown itself a masterpiece of social organization.

In dealing with whatever may belong to a process of organization, or of marshaling a host for a single initiatory purpose, Wesley has never been surpassed by civil, military, or ecclesiastical mechanists. Nor has he been surpassed by any general, statesman, or churchman, in administrative skill;—that is to say, in the faculty of adapting himself, and his movements, to the circumstances of the moment, without compromise of his authority or personal dignity, and with the least possible damage done to his theoretic consistency. Thus far Wesley's praise is entire; and his polity—the polity of perpetual augmentation—went on spreading itself on both sides the Atlantic, from the commencement to the very close of his ministerial life. And during this long period of more than half a century, many very critical conjunctures were encountered by him, and were passed through successfully. The thorough simplicity and integrity of his purpose, as chief of the body, so well corresponded with the elementary simplicity of his views as an institutor, that what had been devised at the first so skillfully, was to the last managed and governed not less ably.

But to found a Church is another sort of work; and it would demand powers of mind, and qualifications, intellectual and moral, quite of another order. Wesley said of himself—truly, not boastfully—and his friends were accustomed to say of him, that, amidst the accumulation of his labors, he was "never in a hurry." A perfect management of his time, his untiring energy, and his self-command, made it easy for him to accomplish tranquilly a vast and various daily task. But if never in a hurry, neither was he ever in repose. Movement, onward and incessant, was the law of his existence; but that repose which, in great minds, or in better constructed minds, is the preparation for renewed action, implies, not merely a *cessation* of movement, but a *retrocession*—a stepping back, and a looking around. Wesley's course gives no indications of any such reduplication as this. As there was nothing of the philosophic quality in his mind, so was there little of the ruminative. Therefore it is, that, while unmatched in whatever has *one intention*, he could have held but a low place as author of a system which should combine complicated impulses, and which should show a harmonious interaction of them.

The work of "Conversion," how genuine soever it may be in any instance, or however unexceptionable in the mode in which it takes place, does not develop the compass and richness of Christianized human nature; nor is it likely that those who, as itinerant evangelists, are concerned only, or chiefly, with the work of conversion, should be much conversant with, or should possess a correct knowledge of the human heart, in the depth and variety of its range of emotions. Then this same limitation of view, which was consequent upon the speciality of the evangelists' function, as awakener of the conscience, brings with it a narrowed apprehension of the Christian system; and the Bible comes to be read and used, mainly, or exclusively, as the preacher's instrument for effecting repentance. But how narrow a view is this!

Wesley made it his boast (the word is not here used in any sinister sense) that Methodism was more Catholic than any other system of Christian combination that the world had ever seen. This was true; for he required from converts no assent to a Creed;—he stipulated for no surrender of religious principles or notions. An expressed concern for the "salvation of the soul" was the one and only condition of entrance, and a *consistent* adherence to such a profession was the only "term of Communion." This was good; but then this largely-worded invitation to enter the Society, was an invitation to walk upon a path as narrow as a sheep track; and not narrow in the sense in which the "narrow way" is narrow. Methodism was straitened by the incomprehensiveness of the aspect under which it took its view of human nature, and of the social economy, and of the Gospel as adapted to both. It was further straitened, too, by some ill-imagined peculiarites of attire and of behavior, which Wesley afterward regretted he had not made ten times more peculiar and more stringent than he did. Strange, or strange until we have looked into the structure of his mind, must it seem that he should have had no consciousness of the deep-seated incongruity of this Catholic invitation, which was to lead to the wearing a straight-cut coat, or a close bonnet without trimmings! Wesley did not perceive that, while his good sense forbade his imposing upon his people the style and costume of Quakerism in all its rigidness, and while thus he he held off from his Institute some extremes of absurdity, those peculiarities upon which he *did* insist, and which in themselves were recommended by no valid reasons, either moral or religious, were greater inconsistencies in *Methodism* than the like, or than much more, would be in Quakerism, which, having neither a proselyting nor a Catholic intention, might be as singular as it pleased, at no greater cost than that of burlesquing solemn truths in the view of the world.

But thus it is, and ever has been, that those who are sent by Heaven to bring about great and necessary movements, which, however, are, after a time, either to subside, or to fall into a larger orbit, are left to the shortsightedness of their own minds in fastening upon their work some appendage (perhaps unobserved) which, after a cycle of revolutions, must secure the accomplishment of Heaven's own purpose—the stopping of that movement. Religious singularities are Heaven's brand, imprinted by the unknowing hand of man, upon whatever is destined to last its season, and to disappear. Put a pin through the wick of a candle at so many inches down as shall insure its going out just before sunrise:—has not this been done, ordinarily, by the founders of sects? The error of attaching a high and religious importance to matters of costume, or of conventional behavior, or of worship, has drawn with it, as an inevitable consequence, the superannuation, at length, of the scheme or system thus unadvisedly distinguished. The instances will occur to every reader. Wesleyan Methodism has, however, in it so much of wick and wax, that it may probably outburn what otherwise would have determined its date.

In delivering one's self fairly into Wesley's Methodism, such as it was sixty years ago, and in making one's self, for a time, one with it, an involuntary feeling arises that there is something in the system, as a social mechanism, that is out of harmony with human nature; or, that there must be at the bottom of it some misunderstanding of Christianity. Nevertheless, when the principal elements of this Institute are singly brought under review, each may fairly claim for itself some warranty of scriptural proofs. It must be on the ground, either of a semi-infidelity (if indeed there can be a halving of that which, where it comes at all, comes entire) that any one of these principal elements of the Wesleyan system, considered by itself, can be excepted against or rejected. Still there is a dissatisfaction remaining with us, standing as spectators in the midst of this economy; and in proportion as the spectator's own religious principles are fixed and deep, this uneasiness will be felt in a more lively manner. It is true that no religious man could sit by the side of Wesley's pulpit, as in the seat of the scorner, and say, "fine sample of enthusiasm this!" nor would he be willing to put himself under guidance, such as that of Southey, who would divert this unquiet feeling by treating the perplexing case of Methodism as a something which is at once admirable and contemptible, genuine and spurious, substantial and unreal, and which is "from Heaven," and "of men." No such style of alternate approval and banter can the serious-hearted looker-on and listener adopt for himself. Instead of relieving any perplexity, such a mode not merely renders this particular case the more perplexing, but it breeds confusion in our own minds, and it tends to bring into peril our best convictions. It may be affirmed that whoever has turned on the heel, jeeringly, as he has left a Methodist meeting-house, is likely to experience a death-like qualm when he looks Christianity itself in the face.

But how then are we fairly to put at rest that disquiet which the spectacle of Wesley's own Wesleyanism generates? To some extent relief may be obtained by looking to the evidence, presenting itself on every side, in proof that this leading spirit—the soul and life of the system—was not so gifted with the reflective faculties as that a comprehensive grasp of human nature could have been possible to him. His earnestness, therefore, and his thorough persuasion of the greatness and the infinite moment of the work he had in hand, and his peremptory mode of thinking, would lead him to drive his theory, with a reckless impetuosity, over the inclosure of human affection. He sees, he hears, he comprehends nothing exterior to the one object of his errand in a world of ungodly men. Wesleyanism did indeed effect a recovery from sin and ruin for myriads of human beings, and in its triumphant course of benficence it "led captivity captive:" nevertheless, in this riding forth to conquer, there was some destruction made of what is genuine and precious.

But there is a view of Wesley's ministry, and of his COMMISSION, which may consist with a serious belief, and with a broad view of the Christian system. If we are willing to adhere to the hypothesis that Methodism, as a heaven-directed movement, had a special purpose, which it was to achieve, and that a season—a term of years—was marked out for it, then it must follow that those features in this system which harmonize imperfectly with Christianity, receive an explanation, if not a justification; for it is implied in the very terms that what is destined to effect a particular purpose, and which is to pass away after a time, will not wear a universal aspect, and that it does not perfectly coincide with that which is enduring and unchanging.

Not merely does Christianity recognize the social sentiments, but it lays its hand upon them, enjoining social exercises of devotion, and it forbids its professors to "forsake the assembling of themselves together." Nevertheless, the *congregational* aspect of the Gospel is not, as it is with Methodism, the prominent characteristic of the system; it was not more than a single element of apostolic Christianity; never was it thought of as the whole of it. But Methodism congregated men upon centres, as the whirlwind brings things into vortices; and it was also a sort of whirlwind-agitation which kept them in company; and even after tempestuous agitations had passed away, it was a vehement cohesion, rather than a genuine cementing of the social mass, that was aimed at, and actually effected. Methodism seemed scarcely to be cognizant of any thing in the divine life that could not be talked of, and proclaimed aloud: the depths of the human heart, when the heart itself has come into correspondence with the Infinite Attributes, were beyond its line. It might indeed take note of things tossed up from the depth of the soul, by the surges of passion; but itself kept on the surface: Methodism did not venture into the recesses of the soul further than where the tongue might be its guide.

And then, if considered as a development of the social principle, Methodism carried itself somewhat shallowly; and thus showed itself to be a system destined for an epoch only. Wesley, apostolic man as he was, and having a heart and a countenance warm and bright as the sun with genuine benevolence—an unselfish, loving soul, a soul large enough to fill a seraph's bosom, himself knew nothing of the domestic affections. He had never learned human nature on that bright side of it, or in that effective way in which it is learned when the yearnings of domestic love melt souls into one, so thoroughly casting down the partitions of selfish thought as that each individual of the home circle exists as if with a multiplied existence.

Let a father, possessing a father's heart, be told, in the way of preparation for such a visit, that he is about to inspect a school that was devised, and that is governed by one of the most benevolent of the human race; and then let him be taken to spend a four-and-twenty hours at Kingswood! This father's rising indignation at the iron rules and the rigid absurdities which he there witnesses, may prompt him to violate all charity toward the founder, while he spends his feelings in intemperate vituperation. But a word of explication may calm this emotion. Wesley knew no more what a child is, what a boy is, what human nature is, than he might have known if he himself had been, and had never been any thing else than a varnished anatomy, lodging an intellect in a corner of its cranium.

If one thinks of Torquemada, presiding at the burning of heretics, and remembers that this man called himself, and was called, a minister of Him whose history we have in the Gospels, the prodigious incompatibility of the two ideas is such as quite staggers the mind. But let us not be too hasty in thinking of the Inquisitor as a fiend: perhaps he was such; but perhaps only a theorist, and a theorist is sometimes a creature as much to be dreaded as a demon: this man had no consciousness on the side of human sympathies: in his view it was logically certain that mercy toward heretics themselves, and toward the world, demanded that he should burn them, and nothing in his bosom rose up to contradict this logic.

Wesley's soul glowed with the truest philanthropy; but he, too was a theorizer. It was in love that he struck the heart with the sledge-hammer of his theological logic; and he brake the flint in pieces; but he did not well understand what this same flint incloses. As he dealt with the boys at Kingswood, so with adults in his Societies, that is to say, with an iron intensity of purpose; and human affections, in passing under his hand, were much damaged, or were forced into a half their volume.

Methodism, such as Wesley made it, was girt about too tightly, and it has, in fact, necessarily assimilated itself since to those principles of the social system which theoretic men may disturb for a time, but can not abrogate; yet it too much retains its characteristic as the Christianity of the preacher, and of the heated chapel; and it is therefore deficient in those elements that might entitle it to be spoken of as a CHURCH. How far such needed modifications of Wesleyan Methodism may already have had place, we are not here called upon to inquire; much less to hazard a conjecture as to the probable extent of those changes which time and experience may still suggest. All that we have now to do with is the fact, related as it is to the Founder's personal character, that his Institute, such as he left it, and whatever praise it may be entitled to, was a dispensation for a season, springing from those qualities in his own mind and moral nature which fitted him to accomplish the great work of his day.

No mind and heart that has ever attracted the eyes of mankind, is more thoroughly transparent than Wesley's. How is it then that, like Loyola's, it can have furnished a problem? To read his journals and letters, or his sermons and polemical writings, is to come into the presence, not merely of a master spirit, and of one who stands unmatched in energy, constancy, consistency; but of a man who was too guileless to think of saving himself from the imputation of inconsistency, and far too fervently intent upon an object beyond himself to entertain any care about that semblance of egotism, or of ambition, which the pursuit of that object could not fail to impart to his mode of acting—acting as he did as the founder, proprietor, and administrator of a society so widely extended. Why is it, then, that, among those who would wish to be thought his apologists (though not his disciples) he has been so spoken of as if some mystery overshadowed that bright head, or as if that countenance, beaming, as it does, with childlike love, was the covering of an abyss? It has so happened because the character and the course of Wesley, as of his colleagues, involves a far deeper problem than that of the individual dispositions and motives of the man.

The Gospel—understood and bowed to in all its depth and height of meaning—furnishes the only possible means of clearing up the perplexities that attach to the motives and conduct of those who from it have received their impulse, and who have walked according to its rule. Wesley perplexes those only who, if they would confess the fact, are still more perplexed by Christianity itself.

One must believe that many of that class of persons whom a writer like Southey represents, and to whose tastes and views he evidently labored to adapt himself, must be conscious that the explications he advances in attempting to unravel Methodism, are as futile in philosophy, as they are false in theology; and, in fact, that most of his solutions of the "phenomena" are nothing better than frigid absurdities. That they were so, was strongly felt by Coleridge, whose far deeper acquaintance with spiritual principles, and whose vastly more acute intelligence, prompted him to protest, in many instances, against his friend's vapid arrogance. And yet even he turned away from Methodism, as an enigma he had not solved in any manner that was satisfactory to himself. In frequent instances, his *first* annotation upon the "Life of Wesley," was the prompting of a generous sympathy, and that of indignant contempt which the flippancy of Southey provokes. But in his *second*, or the note upon his own note, he gropes among the darkness of psychology for what may serve to bring about an apparent agreement between himself and his friend. But that which these distinguished men undertook to do—the one frivolously, the other profoundly—was, to give a reason for the bright greenness and the gay blossoms of May, ignoring the sun.

Those, on the other side, who, with a charitable intention, would labor to explain to the class of persons whom Southey and Coleridge represent, how and why it is that they so misunderstand the persons and events of Methodism, show, in making this attempt, that they have themselves, for the moment, lost sight of their own ground. Human nature, with its beautiful adaptations of intellectual and moral forces, is explicable always *within itself*, even in its lapsed condition;—that is to say, the relation of its parts, one to the other, or to the whole mechanism, may always be shown and demonstrated. It becomes inexplicable only when it is thought of in its present broken or disordered relationship to a higher economy —the economy of Heaven. Seen on this side, an ominous darkness hangs over the human system upon which no earth-born philosophy has ever, or can ever, shed one ray of light.

So far as Christianity has christianized the social system, and so far as it acts as a good influence upon individual men, it is easily explicable; and it is so even if the office of professed candor be undertaken by a Gibbon. But the Gospel itself is a truth of the upper world, and in its very substance it wholly eludes the perceptions of those who have not bowed to it. From every other ethical or religious system Christianity differs absolutely —in its first principles, in its superstructure, in its tone, in its tendency, and in its issue. Individually we either deeply feel this dissimilarity; or, if we do not feel it, we labor to extenuate whatever seems to declare it.

Thus it is that Wesley and Methodism so sorely try the ingenuity of those who, if they knew how, would gladly be just toward him, and his communion—saving their "philosophy." This will never be done; nor can it be well to proffer aid toward effecting that which, in the nature of things, is impracticable.

If he had moved in a private sphere, that for instance

of a parish priest, Wesley's flock would not have known that their minister had so much as one fault; and the admiration and love of his intimate friends would only have been a more emphatic expression of the feeling which would have pervaded the little world whose happiness it was to live within sight and hearing of him. His was a personal virtue that was not merely unblemished, for it was luminously bright. His countenance shone with goodness, truth, purity, benevolence: a sanctity belonged to him, which those near him felt, as if it were a power with which the atmosphere was fraught. If we may imagine—what could not have been—so much energy pent within a narrow circle, how would it have filled that space with abounding labors of evangelic charity! It might indeed have happened that some quiet and discriminating parishioner would sometimes whisper so much fault-finding as this—"Our dear Rector is too apt to think other people as honest as himself; he trusts himself too easily to any who tell him a fair tale; and he is too fond of wonders." Another, perhaps, would have asked leave to think awhile before he should assent to some points of the minister's theology. With some such slender abatements as these, Wesley's praise would have been warmly uttered by every tongue in his neighborhood. Friends would have regarded him with a deep reverential love: foes—he could have had none.

It is a sort of axiom with opticians, that, whereas natural objects (the works of God) will bear enlargement to any extent, and excite always the more wonder in proportion as you apply to them, in the solar microscope, a higher and a higher power; it is otherwise with the products of human skill, which, the more they are magnified, the less are they to be admired. This illustration may aid us a little in the present instance. John Wesley—as to his intellect, and as to his views—had his faults and his infirmities: grant it; but we should not have known so much as this if what was individual in him had not repeated itself, and become a feature of a community that now fills half the world. When thus magnified, each ruggedness or want of finish on the surface of his mind, who can not see it? as to this or that misadjustment of the intellectual mechanism, who may not point the finger at it? These things were of the man; but his virtues were God's own work, perfectly finished—and how well they look, although the bright spectrum has spread itself out to a diameter as wide as the empire upon which the sun never sets! It was Wesley's virtues and piety that gave form and tone to his teaching, and his teaching has embodied itself in the Christianlike behavior of tens of thousands of his people, on both sides the Atlantic.

CHARLES WESLEY.

As his brother's friend, adviser, and colleague, Charles exerted an influence that was almost always corrective and salutary. Less credulous than John, less sudden in his apprehensions, and proportionately more discriminative and cautious, his mind reached its maturity earlier; and this maturity was itself of a riper sort. But then his prejudices, as a Churchman, were less flexible; his reserve and modesty were greater, and unless the superior force of his brother's character had carried him forward beyond his own limit, he must soon have withdrawn himself from public life; and then he would have been known only, if at all, as the author of some sacred poetry of rare excellence. But these very hymns, if the writer had not been connected with Methodism, would have shown a very different phase; for while the depth and richness of them are the writer's, the epigrammatic intensity, and the *pressure* which marks them, belong to Methodism. They may be regarded as the representatives of a modern devotional style which has prevailed quite as much beyond the boundaries of the Wesleyan community, as within it. Charles Wesley's hymns on the one hand, and those of Toplady, Cowper, and Newton on the other, mark that great change in religious sentiment which distinguishes the times of Methodism from the staid nonconforming era of Watts and Doddridge.

Better constituted than his brother for domestic enjoyment, Charles had a happy home, where the gentle affections of a gentle nature found room to expand; and it was thus that he became qualified to shed into the Methodistic world something of a redeeming influence, which John could never have imparted. Charles Wesley's mind was an ameliorating ingredient, serving to call forth and cherish those kindlier emotions with which a religion of preaching—a religion of public services, so much needs to be attempered. His personal ministrations, no doubt had this tendency in some degree; but it was by his sacred lyre, still more than as a preacher, that he tamed the rudeness of untaught minds, and gained a listening ear for the harmonies of heaven, and of earth, too, among such.

Ought not then the disposing hand of God to be acknowledged in this instance, remarkable as it is, that, when myriads of uncultured and lately ferocious spirits were to be reclaimed, a gift of song, such as that of Charles Wesley, should have been conferred upon one of the company employed in this work? To estimate duly what was the influence of this rare gift, and to measure its importance, one should be able to recall scenes and times gone by, when Methodism was much nearer to its source than now it is, and when "Hymn 147, page 145," announced by the preacher in a tone curiously blending the perfunctory with the animated,

"O Love Divine, how sweet thou art!"

woke up all ears, eyes, hearts, and voices, in a crowded chapel. It was, indeed, a spectacle worth the gazing upon! It was a service well to have joined in (once and again) when words of such power, flowing in rich cadence, and conveying, with an intensity of emphasis, the loftiest, the deepest, and the most tender emotions of the divine life, were taken up feelingly by an assembly of men and women, to whom, very lately, whatever was not of the "earth—earthy," had neither charm nor meaning.

Rugged forms were those that filled the benches on the one hand; nor were they the fairest in the world that were ranged on the other; but there was soul in the erect posture when the congregation rose to sing, as well as in the glistening eye; and it was a cordial animation that gave compass to the voices of these, the ransomed of Methodism. Perhaps it was little more than a particle of meaning that some gathered from the hymn. But to the hearts of many, its deepest sense—the poet's own sense of the words—was quite intelligible, and was intimately relished. Who could doubt it, that had an eye to read the heart in the beaming countenances around him? Thus it was that Charles Wesley, richly gifted as he was with graces, genius, and talents, drew souls—thousands of souls—in his wake, from Sunday to Sunday, and he so drew them onward from earth to heaven by the charm of sacred verse!

It may be affirmed that there is no principal element of Christianity, no main article of belief, as professed by Protestant Churches—that there is no moral or ethical sentiment, peculiarly characteristic of the Gospel—no height or depth of feeling, proper to the spiritual life, that does not find itself emphatically, and pointedly, and clearly conveyed in some stanza of Charles Wesley's hymns. These compositions embody the theory, and the practice, and the theopathy of the Christian system; and they do so with extremely little admixture of what ought to be regarded as questionable, or that is not warranted by some evidence of Scripture. What we have here before us is a metrical liturgy; and by the combination of rhythm, rhyme, and music, it effectively secures to the mass of worshipers much of the benefit of liturgical worship. Such a liturgy, thus performed by animated congregations, melted itself into the very soul of the people, and was perhaps that part of the hour's service which, more than any other, produced what, to borrow a phrase, we might call *digestive assimilation.* It would secure this, its beneficial effect, in moulding the spirits of the people, by its iteration, by its emphatic style, and by aid of the pleasurable excitements of music.

Charles Wesley's part in the great results of Methodism has not, perhaps, been duly appreciated. Let us then look to, and analyze the facts—if not as they may now be any where observed, yet as they may be remembered by some of us.

In the magnificent amphitheatre of Gwenap, and at other spots in the mining districts of Cornwall, the Wesleys had drawn around them thousands of the *καταχθόνιοι* of that wild region. What was the intellectual and moral condition of these dwellers in the heart of the earth, before the coming of Methodism among them? Is the Episcopal Church prepared to make her boast of the mining population of Cornwall, such as it had become under her care? But Methodism snatched its hundreds and its thousands from out of this heathen mass; and very soon its unsightly preaching houses speckled the dreary landscape on all the hill sides of the country where there were mines, and in each of the fishing towns along the two coasts. These structures, or chapels as they came to be called, were, for the most part, well filled on Sunday, with a people decently attired, more neat and clean than those of the same rank assembling in other places of worship; quite orderly in their behavior, and among whom, very rarely, any audible disturbance of the solemnities of worship occurred, beyond the emphatic "Amen! Amen!" which served so well to carry the minister forward, from period to period of his extemporaneous prayer.

In all these chapels, in their turn, and in many of them scattered over the country, often the officiating minister was a local preacher of the district; and meagre, too often, was then the preacher's part of the service! The sermon was indeed a heavy trial of patience and candor to the casual visitor; the prayer was a much heavier trial! But at the worst, the soul of Charles Wesley—lofty, tender, pure, intense, was there present in the hymn; and, like a summer's shower in a time of drought, was this hymn sung, on such occasions, and in such places! The preacher could at least read it; and the hymn book was in almost every hand; and enough of the soul of music was among the people to secure for the congregation the benefits of a liturgical worship, animating, elevating, instructive, unexceptionable; and the people were sufficiently alive to Christian truth to qualify them for taking part in such devotional services with pleasure and advantage.

If that breadth of country be thought of, over which Methodism had then stretched itself, far beyond the proportion of its itinerant ministry, and which it could occupy in no other way than by its system of irregular and uninstructed ministrations, then it must be to Charles Wesley that we should assign the place of honor, as the every where present soul of Methodism. It is true that the Hymn Book is his in part only; but then his part in it is the vital part.

In any system of public worship the *constant* element—that is to say, the *liturgical*—will always exercise a great influence over the variable part—the extemporaneous—in giving it tone and direction, and in preserving a doctrinal consistency in the pulpit teaching. It will be so at least wherever this liturgical ingredient warmly engages the feelings of the people, and where it is performed with untiring animation. In communities that have laid aside liturgies, in every other sense, the HYMN BOOK which they use, especially if psalmody be a favored part of public worship, rules, as well the preacher as the people, to a greater extent than is often thought of, or than would perhaps be acknowledged. The Hymn Book, to such bodies comes in the stead of Creed, Articles, Canons, and presiding power. Isaac Watts is still held in grateful remembrance by those who use his devotional compositions: but there may be room to think that, in the course of these hundred and fifty years past, he has rendered services to them, in behalf of which they have not yet blessed his memory, and, perhaps, may never do so.

Benefits the most substantial are often those of which the least notice is taken; and silent blessings are wont to be silently received. Thus putting out of view their adaptation to public worship, "hymns, and psalms, and spiritual songs"—a species of literature in which the English language is more rich than any other—administer comfort, excitement, and instruction to an extent, and in a degree, which never can be calculated. The robust in body and mind, the earthly, the frivolous, and the sordid, know nothing of that solace, of that renovation of the heart which sacred poetry is every day conveying to the spirits of tens of thousands around them. It is not merely when sickness has slackened the cords of life, but also when the heart has become benumbed by the toils and cares of a common day, and when even the understanding is rendered obtuse, it is then that the hymn and psalm, at a late hour, restore the spirit, and give renewed clearness, by giving consistency to the distracted intellect, and so lead the soul back to its place of rest in the presence of "things unseen and eternal." Among those to whose compositions millions of souls owe inestimable benefits, in this manner, Charles Wesley stands, if not foremost, yet inferior to few.

WHITEFIELD.

Whitefield must be allowed to occupy the luminous centre upon the field of Methodism. Besides his personal claim to this distinction, which we think is clear, there is a ground on which those who would award this position rather to Wesley, might be content to relinquish it in his behalf; for, if it be true that *his* ministerial course furnishes peculiar evidence of the reality of the Gospel which he preached, and of the presence of Him who "worketh all in all"—if it be true that Wesley's glory was, as one may say, an effulgence of Christianity itself, the same may more emphatically be affirmed as to Whitefield, whose natural endowments were fewer, and whose success as a preacher of the Gospel was not less, perhaps greater.

Whitefield's natural powers and gifts were indeed extraordinary; nor is it known that the same have been possessed in a higher degree by any one: but then they were of that sort which, if they had been exercised in any secular line, could have won for him nothing more than an ephemeral reputation, and its immediate worldly recompense. His name as an orator might have found a place, casually, on some page of the annals of his time; but no faculty did he possess which could have given him a permanent renown among the distinguished men of his age, whether in the senate, at the bar, or as a popular leader: much less could he have secured a lasting fame in the walks of literature or science. But Wesley might no doubt have earned a great reputation either in the senate or at the bar.

The endeavors that have been made to give a sufficient reason for Whitefield's power over the thousands that crowded around him—while the true and the principal reason is rejected, or is put out of view—are quite futile. His natural gifts, although extraordinary, were yet limited in their range, and were employed upon subjects that move the human mind from its very depths, when they move it at all; but they so move it only when an energy works with the word which no orator, however gifted, can command, and which, again and again, the most perfect pulpit oratory has wholly failed to engage on its side.

If Whitefield had possessed any one of those higher intellectual endowments which might be named as an adequate cause of the unexampled effects produced by his preaching, we of this age should be reading his sermons with delight; but in fact they have sunk out of all recollection—they are never read. Neither the imaginative nor ratiocinative power did he possess in more than an ordinary degree; and as to the fascinations of his voice and manner, a five years' popularity, if resting on *this* basis alone, would have been its utmost term. All instances that might properly be adduced in such a case show this. But Whitefield, with the Gospel message, and that only on his lips, drew thousands around him, go where he might; and he did so from the first year of his ministerial career to the very last.

Powerful causes, wherever they are at work, give evidence of their presence in the continuous uniformity of the effects that follow; and it was a wonderful uniformity of results that attended Whitefield's preaching throughout the many years of his ministry, and under every variety of circumstance. This preacher, occupying as he does a very narrow walk upon the field of thought, yet displays there a mysterious power. Inartificial as to the structure of his discourses, all minds around him, whether the rudest or the most highly cultured, confess him to be the minister of God toward them. He holds MAN, as if in the abstract, or as if whatever is not common to all men were forgotten. The most extreme diversities, intellectual and moral—differences of rank, culture, national modes of thought, all gave way, and ceased to be thought of: distinctions were swept from the ground where he took his position. At the first opening of his lips, and as the rich harmony of his voice spread its undulations over the expanse of human faces, and at the instant when the sparkle of his bright eye caught every other eye, human nature, in a manner, dropped its individuality, and presented itself in its very elements to be moulded anew. Whitefield, although singularly gifted with a perception of the varieties of character, yet spoke as if he could know nothing of the thousands before him but their immortality and their misery; and so it was that these thousands listened to him.

No preacher, whose history is on record, has trod so wide a field as did Whitefield; or has retrod it so often, or has repeated himself so much, or has carried so far the experiment of exhausting himself, and of spending his popularity, if it could have been spent; but it never was spent. Within the compass of a few weeks he might have been heard addressing the negroes of the Bermuda islands, adapting himself to their infantile understandings, and to their debauched hearts; and then, at Chelsea, with the aristocracy of rank and wit before him, approving himself to listeners such as the lords Bolingbroke and Chesterfield. Whitefield might as easily have produced a Hamlet or a Paradise Lost, as have excogitated a sermon which, as a composition—a product of thought, would have tempted men like these to hear him a second time; and as to his faculty and graces as a speaker, his elocution and action, a second performance would have contented them. But in fact Bolingbroke, and many of his class, thought not the hour long, time after time, while, with much sameness of *material* and of language, he spoke of eternity, and of salvation in Christ.

The same subjects, in the same phrases, held the ear of men in the same manner from the date of his first sermon in St. Mary de Crypt to that of his last in New England—a period of thirty-four years. The crowds that thronged the churches of Bristol or London, at his first appearance, were constituted, for the most part, of the constant frequenters of churches and meeting-houses, and they were persons upon whose thickened organs of hearing sermons enough had beat, from Sunday to Sunday, from their youth up. But then from these congregations he passed to Moorfields and Kennington Common, and there found the reckless savages of civilization:—thence he went to Kingswood, where he encountered a ferocity, wild, robust, and unused to simulate civility. From Kingswood one might follow him across the Tweed, and find him preaching the same Gospel in the midst of a people too fully instructed "in the right ways of the Lord" to have any thing to learn, one might suppose, from this raw preacher, who knew nothing of the "Solemn League and Covenant," and who had received episcopal ordination! Yet so it was that alike noble wits, Kingswood colliers, and seceding congregations, broke down before Whitefield! Floods of tears moistened cheeks, rough and smooth; and sighs, suppressed or loudly uttered, gave evidence that human nature is one and the same when it comes in presence of truths which bear upon the guilty and the immortal, without distinction.

The preacher of these truths, wielding a power manifestly extraneous to his natural gifts, thought little or nothing of those means of effect to which so much importance has been attached by a certain class of writers. Or if he had at the first thought of them, experience would have taught him that they might be wholly disregarded Whitefield's journals show indeed that he had a feeling of the grand and beautiful in nature; but he found himself, and his message, and his hearers, the same, whether his voice wakened the echoes of a primeval forest in the New World, or resounded from the near walls of an English meeting-house. Those whose sense of the picturesque is more vivid than their moral consciousness, have labored with their materials in endeavoring to give a reason for Whitefield's power as a preacher. The magnificence of the silvan theatre in which the gathering of the people took place, the stillness, in such a place, of a congregation of ten or fifteen thousand persons—the recollected remoteness of cities—the ardors of the climate—the interludes, not infrequent, of the mighty thunderings and lightnings of that climate, and the forethought of the many perils to be encountered in returning from the wilderness;—shall not the preacher avail himself well of these various and powerful excitements? He does so scarcely at all; he is unconscious of the place, the scene, the time; and so are his hearers, for eternity is opened up before him, and them.

The basis of Whitefield's mind, or that power upon which his singular gifts as a speaker worked, was the CONCEPTIVE FACULTY, as related to those objects that are purely spiritual, both abstract and concrete; and with him this faculty had a compass, a depth, and an intensity of sensitiveness, never perhaps equaled. So it was that while he spoke the visible world seemed to melt away into thin mist, and the world eternal—the real world—to come out from among shadows, and stand forth in awful demonstration. This faculty in him was by no means that of the poet, or the painter, and which is sensuous in its material; for if it had been of this sort he would have left us monuments of his genius—such as a Divina Commedia, or a Paradise Lost, or a series of Michael Angelo cartoons. Nor was it a sensuous perception, as related to the passions and affections of the human bosom; for if it had been of this kind he would have composed tragedies, or epics. Nor was it that faculty in which Italian preachers (and some others) have excelled, and which has enabled them so vividly to paint the scenes and events of sacred history as to draw tears, for an hour, from melting eyes.

The objects, and almost the exclusive objects of this faculty with Whitefield, were those which are in the highest sense spiritual;—the things not of this world, but of a brighter region;—and yet, let us well note it, not an earth-made celestial apparatus, or a scene-painting of heaven and hell, with its artificial illumination, and its mock lightning, and its peals of mechanic thunder. Enough of this sort has been done and attempted in pulpits, and to how little purpose! Truly of such efforts of oratory it may be said, "which things perish in the using." The great preachers of past times, whose sermons retain a place in libraries, produced surprising "sensations" in churches with little fruit—out of church.

If it had been only, or chiefly, the awful future—that infinite of duration toward which the brevity of this life is tending—if it had been only, or chiefly, the idea of immortality, with its alternatives, which Whitefield's mind grasped, he must at an early time, have expended his power, as to stated congregations, or within each circuit of his itinerancy. He might, indeed, have gone about preaching, with effect, a second or a third time, over the surface which he had once visited; but not much oftener. Every where this question and answer would have been heard among the people, "Whitefield is coming again, will you not hear him?" "No, I have heard already all he has to say about the world to come." How unlike this was the history of this preacher's course from first to last! His ministrations were felt to be as fresh, and they took hold of the minds of the people as powerfully, when he left England the seventh and last time, for America, as when he left it for the first time.

In the wide compass of ideas and emotions among which the human mind takes its circuit, those things only seem always new, and those only continue to exert over it an unspent power, which touch that element in human nature which itself is imperishable—namely, the moral consciousness. All other things, bright as they may appear to be, fade; and, as to each in its turn, the mind sickens, and turns from it dissatisfied. But it is not so with whatever bears upon the primary rudiment of human nature—the moral affections. By this, and not by his intellectual framework, man may be shown to be immortal; for it is on this ground that he stands related to eternal rectitude. Christianity lays a hand of power upon this moral consciousness, and troubles it; but the GOSPEL, using this word in its own peculiar sense, sheds life, animation, hope, where dismay had first come. The Gospel brings before the spiritual sense a personal object of love, adoration, and gratitude; and as the heart is that, in human nature, which "lives forever" when thus it finds its immortality assured, by union with HIM who has obtained it for his people, there is no weariness, or impatience of repetition, while HE is spoken of.

The history of Whitefield's ministry is, in a word, this —the Gospel he proclaimed drew men around him, in dense masses, at the moment when he commenced his course; and it was the Gospel, not the preacher's harmonious voice, not his "graceful action," not his fire as an orator that gave him power over congregations to the very last. No intellectual faculty of a high order lent him its aid in sustaining this popularity.

Let those who think they may succeed in such an attempt undertake the task of searching among things real, or among things which it may be possible to imagine, until they find objects (other than those constituting the Christian system) upon the ground of which such a man as Whitefield could have gathered thousands around him—keeping always close to his topic—and could hold them in his hand, time after time, and could do so through a course of four-and-thirty years.

If we were to speak of that phase of evangelic doctrine which Whitefield, as distinguished from Wesley or others, adopted, it must not be pretended, in his behalf, that he reached his position by any legitimate process of induction, or that he won it as a theologian. He came into it by a process more emphatically legitimate; that is to say, by the simplicity and amplitude of his preceptions of spiritual objects. He felt, if he could not prove it, that that sovereign grace whence the redemption of the world took its rise, must be the one law of the Christian system, and the only principle of harmony among doctrines, seemingly antithetical; and he held that this law must be applicable, not merely to the Gospel abstractedly, but to each individual instance in which it takes effect upon the human heart. He felt that this one principle, as it was the spring of Christianity itself, must neither be abated, nor be made subordinate to exceptive rules, nor be subjectea to cautionary restrictions. It must be held entire, or abandoned wholly. Whatever those misinterpretations were which might be put by others upon that first principle of Christianity—SOVEREIGN GRACE—Whitefield's childlike structure of mind compelled him to exult in, and to preach it.

In the same manner that Whitefield's ministerial course, sustained for so long a time—that is to say, to the end—can be understood on no other supposition than that of the truth of the Gospel, so does that course, its circumstances considered, yield incontestable proof of the purity, simplicity, and apostolic genuineness of his character.

If a spark of ambition, or a personal motive of any sort, had lurked in the bosom of the "stripling preacher," the effect produced upon his townsmen by his first sermon at Gloucester was enough to have turned his head; or if there had been by his side some one to whisper in his ear the word of worldly wisdom, Whitefield's career might have been a brilliant one—as the world thinks. Why should it not have been so? He needed nothing but to observe the easy rule of moving always with the tide, and of feeling his way upward toward the high places of the Church. Or, if his early triumphs might have been attributed to accidental causes, the recurrence of the same wherever he afterward appeared made it certain that a preacher, who was not yet five-and-twenty, and gifted in this extraordinary manner, needed only to husband his powers, and to manage his popularity; and every thing bright which the world can offer was before him.

Entirely unlike this was his actual history; and the course he did adopt at the first moment, he pursued, without turning to the right hand or the left, from that first moment, until the day when, broken with excessive labors, he said—"I shall be better and preach again in a day or two" and died. During the months of his first popularity—that is to say, of his first coming before the world, the church walls reeked wherever he had been announced; and the crowds that gathered round him, instead of spending their feelings, in terms of heartless admiration, wept, each for himself, as the preacher passed from their sight. This popularity, of which there had been no example in the Church (or out of it) occurred in good time to allow him to reconsider his purpose of going out to Georgia, as a missionary. Many reasons—most of them plausible, and some of them valid—might have been urged by "judicious friends," in behalf of such a reconsideration. Blame could scarcely have attached to him, if he had resolved to occupy the wide field that had now opened itself before him at home. But to his missionary purpose he did adhere.

Right or wrong in this instance, he broke away from the earnest entreaties of those whose hearts he had won; and he went whither he was carried by that one motive which ruled his life. So far as this sovereign motive mingled itself with any other, that other was a pure and warm benevolence. The Orphan House, with the racking anxieties that attached to it, and the perplexities it involved him in, for many years, gave evidence of the simplicity and unworldliness of his mind. The scheme, whether prudently devised or not, was the scheme of a youth—let it not be forgotten—who had already discovered the secret of his possessing unmatched powers of oratory.

So far as Whitefield's ministerial life and his personal character may properly be appealed to in support of some momentous principles, the inference which is thence deducible is much strengthened, and is not at all weakened, when we take into account, as well the mediocrity of his intellectual structure, as those softnesses of disposition, and that laxity of tone of which his letters and journals give so much evidence. That consistent following of a high and simple motive which marks his ministry was not, as is manifest, the proper consequence of much constitutional nerve and energy. In this instance we have true heroism before us; yet less than a hero. There is greatness—there is moral grandeur; but it is shown in the behavior of a man whose letters and private notes are rendered wearisome, if not repulsive, by a luxurious verbosity—a tautology rarely relieved by any coruscations of mind.

Nor, perhaps, could a paragraph be produced from Whitefield's works, indicative of what might be called a philosophic breadth of view in relation to religion; yet practically, all that such a breadth could imply was his own. His ministerial standing-place was always high raised above middle walls of partition; nor could he, in any instance, be induced to render worship to the idols of intolerance and bigotry. As to those partitionments within which soulless religionists are content to be penfolded, he walked over them unconsciously; nor could he be made to understand how "precious" those things were upon which he thus trampled. "Gentlemen, I hope you will settle these matters to your own satisfaction," said he among zealots,—"my business is to preach the Gospel." But this breadth, this greatness, was not with him the product of philosophy, or the prompting of a powerful intellect; nor was it liberalism, nor was it indifference: it was the greatness of the Gospel, well lodged in a large heart.

The simplicity of his character, the singleness of his views, as well as the rapidity of his movements, and the superabounding variety of his engagements, all tended to betray him, at times, into indiscretions; nor was so much as one of these slidings of his foot lost upon the wakeful hatred of the world. But, like an ingenuous and meek spirited child, he acknowledged these errors, when they were placed in his view; and he thanked his reprovers and then "amended his ways." A nice and exact sense of propriety, and a thoroughly well-bred feeling toward all ranks and conditions of men, supplied in him the place of that sort of prudence which seldom goes hand in hand with a burning zeal and a boundless benevolence. In fact, Whitefield did walk safely among the many snares of that time, when the country had not regained a settled political condition.

The blamelessness of Whitefield's public life is the more noticeable when it is thought of in relation to that quality in which the contrast between himself and Wesley is the most marked. Not at all inferior to his friend in any point of Christian morality, and with a personal virtue quite as resplendent, his spirituality was—if the phrase may be allowed—somewhat loosely garbed. As to the fervent affections of his soul, one could not say that "his loins were always girt about." Never is there ground of apprehension, in following him, lest he should act in any manner unbecoming his professions; nor, if only his sense of discretion be called up, need it be feared that he will greatly misapprehend his line of duty. But there is a feeling, to which perhaps our modern fastidiousness gives undue force, as if the awful majesty of things sacred was in peril in his hands; or as if feelings which should be reverential always, were in danger of being compromised or damaged by his colloquial vivacity.

In connection with the Methodistic revival, or as its consequence, there did in fact come into use a religious style and tone which has given occasion, to those who have sought it, in opposing themselves to evangelic doctrine. In this style there is mingled something of an overweening egotism, something of vulgar levity, something of the taste for antithesis and exaggeration, something of spiritual lusciousness; and much that is quite out of keeping with the chasteness, simplicity, severity of the apostolic writings. It does not appear that to Whitefield *mainly* this faulty style should be attributed, as if he had been its author; but, doubtless, he had his share in giving it currency. There are on record instances of the Christian intrepidity with which he dealt with some illustrious persons; nevertheless, his intimacy with titled folks was not without its effect in softening a little more what was soft in his temperament: so much sunshine did produce upon him a perceptible result. In *him* this melting went no further than the surface; and its only permanent consequence was a vitiation, to some extent, of his religious phraseology. In other instances this honeyed style became nauseating, and it has been the source of serious evils. A book, almost, might be filled with terms and modes of expression for which no warrant can be found in the Inspired Writings; and out of this factitious dialect, a factitious Christianism has often sprung. Yet it may be doubted whether it be possible, in the very nature of things, to originate and carry forward any religious revival, however urgently needed, and though it be the best ordered, without bringing into use a phraseology that must differ in some measure from that of the Sacred Scriptures. To the stagnant part of a community within which such reforms take place, this artificial dialect gives high offense; for with such it is "cant." It should be the duty of the next age to remove from religious parlance these factitious phrases, and to return to a strictly scriptural style.

But did Whitefield show any disposition to linger in the sunshine of "splendid auditories?" It was far otherwise; and his crossing the Atlantic for his last visit to America, was like his crossing it the first time—an evidence of the purity of that motive which had governed his life. In his fifty-fifth year, with a constitution so much broken and spent, he might, without blame, have accepted a position of honor and usefulness at home, along with the agreeable excitement of moderate labor. England was at his command, when he left it to return no more. But although the spring of life was broken within him, the motive power was entire; and it carried him on through his last weeks of incessant preaching, as through his first. It would not be easy to name an instance, surpassing that now before us, of a thorough uniformity of conduct and intention, held to from the moment of a man's coming before the world, to the very last hour of his life.

And now is it not time that the world should deal righteously with itself as to its ancient quarrel with one like Whitefield? The world has a long score to settle in this behalf, for it pursued him, from first to last, with a fixed and furious malignity; and even now, where Wesley is spoken of with fairness, and perhaps with commendation, a line of reluctant praise, coupled with some ungracious insinuation, is the best treatment Whitefield can obtain after he has been eighty years in his grave! No one can dare to say that his life was not blameless; and that his intentions were benevolent is manifest. His temper was not arrogant; for meekly he received rebuke, and patiently he endured so many revilings. It was with the courage of a noble nature that he confronted violence; and with the simplicity of a child that he forgave injuries. Yet among those who by their flagitious vice and outrageous crimes have the most deeply sinned against society, it would be difficult to find a wretch upon whose guilty pate has been showered so much rancorous abuse as, year after year, was heaped upon the head of the love-fraught, self-denying, and gentle-natured Whitefield. There is a mystery here which "philosophy" should do its best to clear up; or not succeeding in this endeavor, should ingenuously acknowledge that as, on the one hand, it can give no intelligible account of Whitefield's motives, so neither can it show reason for the world's hatred of him.

FLETCHER.

The justly venerated name of Fletcher of Madeley brings into prominence, in a peculiar manner, what we have assumed to be the true idea of Methodism—namely, that it was a divinely appointed development of the Gospel—temporary in its purport, although fraught with momentous ulterior consequences. Methodism, in the rise and progress of which we trace and reverently acknowledge the hand of God, it is not easy to regard as the origination of what could, in that form, be permanent.

One must be resolved not to see a providential intention in the Methodistic movement, if it is not to be recognized in the singular adaptation, one to the other, of its principal agents. This company of men neither fashioned themselves individually for their work; nor did any one of them select his colleagues as the men, among others, that were best qualified to assist him in carrying out his scheme. If Wesley had chosen his own Whitefield, *that* Whitefield assuredly would not have been the preacher of "election;" but would have been one as peremptory as himself in adhering to a single rudiment of truth; or if the master mind had looked around for one who should be qualified as a writer to make good, to defend, and to consolidate Wesleyan theology, and to hand it down as an impregnable scheme of doctrine to posterity, Fletcher would not have been his choice.

Nevertheless he was the very man—*now* we may see it—who was well qualified for the part he actually took in the Methodistic dispensation;—that is to say, to write attractive books that could not fail to be read by thousands during the years in which they were needed, but which would not be read, after that season, by a creature. The "Checks to Antinomianism" did their office; and they *have done* it; for, in theological literature, they now hold no place.

Even Whitefield's preaching, and if there had been none of a more exaggerated sort, needed a counteraction, a drag on the wheel. But among those who followed in the same track, or who started independently at the same time, there were several who, with far less simplicity of soul, distinguished themselves by a prurient grossness of taste, by an eager pursuit of exaggeration and paradox; or by a temper which may justly be designated as fanatical (because involving some element of malignity) and who would not fail to put upon Calvinistic theology a guise that must render it an object of mockery or of loathing to the world, and of alarm and reprehension to the seriously minded. To repress this exuberance, to redress this grievance, and to put to shame those who had thus outraged religious propriety, Fletcher came forward, under Wesley's auspices. He was fitted for this task, by the warmth of his religious sentiments, by the acknowledged purity of his personal character, by the Christian meekness of his temper, by his humility, fervor, and love. As a theologian he possessed acquaintance enough with doctrinal literature and with the Scriptures, to give him always a point or two of advantage in relation to his antagonists; but he was no such reasoner, he was no such master of biblical criticism, as might have made it possible for him to overstep the limits of his appointed task, or, as a theological writer, to survive his day. As a writer he held a fluent pen: with much vivacity, and with some faculty of appropriate illustration. he possessed that happy art of diffuseness which, while it does not send the reader to sleep, so dilutes the meaning of each page as serves to adapt it well to the feeble assimilative powers of the class of minds for which it was prepared. Any one who is accustomed to read by a process of abbreviation, might easily make himself master of the entire meaning which Fletcher wire-draws over a hundred pages; and if he be skillful in catching the one hinging sentence of each page, all going before, and coming after, may safely be disregarded.

We should be assigning to Fletcher far too high a place, as a writer, if we were to affirm that his reasoning is sophistical; for in fact he does not *reason*, nor could he do so. What he brings together, are not consecutive propositions, but pointed instances and illustrations, sometimes appropriate, but even then not conclusive in argument; and often they are wholly inappropriate, as well as inconclusive. Often they are such as needed only a little re-dressing to be brought to bear with effect against his own doctrine. With an understanding inferior to Wesley's, he was better fitted to his line of labor in this respect—that he could go on in the mode of cumulative argumentation, without at any stage bringing out in a tangible manner, the inconclusiveness of the whole; whereas Wesley, in that strict and categorical style which he adhered to, was continually in danger of breaking up his own sophisms. Fletcher was always safe in his cork-lined skiff, among the breakers, and riding high upon foam, where Wesley would have run upon the rocks.

Personally, Fletcher of Madeley deserved all that warm affection, and that admiration of which he was the object in his circle; but while it is difficult to find parallels to Wesley or Whitefield, in the catalogue of Christian worthies, he stands as one of a class which, if not very numerous, has not been the most rare. In a genuine sense, he was a saint—a saint such as the Church, of every age, has produced a few samples. Sanctity and purity of manners were his distinctive characteristic: an attenuated temperament, and feeble constitution, attenuated the more, from year to year, under the discipline of ascetic notions, rendered him as unearthly a being as could tread the earth at all. And then if he seemed but as a shadow bodily, an overdone style of self-abasement—a humility, the expression of which inflicts positive suffering upon those who must listen to it, placed him too far beyond the range of ordinary sympathies. It is seldom that an Englishman-born is heard to exaggerate modesty in the style which, to Jean Guillaume de la Flechère, had become habitual. Perfectly assured as one is of this good man's Christian integrity, and of his eminence in every virtue, it is a species of torture to read those letters of his, in which the bathos of lowliness quite exhausts all powers of language. This mistaken style often finds imitators among those who, in adopting, for themselves, such terms of abasement, do not go so far wrong as they would wish the world to suppose.

Among the principal persons of the Methodistic movement every thing (so far as human infirmity admits) was genuine and sincere; but there was much that had not been considered in its consequences. Whitefield, as we have said, opened a vein of English—luscious and colloquial, which, as flowing from the lips and pens of his imitators, would, if it had not met correction, have covered Calvinistic Methodism with an offensive and pestilential deposit. On the other hand—the Wesleyan side—there meets the eye an expanse of fragmentary verbosity—dry and friable, and of which, as one of its originators, Fletcher must be named. To any one who might be capable of such a task, we should much rather recommend the writing a book of his own; otherwise one so qualified might give to our religious literature a serviceable compendium within the compass of a hundred pages, which should embody, in a biblical and logical sense, the entire substance of the ten volumes of Fletcher's works. What this copious writer has to say, might soon be said; and in truth it is little more than this, that, throughout the Inspired Writings, men are dealt with by their Maker, their Judge, and their Saviour, such as we all feel and know ourselves to be;—that is to say, suasible, accountable, and free; and not such as theological theorists, or as metaphysical sophists, or as some popular declaimers, catering to a debauched taste for paradox and exaggeration, have pictured men to be. This is nearly the whole pith of the "Checks to Antinomianism." But Fletcher had not grasped that key of biblical interpretation which allows the devout and ingenuous reader of the Scriptures to possess and to enjoy principles, among and between which the connection of abstract consistency can never be traced, or at least has not hitherto been laid open. If a simple and reasonable question could have penetrated so far as to the still interior of this good man's heart his answer to it might have been followed by his drawing the pen through very many pages of what he had written in attempting to botch up a sort of consistency for his own theology. This question would be of this sort, "If Antinomianism were quite gone and forgotten, would Arminian theology give you entire contentment?" One might answer for Fletcher that he would in that case have gladly dismissed it, as a man returning to health and appetite rejects the meagre diet that had been imposed upon him by his physician. But he wrote his "Checks" with a feeling like that of those empirics who labor to convince us that animal food is poison, that vegetable substances are much to be suspected, and that, in fact, nothing is quite safe for the stomach but medicine.

Nevertheless, Fletcher most usefully and ably discharged his function as Wesley's polemical attendant and champion; and his writings had great influence, no doubt, in waking up, and in calling into exercise, that right-hearted good sense which is a characteristic of the English mind, and to which some few demagogues and fanatics in Whitefield's train were then doing much wrong. It is long since this good sense and better religious feeling has swept the religious field nearly clear of those Antinomian paradoxes which sprang out of the Methodistic heat. A few notorious preachers and obscure writers, whose names it is a happiness to forget, rendered perhaps a more effective service than even Fletcher and his "Checks," to the severity of Christian truth, while they were doing their utmost to dress up their corrupt theology in a harlot's attire; for the best check to Antinomianism is given by those who themselves are held in check, neither by the fear of God, nor any sense of shame in giving utterance to their absurdities.

Fletcher's part in that unedifying controversy which sprang out of the Minutes of Conference for 1770, while it consists well with his repute as an eminently holy, conscientious, and peace-loving man, brings to view a feature of Methodism which will demand further attention—we say a feature of *Methodism;* for although the same appearances have attached, in greater or less degrees, to all seasons of religious excitement, yet in this instance there is observable a marked sequence of causes and effects. Little thinking, or thinking not at all, of what must inevitably be the consequence when the style they indulged in should reach the rude mind of the people, and be imitated by the false and the foolish, some of Whitefield's followers—Berridge by eminence—so wrote, one to another, and so penned their journals, and, too often, so preached, as if, in their minds, there had been resident a very faint consciousness of the infinite perfections and majesty of Him with whom man has to do. What it is usual to call the natural attributes of God, and of which the Inspired Writers never lose their recollection, had, with some of these good men—or so it seemed—fallen out of place, or had got beyond the range of their vision. When blasphemy assails the ear, the blood curdles; but it is even a deeper and a more lasting distress that is endured when, from the lips and pens of religious persons, there flows a copious irreverence, an indecent easiness, a flippant buffoonery, in the utterance of which before the world, the religious sentiment in all men's minds is outraged, in a manner which no mere blasphemy can effect. Extremes, such as these, were not reached by any of the leading preachers.

These abuses had attached, principally, to the Calvinistic side of Methodism. Wesley's firmer tone of mind, and the brighter complexion of his feelings, held him exempt from all such exorbitances; and so was it with Fletcher; nevertheless, a reverberated influence from faults which they themselves avoided and abhorred, affected them also, when they were drawn into controversy. As to their opponents, it was only according to the ordinary course of things that men who, in a time of love and fervor, fell into a style of luscious irreverence, should, when roused by controversy, and when irritated, exchange, in a moment, honey for venom. The suddenness of the change is startling; but it is not in fact wonderful, for it is quite in human nature.

Fletcher, although his style had shown much of what was overdone, did not at any time render himself offensive in the way that had become characteristic of some of the Calvinistic preachers; nor did he, when he rushed into controversy, fall, as did his assailants and opponents, into virulent and rancorous buffoonery. The reaction upon himself, and so upon Wesley, was to hurry him beyond the limits of religious propriety in giving his portraiture, or caricature, of Calvinistic Antinomianism. Wesley had set a very bad example in his noted apostrophe to the Devil, and Fletcher made an ill use of this pattern. He and his friend seemed unconscious of the awful risks that are incurred by those who indulge, as he so often did, in this species of rhetoric. Nothing can be of worse consequence, in controversy, than to paint the Devil, and then to say to an antagonist—"There! that is *your* god!" What place will there be left in the minds of men for any religious reverence, when the same impropriety comes to be retorted, and when thus, between the combatants, the entire disc of the sun has been blackened? Fletcher's antagonists in this controversy (one does them an office of love in avoiding to name them) wrote in a style which involves its own antidote: offensive beyond endurance, it is quickly forgotten; and so Fletcher's "Checks" are by this time forgotten; yet through a longer course of time they wrought a real, although indirect mischief, for within the Wesleyan pale they continued to shut out the light, both of charity and of Scriptural doctrine; the mass of the people, and even the preachers, taking Fletcher's word for it, religiously believed that the contrary of the Wesleyan theology was a worship not much better than that of the Principle of Evil.

This ill-conducted controversy, which did not redeem itself by calling forth so much as one accomplished theologian, or by giving birth to so much as one book which, in itself, is now worth the reading, not only broke the force of Methodism as related to the open irreligion of the times, but it turned off a thoughtful and favorable regard toward it, in the instance of many whom it had nearly won.

And yet how uncharitably, or, let us rather say—for we ask no *indulgence* on this ground—how incorrectly and unphilosophically should we think, even of those who sinned the most egregiously in this controversy, if we were to take our idea of them, personally, from their own pens! As to Fletcher indeed we might very safely do so, for his worst offenses arose only from that bad taste which the slender build of his mind allowed him to fall into. Great intensity of feeling he had, but little depth;

some elevation, but no soaring—no grandeur—no grasp of general principles. The most unseemly things he could coolly write, much in the way in which the blind sometimes trample innocently over things that are sacred and precious. Intending every thing that is right and pious, this good man makes the blood run cold while, with an apparent insensibility, or unconsciousness of what is due to the awful realities before him, he accumulates illustrations, showing the blasphemous import of his adversaries' doctrine. It is consolatory to believe—as we justly may—that nothing so unwise and unseemly would now be tolerated, or even attempted, in religious controversy.

Whatever service Fletcher may be thought to have rendered to Wesley, as a controversial writer, a far more important and more lasting benefit was conferred upon Methodism by his holy conversation, and his laborious course, as a Christian man, and a parish minister. Madeley has been shedding a lustre upon Methodism now these hundred years. It is true that the books which thence issued may well rest in their oblivion; but the virtues which there bloomed and bore fruit, are of immortal fame, and this fame is not merely that of the man individually, but it is fairly the property of the community in the bosom of which he was reared, lived, and died. If it be asked what this Methodism is, about which the world, even now, has come to no settled opinion, an equitable reply, inclusive even of some Methodistic mistakes, may be obtained by any honest inquirer—at Madeley. The Methodism of Fletcher was Christianity, as little lowered by admixture of human infirmity as we may hope to find it any where on earth.

COKE.

The position we have ventured to take, namely, that Methodism was "from Heaven," receives its confirmation in two modes in each separate instance, when we look to its first movers; for there then becomes manifest at once the peculiar fitness of each to accomplish his destined work, and also the disproportionate vastness of the result, when we think of it as related to the natural powers of the agent. This kind of proof, coming in as it does from opposite directions to bear upon the same conclusion, is the characteristic, as of other religious movements, yet in none so remarkably as in the Methodistic revival; and among its instances of this order, that of Coke is as significant as any.

Rightfully called an "apostolic man," and the father of the Wesleyan Missions, and so the originator of a work which has been incalculably beneficial, one might wish to think of him rather in the vagueness of an imaginary personality, than precisely according to the un-heroic truth of his individual form and style. And it might be better, too, to have heard of him, as an unwearied and successful evangelist, than to have listened to him, as addressing a home congregation, in his own formal, operose, and iterative manner. We might say, let the man be measured by the extent of his achievements; but it is better to say—and he himself would so have said—let the Wesleyan Coke be thought of as the honored servant of God, faithful in the employment of the gifts that were intrusted to him, these gifts being such as well fitted him for his part; and yet wholly insufficient if named as the proper causes of his success.

Absolute devotion to his one object, a devotion which spared nothing of personal welfare, or ease, or fortune, or worldly repute, was Dr. Coke's distinction. As to the entireness of this devotedness, he was not inferior to

Wesley, or to Whitefield, or to Fletcher; and the sacrifices he thus willingly offered to God included more than had been surrendered by any other of the founders of Methodism. The "all things" which he accounted as dross for Christ's sake, embraced the materials, or the means of obtaining, whatever is most desired and sought after by mankind. On behalf of Xavier there may fairly be claimed the praise of having sacrificed himself—his rare talents, his personal advantages, and an unquestionable career of ambition at home, to the high purposes of Christian benevolence. But then, beside his zeal and devotedness, Xavier's soul was large as a hero's soul could be. He was borne to the East as on the eagle's wings of an innate and boundless ambition, which, on any other course, might have carried him to the pinnacle of power or fame—political, military, or sacerdotal. Can any thing of this sort be alleged as to Dr. Thomas Coke? It does not appear that the "high destiny" sentiment had any lodgment in his bosom. It would be doing him in every sense a wrong, to paint him as one of the giants. His habits and his consciousness as a gentleman, and as a man of fortune, and as a scholar and clergyman, gave him an air which, in all positions, saved his diminutive and rotund person from contempt. His ardor, his disinterestedness, his courage, his devotedness, which were always conspicuous, secured him, in most instances, a fair treatment from the world. But beyond this—that is to say, all the impress of power and greatness attaching to this evangelist's character and course, and to the work he accomplished—was the greatness and the power of the Gospel which he preached, and of the Divine energy that went with him.

Not to speak of the important—the indispensable services that were rendered to the Wesleyan community at home, that is to say, throughout England and Ireland, by Dr. Coke, as Wesley's second and representative, and which no other clerical minister in his service was at all qualified to afford, it was he, if not absolutely as the earliest instrument, yet as immeasurably the most efficient, that carried organized Wesleyanism across the Atlantic, and laid the foundation—broad and firm, at once of a missionary work, and of a settled religious community, which perhaps may outlast the parent body.

Dr. Coke, not abjectly, but in a manly spirit, surrendered himself to Wesley's guidance; and, avoiding to risk any thing as to the onward movement of the evangelic enterprise, by an unseasonable obtrusion of his individual notions or opinions, he gave himself to the work—that is, to *Wesleyan* Christianity, without distraction, disturbance, or exceptive protest; and it was such a colleague as this that Wesley needed. But as a consequence of this (it should not be called *subserviency*) it followed that although entitled to a foremost place among the founders of Methodism, he can not be thought of as having imparted to itself any peculiar characteristics, springing from his own mind or temper. In this respect, incidental as it is, a ground of comparison might again be made good between the apostle of the East Indies, and the apostle of the West. Xavier illuminated the early Jesuitism by the world-wide splendor of his virtues; but his genuine fame stands clear of any direct implication with Jesuitism, as a scheme.

To render to Dr. Coke—in a word—the tribute of praise that is his due, as Wesley's most efficient coadjutor, completes what need be said of him in relation to our present purpose.

LADY HUNTINGDON.

The broad facts of this noble lady's history afford ground enough for the repute she has enjoyed as a woman of much tact and ability, of great energy, and of a munificent temper; while the use she made of her influence and fortune for the promotion of the Methodistic movement—that is to say, of Christianity itself, sufficiently attests her piety and zeal. It must also be inferred from the circumstance of her having retained the friendship and regard of many among the leading persons of her time, through a long period of years, that she possessed qualities of mind and attractions of manner, that were of no ordinary sort; for it is certain that those who ridiculed, or even hated her Methodism, still yielded themselves, in frequent instances, to her personal influence. So far, an idea of Lady Huntingdon may be gathered from facts that are beyond doubt. There is, however, so little that is discriminative in the extant eulogies of her friends and correspondents, or of her biographers, and there is so little that bears a clearly marked individuality in her own letters, that a distinct image of her mind and temper is not easy to obtain.

As to the position assigned to her among the founders of Methodism, it is due to her rather on the ground of what she did for it, as its patroness, which was almost immeasurable, than because she imprinted upon it any characteristic of her own mind. Calvinistic Methodism was not of her creation. In the centre of the brilliant company of her pious relatives and noble friends, and with a numerous attendance of educated and episcopally ordained ministers, and—beyond this inner circle—a broad penumbra of lay preachers, chosen by herself, and educated, maintained, and employed at her cost, and acting under her immediate direction, she seems to sit as a queen. Something of the regal style—something of the air of the autocrat, was natural to one who, with the consciousness of rank, and with the habitude of one accustomed to the highest society, was gifted with a peculiar governing ability, and was actually wielding an extensive influence over men and things. It would have been wonderful indeed if nothing of the sort had been perceptible in her manner and style; yet that her main intention was pure and beneficent, and that ambition was not her passion, will be felt and confessed by every candid reader of her letters.

These letters, or so much of her correspondence as has been given to the world, amply attest what is here alleged in her behalf, namely, that Lady Huntingdon, like Wesley, and like Whitefield, and others around them, was governed by a motive of the highest order, and that she has a rightful claim upon our sympathies and admiration. Thus far these documents are clearly available in her behalf; but they do not afford the means of giving distinctness to a portraiture of her mind and temper; and they are such that a continuous perusal of them can be accomplished only as a task. They indicate much business-like ability, and they show always a pertinent adherence to the matter in hand; they are therefore more determinate, by far, than Whitefield's, and, indeed, are little less so than Wesley's, whose letters are eminent samples of succinct determinativeness: they bespeak an unvarying and genuine fervor, and a simple-hearted onward tendency toward the one purpose of her life—the spread of the Gospel, and the honor of her Saviour. Lady Huntingdon's letters are moreover marked by often repeated, but not to be questioned professions of the deep sense she had of her own unworthiness and unprofitableness. Such are the ingredients—few and perpetually recurrent—of these compositions: a severe monotony (not severe in the sense of harshness) is their characteristic. But then when it is recollected in what society she had passed her early years, and from which she was never entirely separated, and that she possessed mind enough to maintain her place in the regard of some of the most distinguished persons of that age, it may seem surprising that the uniform color of these letters is relieved by no sparkling of wit, by no flashes of intellect, by no allusive references to the events of the time; and that they do not put us into connection with the great world by one casual hint, or a single discursive observation; and yet of that world she knew much; nor was she ever far from it.

This monotony, and this absolute exclusion of whatever was merely secular, had, however, its meaning, and we may see in it, not simply an indication of that fixedness of purpose which may be expected in such an instance, but something more, and which, as we have noticed, is a characteristic of Methodism. A straitened and rudimentary style of thought attaches to every thing that has survived of the Methodistic literature—if literature it can be called. Although voluminous, it has little volume, and might be compressed within very narrow limits: it is theological, but it does not constitute a theology. This mass of letters, journals, minutes, experiences, or of controversial treatises, does indeed furnish much evidence illustrative of the rise, progress, and characteristics of Methodism; yet there is little in it that would now attract an eye not in search of *mere evidence* touching this course of events. So fitted for their part were the originators and movers of Methodism that, while amply furnished with gifts proper for the great work they were to accomplish, they were not so qualified as might have enabled them to go beyond their allotted task.

This law of the Methodistic dispensation receives peculiar illustration in the instance now before us. If Lady Huntingdon, along with the advantage she drew from her rank and her command of fortune, and enjoying, as she did, access to statesmen and official persons—if she had possessed a wider compass of mind—if she had been so far the Elizabeth as might have prompted her to call a Walsingham and a Cecil to her counsels, she might, at that time, have put forward an ecclesiastical movement the consequences of which we, of this time, should have seen and felt in every thing around us. The Church, at that time, although it had *animus*, had no soul, and no concentration, moral or spiritual. It had slid far away from the Reformation-ground. In reply to its assailants—the Methodists—it dared not make its appeal, as they did, to the Articles and Homilies, nor did it even retain more than a very feeble devotional sympathy with the liturgy. Scarcely at all, in a religious sense, or otherwise than from motives of interest, was the aristocracy of that age attached to the Established Church: the mass of the upper classes was utterly indifferent, or was avowedly infidel; while among those persons of rank who might be religiously disposed, more than a few were openly or implicitly connected, either with Nonconformity, or with Romanism. Upon this class Whitefield's preaching had made a decisive impression. As to the masses of the people, they were nearly lost to the Church, except when a parson or a magistrate could gather them as a mob, to carry some purpose of violence.

If at that time a head and leader, occupying Lady Huntingdon's high position, and surrounded, as she was, with ordained ministers, not wanting in endowments as popular preachers, had devised and planted—not a Society, but a Church; and if, instead of building and opening chapels, here and there, without polity or plan, she had employed, in a politic manner, the means which were in fact at her command, it may be doubted if the Established Church, or the hierarchy then in possession of it, could long have held its own. Toward the people a body of Calvinistic clergy might easily have made good their own position as the true successors of the Reformers: those few phrases in the Offices which had a discordant sound, were not enough to have constituted a barrier, resisting such a force as that which Methodism had then at its command. The people, crowding into the churches, if a plan had been concerted and held to, would have borne their favored preachers forward, high lifted above the obstructions which these few obsolete forms could have been made to supply.

Or let it be imagined that a politic or statesmanlike comprehension of the relative strength of whatever was, or might have been opposed to it, had brought the Calvinistic and the Arminian bodies to combine, and to act in concert; in that case could those things have come down to us entire, which have come down? It is hard to think they could. But Methodism was not a scheme devised by man; it was not, at any moment, earlier or later, a foreseen movement. It did, in its day, the work of God, and it possessed neither the innate powers, nor the ambition to do more.

Whether the chapels in Lady Huntingdon's Connection are at this time few or many, is a matter of no general moment to inquire; for whether few or many, the "Connection" has subsided into its place as one among the religious communities that hold orthodoxy and evangelic doctrine; and probably it is efficient in a full proportion to its statistics. But with this we have here no concern. What does concern us is the fact that much that has become characteristic of evangelic Christianity, at the present time, had its origin in Lady Huntingdon's drawing-room;—that is to say, in the circle of which she was the centre, and her house the gathering point. In a diffusive or undefined manner this religious style has pervaded the non-episcopal religious communions, where it has easily commingled itself with existing homogeneous elements. But within the Episcopal Church the transmission was more determinate, and more sharply outlined, and it may there be traced with more precision, and is pregnant with further consequences.

The fact of this religious transmission, which connects the venerated names of Venn, Newton, Scott, Milner, and others, in no very remote manner, with the Founders of Methodism, might, to a reader of its history, seem too conspicuous to be called in question; nor does it very clearly appear what those manly and Christianlike feelings are which should prompt any parties, at this time, to repudiate it. A wiry task surely is it which those undertake who labor, thread by thread, to disengage the modern episcopal evangelic bodies from the ties of filial relationship to Wesley, Whitefield, and their colleagues. Instead of pursuing an attenuated argument of this sort, one would boldly—as cordially affected toward the Episcopal Church—rejoice in contemplating this (assumed) fact that the Methodistic revival, instead of its turning aside from the Church, as if adjudged to be undeserving of the heavenly benefit, did so largely partake of it, and that the consequences of this revival have centred upon the Episcopal Church, far more decisively and more permanently than it did upon any of the dissident bodies around it. It is the Episcopal Church that has inherited the main part of the religious animation and refreshment which has come down from that band of ordained ministers of which we are now speaking. Besides those already named, and who stand so nearly related to the present times, in ascending a few years we reach, without a break, that company of men, less regular in their ministrations, but not less deserving of affectionate regard, whose names can by no means be disconnected with Methodism—names which, so long as the Church retains its Articles and Homilies, it would be a treason to disown. Let Fletcher lead the way, and let him bring with him Hervey, Grimshaw, Berridge, Romaine, Toplady, Talbot, Walker, Shirley. Is it easy to imagine that the twelve or twenty clergymen who must stand or fall together, as the true representatives of the Reformers, would have been spurned and condemned by Cranmer, Ridley, Latimer, Hooper; or that Jewell and Hooker would have turned from them with cold disdain? Can we think this? Certainly those can not think it who, with no interests at stake, and no prejudices in peril, are accustomed to follow the devious and perplexed track of religious history by the guidance of principles applicable to all ages.

It may well be granted that the rise of Methodism brings to view many instances of what may be called independent origination; and it is true that the minds of men who were unknown to each other became, about the same time, similarly affected toward the first truths of the Christian system; so that when accident or sympathy had brought them into contact, they readily coalesced, and thenceforward thought it their duty and happiness to act in concert. So acting, and so associating, Lady Huntingdon gathered them around herself; and she aided and, to some extent, she directed their movements. But this company, thus for a while concentrated, and thus governed, at length diverged in the two directions of a new Calvinistic form of dissent; and of Calvinistic conformity; and while the one has become a variety only, within the dissenting mass, not materially affecting its position or prospects, the latter has been the principal means of recovering the long-lost influence of the Episcopal Church over the laity, and of bringing down to these precarious times a firm Protestant feeling, which is not unlikely to burst forth anew, and to lead the way in a time of less ambiguity than the present.

As with Wesley, so with Lady Huntingdon, a formal separation from the Established Church was, in each act and instance, submitted to with extreme reluctance, and not until it was felt to be inevitable. When at length the irregularities of the Methodistic clergy could no longer be winked at by the Church authorities, the greater number of them fell back into their places, as parish ministers; and this defection, while it give rise, necessarily, to a new order of ministers in the "Connection" whose ordination placed them on a level only, with the dissenting ministry, it took place at a time when no alternative was left to Lady Huntingdon's congregations but to seek protection under the Toleration Act, as dissenters.

This double illustration of a conspicuous principle, as afforded by the Wesleyan and Calvinistic movement, might be enough to preclude the necessity of any future experiments, attempted with the hope of constructing a platform outside the Episcopal Church, but yet resting against its walls: it is evident that the reforming energy must henceforward take an inward direction. But at the moment when any such reform does take place, unless a constitutional renovation of the two nonconforming masses—the Wesleyan and the Calvinistic—shall avail to preclude so natural a result, an extensive absorption will be imminent to both; for it can not but happen that the renovation, or the more effective adjustment of a body near to us, consigns ourselves to decay unless we fully partake of the same benefits.

Lady Huntingdon was always the object of a warm personal affection with those who were nearest to her. With them, it is always "our *dear* Lady Huntingdon;" and putting out of view formal eulogies, it is unquestionable that, if she governed her Connection as having a right to rule it, her style and behavior (like Wesley's) indicated the purest motives, and the most entire simplicity of purpose. This, in truth, may be said to have been the common characteristic of the founders of Methodism, especially of the two Wesleys, of Whitefield, Fletcher, Coke, and Lady Huntingdon—a devotedness to the service and glory of the Saviour Christ, which none who saw and conversed with them could question.

The same praise, and in the same degree is undoubtedly the due of many of those who were the associates and colleagues of these principal persons. It is as bright a company that we have before us, as we find any where on the page of Christian history.

THE METHODISTIC COMPANY.

The names that would claim a place in a history of Methodism, on the ground of personal connection with its founders, and of important services rendered to this evangelic movement, may be as many as a hundred;—a company large enough, assuredly, to attract an eye that is looking over the wide field of Christian history; and why should it not attract as much regard as we are used to pay to any other band of men whose names are conserved with affection and respect?

It would not be easy, or not possible, to name any company of Christian preachers, from the apostolic age downward to our own times, whose proclamation of the Gospel has been in a larger proportion of instances effective, or which has been carried over so large a surface, with so much power, or with so uniform a result. No such harvest of souls is recorded to have been gathered by any body of contemporary men, since the first century. An attempt to compute the converts to Methodistic Christianity would be a fruitless, as well as presumptuous undertaking, from which we draw back; but we must not call in question, what is so variously and fully attested, that an unimpeachable Christian profession was the fruit of the Methodistic preaching in instances that must be computed by hundreds of thousands, throughout Great Britain, and in America.

Until the contrary can be clearly proved, it may be affirmed that no company of men of whose labors and doctrine we have any sufficient notice, has gone forth with a creed more distinctly orthodox, or more exempt from admixture of the doctrinal feculence of an earlier time. None have stood forward more free than these were from petty solicitudes concerning matters of observance, to which, whether they were to be upheld or to be denounced, an exaggerated importance was attributed. None have confined themselves more closely to those principal subjects which bear directly upon the relationship of man to God —as immortal, accountable, guilty, and redeemed. If we are tempted to complain of the unvaried complexion of the Methodistic teaching, it is the uniformity which results from a close adherence to the very rudiments of the Gospel. Uniformity or sameness of aspect, as it may be the coloring of dullness and of death, so may it spring from simplicity and power; but can it be a question to which of these sources we should attribute that undiversified breadth which is the characteristic of Methodism?

To dispute the claims of the Methodistic company to be thus regarded, on the ground of any errors of an incidental kind that may have attended their teaching, or of the follies or delinquencies that may be chargeable upon any of them, individually, would be a frivolous as well as an ungenerous mode of proceeding. Need it be said that these Methodists were men "of like passions with ourselves?" and such, too, were those who, in the Apostolic age, carried the Gospel throughout the Roman world, and beyond it. Taken in the mass, the one company of men was as wise as the other—not wiser—as holy, not more holy. If it be affirmed that the Christian worthies of some remote time were, as a class of men, of a loftier stature in virtue and piety than these with whom we have now to do, let the evidence on which such an assumption could be made to rest be brought forward: this can never be done; and the supposition itself should be rejected as a puerile superstition.

Yet there is one plea on the ground of which, if it be valid, the Methodistic company might be cast down from the place of honor which is now claimed for it. This ground of exception is that occupied by those who, with strictness and consistency, hold the doctrine that, apart from the line of episcopal ordination, unbroken in its descent, there is and can be no Church, no ministry, no sacraments, no salvation. It is much to be desired that those who profess thus to think would take up the case of Methodism, and deal with it thoroughly, flinching from no consequence toward which their theory may lead them. The instance is every way well adapted to such a purpose; nor does it offer any color of evasion, nor admit of any way of escape from the one conclusion which the premises demand, if those premises be valid. The conditions of this very definite case preclude an evasive reply, such as this—"We can not tell whether Methodism was from Heaven or of men." Neither Wesley's episcopal ordination, nor Whitefield's, could, on the ground of the "historic succession," carry with it a power of ordination; and certainly it could not excuse or palliate their insubordination, as presbyters of the established Church. It is not as if Methodism had sprung up in some remote quarter of Christendom, where it could not have connected itself with the Apostolic line, or where ignorance, on questions of this sort, was involuntary. Nor is it as if Methodism had been a revival, taking place within a body which claimed for its ministry a high ecclesiastical ancestry, so that its original irregularity was shrouded by the mists of centuries. Methodism took its rise in the very bosom of the Apostolic succession; and it was carried forward by men who were fully informed as to all subjects bearing upon the course which they pursued. The offense—if an offense—was committed in broad day, by men with their eyes open; and these men had cut themselves off from the benefit of pleading an abstract conscientious opinion, analogous to that of the Presbyterians or Independents: they declared themselves Churchmen and Episcopalians.

On every side, therefore, this Methodistic problem is clearly defined; and the more we think of it, the more exempt will it seem from ambiguities, or ways of escape. No one who is accustomed to pursue principles with logical severity into their consequences, will deny that the Apostolic-succession theory, such as it has been enunciated and defined of late, must either break itself upon Methodism, or must consign Methodism and its millions of souls to perdition, in as peremptory a manner as that in which the Church of Rome fixes its anathema upon heretical nations.

No doubt there are more than a few sincere, seriously-minded, and kind-tempered persons, holding this theory, who would find themselves wanting in the nerve and hardihood required of them, on an occasion like this, when challenged, by the clearest rule of consistency, to take their places, as spectators, while men, such as Wesley, Whitefield, Fletcher, with millions of their proselytes and spiritual progeny, are to be sent down alive into the pit! The one precise ground of this *auto da fé* should not be lost sight of. Let it be stated;—the Methodistic preachers, even if they held some questionable subsidiary notions, yet professed, in the most decisive terms, their adherence to the doctrine of the Three Creeds; therefore they were not heretics. They declared their approval of the Thirty-nine Articles: they threw themselves upon the Book of Homilies: they frequented the liturgical worship of the Church; they partook of its sacraments; they acknowledged its orders.

It can never be thought a Christian-like act to consign masses of men to perdition on the mere charge of enthusiasm, or of some extravagance in behavior. As to the general good conduct of the Methodistic converts, it is not pretended that it was not fully equal to that of other men—reputed Christians. Nevertheless, there remains this one ground of exception against the Methodistic body, which the Apostolic-succession theory brings forward, and which it must continue to bring forward and insist upon. Whoever, while he holds this theory, flies off from its application in a case so flagrant and so thoroughly unambiguous as this, implicates himself in the sin of schism, and comes within range of that anathema to which he has not the conscience and the courage to respond.

But if Methodism be cut off from one line of succession, it may claim another, or more than one other. If there be any difficulty in connecting this body of evangelists with those, in other ages, who, in a like spirit, have borne testimony to the truth, that difficulty attaches much rather to the obscurity of the extant evidence on the ground of which the claim of the more ancient witnesses is to be established, than to any ambiguity as to the latter. To trace the true Apostolic line, from Methodism upward, would lead us over ground not merely too extensive, but which might be passed over to more advantage apart from our immediate purpose. Already we have claimed for Wesley, Whitefield, and others, a genuine relationship to the Protestant martyrs and founders of the English Church, between whom and themselves no important difference of doctrine or of feeling can be made out. The question is not whether the English reformers would have formally sanctioned the Methodistic secession, for to this question no answer can be obtained, even by inference; but it is affirmed that these Methodists, rather than any other Churchmen of their times, may make good their pretension to have been, in doctrine and in spirit, the genuine sons of the English Reformed Church.

But the Methodists took orders in another manner, less direct and explicit indeed, but yet—so bold are we—not unauthentic or unimportant. Methodism, in a deep and genuine sense, held on to Nonconformity, and to whatever had been good in Puritanism.

Wesley, Whitefield, Fletcher, and their colleagues, if placed by the side of Howe, Baxter, Charnock, Manton, Bates, Flavel, and others, must be thought to rank below them, in theological attainment, in compass of learning, in intellectuality, and in discursive power, as preachers and writers; as well as in the depth and elevation of their devotional style. In blamelessness of life, in devotedness, and on the ground of doctrinal integrity, the balance stands even between the two companies. But then, even after allowance has been made for the obstructions that stood in the way of the Nonconformists, the Methodists had much the advantage on the ground of expansive and adventurous Christian philanthropy: on *this* ground, in fact, the founders of Methodism have no rivals. Yet besides their warmer zeal, as evangelists, the relation in which they stood to the ecclesiastical authorities of their time gave them a signal advantage: to this an allusion has already been made. The energies and the *animus* of the Nonconformists, as also of the Puritans, had, to a great extent, been employed and exhausted in resisting, and in protesting against, the despotic measures of the Court and Church of their times: hence it was that they were always too much occupied with matters which were either altogether frivolous, or of very inferior moment. But a protesting and a resistant function of this sort does not favorably develop the symmetry of the Christian character; much less does it auspiciously affect the course of the evangelist; for even if his temper has not become soured in controversy, his zeal for the conversion of souls will scarcely hold itself clear of impatience to make proselytes to his party. Resistance to Church despotism may be the duty of Christian men, at some seasons; but such seasons will not be the times that are made glad by the triumphs of the Gospel.

The Methodists stood in a far better position than this as evangelists. Reviled, pelted, and hooted by mobs, as they were, sometimes mistreated by magistrates, and generally unwisely and unkindly dealt with by the Church authorities, they themselves had no quarrel, either with Church or State; in all points they were loyal men: they cherished also a filial regard toward the Church; and they themselves were of it. As to the civil power, they knew and found that its feeling and arm were always on their side. In their bosoms there was no rankling grudge against authorities—there was no particle of that venom which, wherever it lodges, infects and paralyzes the religious affections. Their sole quarrel was with sin and Satan; it was not with the visible powers of this world. Men may wage war with the Devil, without hatred; but not with their fellow men. Whitefield's face, while denouncing all the powers of darkness, still wore its usual loving smoothness; not so the Puritan, when Prelacy was in his eye.

We may well recognize that providential ordering of the Methodistic revival, which kept it clear of all sympathy with the bitter "vestments and gesture" feeling of the preceding century; and if required to name that one adjunctive circumstance which most favored its progress, as a proclamation of the Gospel, we should not hesitate to say—the Church training, and the Church feeling of the Wesleys, and of Whitefield.

The Puritan temper had nearly ceased to attach to the Nonconformists of the times of Watts and Doddridge; and they and their predecessors had done their part well in preserving evangelic doctrine from the extinction which then threatened it. It was a witness-function which they had discharged, and which had more of a passive than of an active character; invasive it was not in any degree; yet the true-hearted among the Nonconformists affectionately greeted their more enterprising successors, and cordially bid them God's speed. When Whitefield sat at the bedside of Watts, and in his frequent intercourse with Doddridge, and when he and the Wesleys, as often happened, were welcomed in the homes of the dissenters—that is to say, such dissenters as Williams of Kidderminster, they may be thought of as then tacitly receiving a charge, and as being invested with a commission to do effectively what these good men had not been in a position to attempt. Yet it was with a lively satisfaction that they hailed the dawn of a brighter day! They gave the rising Methodism their blessing, and died, rejoicing in hope. Thus did this new ministration of Apostolic Christianity receive a double authentication, first and formally from the Episcopal Church, and then virtually, from the Nonconforming Church. It was in a manner not altogether unlike this that the Reformers—German, Swiss, and English—united in themselves, officially and personally, the double continuity of a formal, and of an occult ordination. Visibly, they were ministers of the Church from which they separated, and which cast them out: at the same time, by personal intercourse and correspondence, by congruity in doctrine, by sympathy as martyrs, or as sufferers for the same Gospel, they stood related to the Bohemian and the Waldensian bodies, and were honored by the opprobrium that attached to the names—Wickliffeites and Lollards.

That law of continuity which is seen to prevail in the history of Christianity, has hitherto always shown itself under this twofold aspect. That is to say, revivals and renovations, whenever they occur, so arise as to render homage, first, to the visible or hierarchical transmission of Christian ordinances and ministrations; and at the same time they do not fail to connect themselves with that which has come down from an earlier season of reform and refreshment. Although an ample comment upon this biform law of religious history might seem, in some of its instances, to be too elaborate, or in a degree precarious, yet, when the course of events through long periods is broadly regarded, it presents itself too frequently not to attract notice, and to establish itself silently in our convictions.

Those whose own religious temperament is tranquil and devout, and who had always rather love than hate, will, while reviewing any separate portion of Christian history, or when contemplating the whole of it, draw much comfort from the considerations which this general principle suggests; for these considerations avail, not merely to discharge ecclesiastical virulence, if it has had any lodgment in our minds, but to abate that antagonistic vehemence to which we so easily give place, in matters of religion; and in a word, it will aid us in the endeavor to look calmly upon the troubled arena of this present scene, as from a higher level.

Further from our immediate purpose we must not travel than may be needful thus to bring the METHODISTIC COMPANY into, what we think, is its rightful position on the field of religious history. How comforting is it, and how consoling, and how does it purify, ennoble, animate, and elevate our own feelings when we consent to think and speak of these good men as taking their place in the host which "no man can number" of those who are constituting, and shall constitute a social economy, unearthly, and never to be dissolved!

We cast from us therefore with pity (and with shame if ever it have found a lodgment in our own heart) that hierarchical arrogance which would impel us to look upon the Methodistic band with scorn, and which mutters its anathemas against schismatics. On the other side, we put as far from us the dissident's glorying in the same company, when he points to them as the successful leaders of a great and permanent revolt from the Episcopal Church. In the place of either of these contracted feelings, we recognize, upon the front of Methodism, that special characteristic which has attached to Heaven's own servants, from age to age, as the authentic representatives, first, of an existing and visible order of things; and then of that always extant, remonstrant energy which took its rise in some anterior season of renovation. Let us be shown any where a company of men whose office it has been to reanimate what has become lifeless, and to purify what is corrupt, who have not stood related, in this twofold manner, to the present and to the past.

THE SUBSTANCE OF METHODISM.

THE FIRST ELEMENT OF METHODISM.

INTENDING to confine our view to its most distinctive features, we inquire concerning the Methodism of the last century, what is it which distinguishes it on the one hand, from that religious condition which it found existing, and on the other, from that which has come into its place, and which now surrounds ourselves.

Methodism was not a NEW THEOLOGY, or a polemical affirmation of dogmas, contravening or adding to that system of belief which had been embodied, two centuries before, in the articles and confessions of the several Protestant Churches. Those few points of doctrine which Wesley individually appended to the existing Protestant faith do not materially affect our present allegation, namely, that the Methodistic preachers held and taught, substantially, the doctrine that had been professed by the Reformers; and, as to Whitefield, and those who followed with him, he advanced nothing, in doctrine, that was new to Calvinistic theology.

Nor was Methodism, as to its primary intention, the promulgation and enforcement of a new religious mode of life, or an order, or factitious institute: it was not the gathering of a body of Regulars. Wesleyanism did indeed issue in the constitution of a new society; but this was an incidental consequence, resulting from the Founder's success in effecting his original and always principal purpose—"the conversion of the ungodly."

Setting off then from the mass of facts before us some incidental and unimportant peculiarities of opinion, as well as that which belongs to its external organization merely, we are to find in Methodism only that which is identical with the sense of all the Protestant communions, as expressed in their several confessions, creeds, and articles of religion, and which is held by all to be of the very substance of Christianity itself. And yet, while the theology is entirely what we recognize as the authentic belief of the Protestant Church, the product of the Methodistic ministrations, that is to say, the general or average product, apart from what might be attributed to the oratorical powers of individual preachers, was such as has no parallel, even in the most exciting moments of the Reformation; nor has it had any parallel in these later times. We are called upon therefore to show what it was which constituted the visible difference—vast as it is.

In what proportion of instances the Methodistic movement, which affected so many thousands of hearers through its forty years of primitive energy, did in fact issue in producing a "godly, righteous, and sober life," we are not now concerned to inquire, nor could such an inquiry, however laboriously instituted, yield any satisfactory result. What we have to do with is not that which can be known only in Heaven; but that which is patent and unquestionable, namely—that Protestant doctrine, proclaimed by men variously gifted and qualified, did, through a course of years, and wherever carried, affect the minds of thousands of persons, not in the way of a transient excitement, but effectively and permanently. The very same things had been affirmed, from year to year, by able and sincere preachers, in the hearing of congregations, assenting to all they heard—not indeed altogether without effect; yet with no such effect as that which ordinarily, if not invariably, attended the Methodistic preaching. Nor, if we look beyond the pale of religious influence, had any previous ministrations of the same Protestant doctrines taken hold, as this did, or in any remarkable manner, of the untaught masses of the people—the non-attendants upon public worship—the heathen million that circulates every Sunday around churches and chapels.

Let it be said—and we hold it as an undoubted truth, and a truth apart from which the facts before us must be wholly inexplicable—that the Methodistic proclamation of the Gospel was rendered effective by a Divine Energy, granted at that time, in a sovereign manner, and in an unwonted degree; but this truth remembered always, as it ought, the question returns—What were the principal elements of that religious impression which the Methodistic preaching so generally produced? This question must, for convenience sake, be answered in a distributive order, or under several heads, although in fact what we have to consider separately, constitutes a whole that is indivisible.

There are principles in human nature—as well intellectual as moral—which, although inherent in its structure, may, and often do, remain latent as to any effect, not in individuals merely, but in entire races of men, and that through long centuries, and even where civilization has wrought its effects partially upon them. Those vast diversities of condition, moral, intellectual, and social, which affect the several branches of the human family, resolve themselves, for the most part, into instances of this kind: that is to say, of the activity or the quiescence of certain elements of human nature. Man is the only one of the animated orders that is liable to any such obliteration of his original faculties—and so, he is the only being that falls out of his place, and fails, in so many instances, to reach the average level of development, proper to his order. A striking instance, illustrative of what is here affirmed, is afforded in that faculty which, among cultured nations, is the source of the arts of life, of the sciences, and of philosophy, namely—the abstractive. This faculty—we see it when once it begins to be developed—is of the very substance of the mind: it is man's distinction as head of the animated orders; and it is also his distinction as an intelligent inspector of the mechanism of the material universe, and so, in a sense, the consort of the Creator. Nevertheless, there are vast regions on the surface of the earth—regions that have been occupied during thousands of years by races of the human family, among which this master-spring of the mind has scarcely at all got into play. Man has there stood only a few steps raised above the level of the brute;—he has been a wretched troglodyte, or the tenant of a bush or hut; and he has so remained unchanged, while four or five empires, near neighboring to him, have risen, and flourished, and disappeared in their turn. And yet it is certain, that if at any moment during that long reckoning of silent centuries there had come among these tribes, the civilized man—protected and favored—carrying with him his implements, his arts, and his science, he might have woke up the dormant power, so that a nation might have been born in a day. If the civilization, the refinement, and the philosophy of the civilized nations be a wonder, is not the barbarism of races that are capable of the same by structure, and which yet is perpetuated through cycles of time—a still greater wonder, or we may say, a deep mystery? With an instance such as this before us, there can be no room to think it incredible that some principal rudiment of the moral structure of human nature, should *also* be liable to a like dormant condition, or that whole races of men, civilized or barbarous, should, through perhaps the entire period of their national existence, show only the feeblest indications of the presence of such a moral power. It is certain that if the abstractive faculty were not a rudiment of man's intellectual structure, no modes of excitement, no stimulants, how powerful soever, would avail to convey, or to confer it. It is manifest, therefore—perplexing as the fact may be—that so principal a faculty may, in the instance of nations, and through the longest periods of time, be, as if it were not. If this fact be perplexing, when thought of in its relationship to such notions as we are apt to form of the Providential government of the world, so, and in a deeper sense, is the fact perplexing that races of men, millions strong, have passed through their allotted cycles, and have counted out their destined centuries, barely conscious, if at all, of their immortality, or of their future encounter with inflexible justice. Yet to infer hence that the religious consciousness is no part of human nature, or that man is not born to live again, would be a conclusion equally unphilosophical and dangerous.

The religious sense, that is to say, a vivid feeling of our relationship, individually, to invisible government—hereafter to be reckoned with, requires to be distinguished from some other principles of our nature with which it usually commingles itself, and with which it may easily be confounded. Thus, in the first place, the religious sense is distinguishable from the moral sense, or that consciousness of right and wrong, which may be fully developed as far as it is related to the good and evil of our present term of life, and yet may bring with it no reference to a future life. Although the belief of a future life will not fail to stimulate the natural conscience, this power, as the basis of secular morality, does not spring from any such belief, and is often entirely independent of it.

Then again, the religious sense has no inseparable alliance with that tendency of mankind, so universally displayed, to surround themselves with invisible powers—the objects of immediate hope and dread, and which are the creations of the imagination, rather than of the moral sense. Nations the most addicted to polytheistic worship have shown themselves less alive than others, either to the moral, or to the religious feelings.

While in the midst, as we now are, of another argument, it would carry us too far to attempt to illustrate the independence and the sejunctive tendency of the religious and of the moral sense, by taking even a glance at the religious history of the Jewish people, and of the Christian Church. Instead of entering upon so various and heavy a task, we may find, nearer home, sufficient exemplification of what we have just now to do with, namely, that first element of Methodism which continued to be a prominent characteristic of it, through a course of years.

Taking an ordinary instance as sufficient for our purpose, let it be asked what it is that a Christian minister may believe that he sees before him on a Sunday? He may be sure that there is always much of the diffused and salutary influence of Christian doctrine within the compass of his stated congregation. With a few exceptions (probably) he addresses those who, whether in the way of a passive acquiescence, or as the result of reading and reflection, have come sincerely to accept Christianity as true:—they *do* "unfeignedly believe the holy Gospel." They *do* "look for the resurrection of the dead, and the life of the world to come." In this pulpit-prospect there is therefore a wide range for charitable hope, and ground enough on which the pastor's consolation may rest, that he has not altogether "labored in vain."

Or to vary the instance, we can many of us recall the recollection of those over-crowding times when a preacher of unmatched power and grace—a perfect orator, used to fix every eye upon himself, through his hour of fluent and affluent sublimities. How did all faces gleam with an intensity of intellectual enjoyment, longing to vent itself in loud acclamations at every pause! And when that hour of fascination was over, what looks of gratulation were exchanged among friends, from pew to pew! what shaking of hands, and how many smiles and nods passed to and fro, among the delighted people!

But now all these pleasurable indications must be dismissed, for it is a Methodist of Wesley's, or of Whitefield's order that is in this same pulpit. As a preacher he is not more sincere or right-minded than the last; and as an orator, he is far less highly gifted; he is not so accomplished a theologian, nor in any sense is he rather to be chosen than the other, as to his dispositions, or endowments, or as to his creed; but he is a Methodist, and his words sink into the hearts of those that hear. While he speaks, a suppressed anxiety rules the spirits of the crowd, and this feeling breaks forth into sighs, on every side:—the preacher's style is not, in itself, oratorically affecting, and yet many weep, and an expression, not to be simulated, of anguish and of dread, marks many faces. What is it then that has taken place? It is this, that a sense, deep seated in the structure of human nature, but which hitherto has slumbered, has suddenly woke up. There is a tumult in the soul, while a power irresistible is claiming its rights over both body and soul. Instead of that interchange of smiles which lately had pervaded the congregation, while the orator was doing his part, now every man feels himself, for the hour, alone in that crowd. Even the preacher is almost forgotten; for an immortal and guilty spirit has come in to the presence of Eternal Justice. Within the dismayed heart it is as if the moral condition, hitherto unheeded, were spread abroad for strictest scrutiny. Quite gone from the thoughts are all those accessories of religious feeling, which so often in times past, had been the source of agreeable devout excitement. It is a dread of the supreme rectitude that now holds the mind and heart.

To many who had honestly thought themselves religious persons for twenty years or more, the feelings are quite new which now have come into exercise; and such persons are willing to acknowledge that, whatever impressions of a religious kind may have been produced upon them heretofore by eloquent preachers, those which the voice of this Methodist has enkindled differ from such feelings, not merely in degree, but in kind: to them it is as if a lost rudiment of the moral nature had sprung into activity. It is a sense of the soul's relationship to God —a relationship which nothing can dissolve, and which demands the immortality of its subject. This awakened sense, at the first, can be painful only; and its activity is an anguish—an agony. The belief, or rather the vivid consciousness, of a future life, results involuntarily from this new perception of the infinite import of good and evil.

When it is affirmed, as now, that the feeling excited by the Methodist preacher, and which so powerfully affects the mass of his hearers, differs not only in *degree* but in *kind* from ordinary religious emotions, what is intended may be made clear by a familiar illustration; as thus:

A man has been trained from boyhood to the military profession, and he has spent the years of youth and manhood in camps, barracks, and garrisons, and all that belongs to a soldier's life, or that can belong to it, in time of peace, whether in the way of reading, or of converse with veterans, or of martial movement and circumstance, has become part and parcel of his nature. But at length actual war sounds its note in his ear; and he joins his comrades on the field, and moves to his position in the ranks while yet the morning mist hangs upon the slopes in front of the lines:—in a moment a flash of fire and its thunders is followed by the fall of men on either hand: blood and moans begin this long new day of his life: battle is a reality; and although the same subjects fill his thoughts now, as have filled them heretofore, his state of mind, now and then, differs not in degree of feeling merely, but in kind.

Whoever has lived through hours or moments, of extreme peril or anguish, will know how to find analogous instances. Even to witness a fatal shipwreck from the shore, or a conflagration, in which several perish; or to stumble in one's path through a copse upon the weltering body of a murdered man—any of these less frequent incidents may have made an impression so deep and indelible upon a sensitive mind, as that the years preceding such an occurrence seem to belong to a state of existence essentially unlike that of the years subsequent to it.

Preaching, in ordinary times, produces an effect upon practiced congregations analogous indeed to the subjects that are at any time brought forward;—that is to say, the feeling of the people is in harmony with the feeling and intention of the speaker; and beyond this rippling of the glassy surface, an individual, here and there, is more deeply affected. But, as to the mass, there is no proportion whatever—there is no approach toward a proportionate feeling, as related to the import of the principal facts upon which the preacher insists. The difference, then, between this preacher and the Methodist of the time gone by is of that sort which the instances above adduced illustrate: the one is listened to with assent and approval—every word of the other is as a shaft that rives the bosom.

Whether Wesley and Whitefield, and others of their class, addressed Christianized congregations, or the lowest of the people, a wonderful uniformity marked the effect produced, where any effect at all was produced; and whether the hearer was one who had listened to ten thousand sermons, or was now hearing his first, the two hearers stood almost undistinguished side by side. But this could not have been if the preacher had gone about to produce conviction by a circuit of reasoning; for in that case what might have swayed one mind, would not have touched the other. What the preacher advanced ordinarily, was a bare affirmation of that which the human mind, by its very structure, assents to as true, when it is so affirmed as to take hold of the conscience. Having won this first advantage, that is to say, having lodged in the conscience his initial principle, he went on to improve his conquest. In doing so he sometimes used a style which modern congregations could not easily be brought to tolerate, and against which some reasonable exceptions might no doubt be taken. Nevertheless, it must be the phraseology only, or the preacher's manner, and his undue vehemence, that could be resented, at least by those who are the frequenters of churches; for he does nothing more than insist upon, and expound, that very language which is on the lips of all such persons habitually, or of all who profess any form of Christian belief.

When that which is so momentous is in question, the mere adjuncts of the Methodistic preaching—its rudeness, perhaps, or its harsh phrases, or its obsolete dialect, should be disregarded. The Methodist asks for no assent reaching beyond the range of our own constant acknowledgments. But if these things be granted, then he expounds to us what, without his asking, we have confessed often;

but now the mind's habitual complacency has been rent away and dispersed, and the affrighted hearer finds that he can not, if he would, "cloke or dissemble his sins before the face of Almighty God;" he feels and knows that he is indeed one who had need deprecate the "wrath of God," and pray to be delivered from "eternal damnation." Now, if never before, he admits it to be true that he has "most justly provoked" that "wrath and indignation;" and now he feels the "remembrance of his multiplied offenses to be grievous, and the burden of them intolerable."

If then it be asked "What was Methodism?" our first reply must be—it was the waking up of a consciousness toward Almighty God, which gave a meaning to expressions such as these.

But the Methodist preacher advanced further on this ground; and he spoke, without scruple or abatement, of the future retribution. Why should it be required of him to evade the meaning of terms so well authenticated, and that were still in use? "Eternal damnation" was not a phrase of Methodistic origin; nor was it new to affirm it to be the "just reward of our sins." Nothing on this ground was added by the preacher to the universal belief —or the *professed* belief of Christendom. The fact, however, is to be well observed that, while insisting with unwonted urgency upon this dread article of catholic belief, the personal temper, neither of the Wesleys, nor of Whitefield, nor of any of the more noted preachers, was in any degree morose, gloomy, acrid, or wrathful. A temper the contrary of this was the characteristic of this band of men. If some few of the lay preachers were fierce or stern in their dispositions, it was not so with the chiefs. Methodism—let us note the fact—was not ushered into the world by a company of brazen-tongued and fiery zealots. Wesley by temperament was joyous, Whitefield loving, and in respect of mildness of temper and benevolence, they and their colleagues stand in very favorable contrast with the Puritans, as well as with many of the German, Swiss, and English Reformers. In speaking as they did of the "wrath to come," they are exempt from the imputation either of a malign fanaticism, or of a presumptuous exaggeration of the existing doctrine thereto relating; nor does it appear that they were in fact ex cepted against by their contemporaries on this ground. They thought and spoke as Baxter, and as Luther, and as the divines of earlier times had thought and spoken.

If we are willing to trace the hand of God in the Methodistic movement of the last century, we should acknowledge it in this instance, that it took place at the very verge of that period when the ancient belief as to future punishment was still entire. These preachers therefore employed the doctrine they found ready to their hand, without thinking themselves obliged to maintain it against any prevalent gainsaying. Any such feeling would have given a controversial air to that which, to produce its direct and proper effect, must be affirmed peremptorily, and as if assented to by the hearer. If the preacher had abated these affirmations, in compliance with a known contrary opinion, he would have forfeited his power: if he had gone about to sustain them with argument, he would often have failed, and often have run into exaggerations.

A new Methodism—a Methodism confronting the Christian, and the unchristian mind of this present time, would find itself in a very different position; but we here touch a subject which may be better considered in another place

---

THE SECOND ELEMENT OF METHODISM.

As the FIRST element of that revival which Methodism so extensively effected, we have thus alleged to be an awakening of the dormant religious consciousness, or innate sense of our relationship to God, the righteous Judge. This religious consciousness, as it goes far beyond the range of that moral sense which regards the obligations of this life, so does it vastly exceed, and much differ from the feeling which in ordinary times, pervades Christianized communities. But then, how deep soever and intense for a time, this awakened consciousness may be, there does not necessarily result from it any permanent spiritual renovation of the minds in which it takes place. The tumult of his new sense toward God may wholly subside, and all the anguish and the terror attending it may be allayed, or may be diverted by the return of earthly passions, and the soul may thus relapse, and often does so relapse, into its slumber. But if not, and if this quickening proceeds, there supervenes a deeper feeling still—a consciousness of the relationship of God, the Father of spirits, to the individual spirit, which is thus beginning to live a life divine. This reflex idea is the proper consequence of that which had already taken possession of the soul; and we find in it what we name as the second element of the Methodistic revival.

From the commencement of our Lord's public teaching, the spiritual system He proclaimed stood out in bold contrast with every other scheme of religion, or of philosophy—first, by presenting to the minds and affections of men—not a pantheistic idea, not a vague abstraction, not a "Deity," but "God the Father"—an idea which embraces all perfections, natural and moral, and represents them as centring upon a Personality, distinct, independent and individually defined. The consequence of fully admitting this Christian idea, was a belief and feeling of the *individual* relationship of God toward the soul individually. The main purport of our Lord's discourses, especially of those which were addressed to his immediate followers, was to imprint this one idea upon their minds and hearts. Thus it was that he "manifested the Father;" and, in the use of symbols the most peculiar, he encouraged each of his disciples to confide in the Divine regard toward *himself individually*. This doctrine, then so new, and so powerful always in its effect upon the human affections, imparted to dogmatic Christianity its force, its animation, its warmth; and a renovation of this belief has attended every remark-a●le season of religious refreshment. In a most decisive manner it attached to the Methodistic revival.

While, however, the personal ministry of Christ, and its intention, as embodied in his discourses, seemed to relate mainly to this principle of the Divine regard to each soul, and the tendency of which, if not otherwise counterbal anced, would be to insulate the human spirit—the Apos- tles, in giving Christianity to the world as a visible scheme, or Church system, brought foward another principle, namely, the relative and social, in giving effect to which men are considered and treated less as insulated beings, and more as members of a body, embracing all those who are embraced in the affections of each, and comprehended in the circle of domestic obligations.

This is a rudiment of that CHURCH IDEA which we assume to be as undoubtedly apostolic in its origin, as the other just named. Now the various, or, as one might say, the multifarious forms under which the Christian system in the lapse of ages has put itself forward, might conveniently be classified on this very ground; that is to say, as having either given expression, *chiefly*, if not exclusively, to that in the Gospel which concentrates the religious affections upon the individual relationship between God and the soul; or to that which diffuses the religious feelings and renders them less immediate. In a classification such as this, Methodism would take its place along with instances of the former class. Yet an objection starts up against such a decision; for it may be said—"Has not Methodism shown itself to be eminently a *social* scheme?" We grant that it has, yet it is social only so far as the individual convert is individually considered: of the apostolic Church Idea it has seemed to be little conscious, or too unmindful. It was on this ground that Wesley innovated the most, where least he is thought of as an innovator.

If the distinction we have now to insist upon be of a kind that is less obvious than some, it is far from being of inferior moment; and in truth, at this time, it is precisely tnat distinction which most urgently needs to be well understood, and attentively regarded. If we imagine each of these modes of Christian piety to be carried to its extreme point, and even to be a little exaggerated, then we shall have before us two broadly-marked religious styles, as well of feeling as of behavior, and between which the reconciling principle has not hitherto been discovered, or not applied. That it will be discovered, and applied too, and that thus an entire Christianity shall at length exhibit itself, we hold to be certain.

Taken, therefore, somewhat in its extreme form, for the sake of obtaining a more decisive contrast, the Church Idea of Christianity—beyond which the Church of Rome knows of nothing, and to which the Church of England has given more prominence than has been allowed it by any other of the Protestant communions, and more prominence than to the opposite, or counteractive idea, upon which Methodism wholly rests—this Church Idea lays its hold of all that are born within its circle, and it seals them as the property of the Church, and treats them as passive subjects (not individually, indeed, but *seriatim* rather) in its own appointed manner, as they arrive at each epoch of their mortal journey, from the womb to the grave: it duly engages for their safety and welfare, certain conditions being complied with; and it sends them forward, authoritatively countersigned, or endorsed, not merely into the unseen world, but beyond its entrance.

Now it must not be denied that, within the limits of even a system such as this, the religious affections may find room for exercise, and may become intense, profound, and ecstatic. Nevertheless, it is manifest that, so long as this Church Idea is held entire, or where it is open to no disturbance from the contiguity of more animated religious systems, there must belong to it a reserve, a distance, and a sense of remoteness from the object of worship. Piety, under this form is mediate always, more than immediate; and whereas the individual adult worshiper has reached, as a matter of course, and as if according to an invariable rule of official promotion, his actual place in the marshaled host that is moving forward with a steady tread toward the world eternal, he is not likely to entertain the thought of his own individuality; nor has he been encouraged to cherish the animating belief that he, individually, is the object of the Divine complacency in a peculiar sense.

How unlike this, on every side, whether of feeling, or of behavior, or of customary phraseology, is that Idea of Christianity which, in connection with our immediate purpose, we must call the Methodistic! Nor is the force of the contrast abated, in any sensible degree, when we select our Methodistic samples from out of the very bosom of the Church; nay, when we not only find our instances within its pale, but leave them there! Methodism may indeed flourish within the Church; but it will not be of it in a thoroughly homogeneous sense; or it will not do so until that harmonizing principle has come into operation, which shall give play to the two counteractive, but not incompatible, rudiments of Christianity itself. Until then, even if every phrase and every rubrical usage that hitherto has stood in the way of unanimity and conformity were removed, there must still exist a Christianity within the Church, and a Christianity out of it—whether Methodistic, or dissenting. Those phrases and those usages have hitherto served as the means of conserving among us that other Christian element which the Church does not recognize so distinctly as it might, and to which, in the last century, Methodism gave so broad an expansion.

The pulpit style of Wesley, and of Whitefield too, although in another tone, if it might be characterized in a single phrase, must be called the *individualizing*. These preachers, whose eye sparkled with a fiery energy, and whose hand, in every movement, seemed to have an aim, as if at a single bosom, spoke to the soul of every hearer, apart from the thousands around him. "My message is to *thee*, sinner! I stand here to-day to bring *thee* to bethink thyself of thy past ways. *Thou* who dost now appear in the presence of thy God—loathsome in thy sins—I challenge and command thee to bow thy stubborn neck, and to bend thy knee. Dost not thou—even thou, ungrateful as thou hast been these many years—yea a hardened rebel from thy mother's breast until now—dost thou not hear the Saviour calling to *thee* to repent and turn? Was it not for thee that he shed his blood? Did he not carry thy sorrows to Calvary, even thine? Was he not wounded for *thy* transgressions? Did he not think of thee, of thy soul, and of all its abominations, that dark night when he lay in agony on the ground? Yes. It was none other than thy sins that made him sweat blood in that garden. But now, with a purpose of mercy in his heart toward thy wretched soul, he calls thee to himself; and says, yes, he says, it to thee, 'Come now, let us reason together.'"

It was thus, and often in phrases far more emphatic and awakening, that a firm hold upon the human heart was taken, and that a commencement was made of that life divine—of that converse of the soul with the Shepherd of souls, to which it is the purport and end of the Christian dispensation to give effect.

As the proper and inevitable consequence of a commencement such as this, all those personally intense affections come into exercise, which in their variations of vividness give a history to each Christian singly, and which may be narrated by him. It is the development, and the subsidence, and the renovation, and the progression, of this theopathy that constitute the "experience" of each, and which is customarily spoken of under the comprehensive phrase of "the dealings of God with the soul." It is this individualized piety which furnishes materials to what is called "experimental preaching;" it is this that becomes the topic of conversation in classes and bands; it is this that has shed life and fervor into the diaries and letters of so many eminent persons, who have been the ornament of the several Protestant communions; and in a word, it is on this ground that the exercise of a pure taste and of Christian discretion are so much to be desired, and have so often been lost sight of.

Now although this individualized spiritual life is much older than Methodism, yet it must be named as having been peculiarly its characteristic; and can we read the Book of Psalms, or our Lord's discourses with his disciples, or the apostolic epistles, and then denounce this rudiment of Methodism, as if in itself it were spurious and unwarranted? Surely not; nevertheless, when this order of religious feeling has been left to expand itself unchecked, and when it has received encouragement, and has been exposed to stimulants, it has come to present an aspect differing essentially from that Christianity according to the Church Idea, of which already we have spoken; and how incongruous do the two forms of piety appear when, as sometimes has happened, the one has sprung into existence upon the very lap of the other! or when Methodism has courted the maternal caresses of the Church!

The most important innovations are often those which attract little or no attention while they are taking place. Wesley earnestly deprecated, for instance, the interference of the preaching hour in his chapels with the hours of divine worship in the parish church; and he also long resisted the administration of the sacraments by his preachers. In such things he dreaded innovation; and yet *these* invasions of Church order were of small moment, as compared with that mighty revolution in Christian feeling, language, behavior, which every word almost of his sermons, and of his personal converse with his people, was bringing about. He did indeed vehemently enjoin his followers to hold to their parish churches; but in the very same breath he woke up in their hearts a vivid individual feeling, which would inevitably withdraw them from it; and this result would take place, even where the ministrations of the Church itself were animated by the Methodistic spirit! Thus it is that, at this time, and irrespective entirely of all questions of ecclesiastical polity, or of external conformity, or of non-conformity, the religious commonwealth (in the Episcopal Church, and out of it) subsists under these two types, that is to say, of the Church Idea, and of the Methodistic. Great changes must have place before the two shall coalesce, or work well together.

The writings of the continental Reformers, as also of the founders of the English Church, abundantly prove that they were themselves alive to that great Christian principle which imparts its individuality to piety. Their own earnest style in the pulpit implies this; and upon it rests the Protestant principle—the right of private judgment, as well as the sacred obligation of witnessing to the truth, even unto death; together with the privilege and duty of every man to read and study Holy Scripture for himself. It was from this solid standing that the Reformers made head against Rome. Nevertheless, in their reconstruction of the Church, it was the Church Idea that became predominant, which thus was left liable, at all times, to those internal discords, and to those convulsions and invasions which, by a deep necessity, must bring it into peril, as often as any great religious revival takes place within, or around it. The next season of religious reanimation may not perhaps take to itself, or bear, the name and guise of "Methodism," but inevitably it will convulse a communion which does not distinctly recognize what is not included in its own Idea of Christianity.

It is of the very nature of animated piety that it should pass into the form of an individual history; and the more profound this piety is, the more decisively *personal* will it become. And then further, when he who, in this intimate manner, surrenders himself to the influence of the loftier revelations of the Christian system, and learns to think of himself—albeit as one of the most unworthy, yet as the object of an eternal purpose of mercy—when, in a word, he has learned to read in the Scriptures far more than what, as a convert, he had thought of—when he has passed beyond the use of milk, and knows how to assimilate stronger aliment, then will "the life he lives daily" be the treading of a path which must be trod alone. What is meant is not a mystic absorption in the Divine Essence but an animated correspondence, from day to day, from hour to hour, carried on between the redeemed and restored human spirit and the PERSONAL REDEEMER—the Shepherd and Bishop of souls, who, in terms the most significant, has invited and has given ample warrant to this "boldness of access" to Himself. Thus it is that a ripened Christian piety is always in a sense seclusive; and thus is it spoken of as a "life that is hid with Christ in God."

Nevertheless the most profound and elevated piety can never be unsocial—far from it; and, on the contrary, it will seek and find sympathy and communion. Yet it is always a question to what extent, and under what conditions, it will or can do so. Or the same inquiry, in substance, might be set forward in other terms—as thus, in relation to our immediate subject it might be asked—Can that religious individuality, which it was the very object of the Methodistic revival to call forth and cherish—can it advance beyond a rudimental condition when, in a compulsory and mechanical manner, it is drawn forth from the bosom, and subjected to formal regulations, and when it is to be registered and reported weekly? This is a grave question, and it seems to bring into view an incongruity in one at least of the forms into which Methodism has passed.

Christian piety, developed according to the Church Idea, will not often, if ever, take to itself this character of individuality; but when developed according to the Methodistic, or, as we now say, the "Evangelic" idea, it seldom fails to do so; and this is that point of difference between the two, on the ground of which the imputation of enthusiasm is used to be thrown by the profane world, and by the formalist adherents of the Church principle, upon those who profess a piety that is less abstract, and more subjective, than their own.

A faulty style, easily fallen into, and not easily avoided, and from which Methodism has never held itself entirely free, gives color to that imputation of enthusiasm of which we now speak. In truth this imputation is more than colorable—it is warrantable—when brought against very much which has received the sanction of Methodistic and of Evangelic usage. What is here intended ought to be clearly understood.

That conscious personal relationship to the Saviour Christ, which we have assumed to be of the very substance of mature Christian piety, and which can never be warrantably rebuked as enthusiastic, is by no means identical with the introverted spiritual sensitiveness, or the overweening religious egotism, or the hypochondriac moodiness, which so often comes in its place, and is inconsiderately accepted in its stead. The one rests upon a clear and ample foundation of scriptural encouragements; the other must go far before it finds any substantial support, either of precept, promise, or example, any where within the compass of the inspired writings. The immediate objects and excitements of the one are those unchanging perfections of the Divine nature, the habitual contemplation of which imparts stability, serenity, dignity to the human spirit, prevailing over its own momentary variableness. But, as to the latter, its objects are concentred around that same variableness. The fitfulness of every hour, the sombre color of one mood, or the gayety of another, the nameless ills, the dim surmises, the absurd fantasies, which perturb misgoverned minds, these are the objects, the occasions, the springs, of that alternately murky and giddy temper to the variations of which the phrase "religious experience" has so often, and so grievously, been misapplied.

That a substitution of the spurious for the genuine should so often take place on this ground, can excite little surprise; for the genuine "hidden life" implies a depth of soul and a tranquil fervor that are not the most common; and it implies instruction, and a well-formed habit of meditation and prayer: it implies, moreover, consistency and moral tone; but as to the other, its counterfeit, nothing more is required for its production than so much religious perturbation as shall suffice for working upon the disorders, the inconsistencies, the waywardness, the ungoverned tempers, the vanity, the pride, the vexations, that are incident to the commonest order of minds. In any community of Christian people, therefore, where we might find one who is qualified, if he could be induced so to do, to speak of that hidden life which gladdens his own heart, scores may be met with who are full of their "experience," and who may easily be encouraged to say much of it, and so of themselves.

Nevertheless it would be a serious practical error on the part of any who should incline to treat these instances as cases of hypocrisy, or of delusion. The world must, perhaps, be indulged in the license it will take, to deride that which, wanting substance as it does, yet contains a germ which, to the world, is a problem always. A wise instructor, and one who is loving as well as wise, and whose wisdom has nothing in it of vulgar shrewdness, will know how to turn the eye from objects that are sullied and marred, and that can yield no peace, and insensibly fix it upon that which is ever bright and constant. But how shall any such office of charity be performed by those whose own piety is fervent perhaps, but superficial and uninformed, and whose habit of mind and language is egotistical? When, in fact, an instructor or spiritual guide of this order puts his stated question to his class, "What have been the Lord's dealings with your soul, the last week?" he invites the utterance of that which not only would be better not uttered, but better not remembered or thought of.

Too easily it has been assumed as certain that this style of spurious "experience" is sustained by example and precept of Scripture. Those who have allowed themselves to think so would do well to make search, and to bring together—if indeed so many are to be found

—five texts from the gospels, or epistles, which, when fairly interpreted, might serve the required purpose. It is granted, indeed, that the soul will have its alternations of hope and fear, of joy and despondency, of elation and depression. This is certain; but let the question be asked, how much regard is paid by the inspired writers to these fitful diversities of individual feeling? So much as this—to enounce a comprehensive admonition—"Is any among you merry, let him sing psalms; is any afflicted, let him pray." To every joy and every woe, to each mood, to each affection the alternations of which checker the course of man, the Gospel furnishes what we need for our comfort, or correction. But these alternations, having sometimes a real, and sometimes an imaginary or factitious origin, become exaggerated when they are habitually regarded, and when they are made the subject of formal question and answer.

It was the proper consequence of the Methodistic preaching to call into activity that life of the soul, as individually related to God, of which now we have spoken, and which must be named as one of its distinctive elements. But it was a consequence not to be desired, and yet not easily averted, that this preaching, and the social economy which sprung out of it, should have the effect of diffusing among all religious communities an unreal style which the Scriptures do not authorize. This mistaken pietism has, however, received some check, and in an effective manner, for amid those various labors of Christian benevolence which have become the characteristic of these times, the religious thoughts and affections of Christian people, and especially of the young, meet their legitimate objects, and are healthfully engaged. In the place of an introverted spiritual egotism there has come in among us a laborious, and often a self-denying and warm-hearted, philanthropy—a good exchange indeed! and if Methodism must bear the blame of having generated the former, it may fairly challenge as its own a large portion of the praise, or the humble gratulation, which is the due of the latter.

THE THIRD ELEMENT OF METHODISM.

THERE may have been, in some instances, more than a colorable pretext for the opprobrium thrown upon Methodism, that it has produced insanity; for if we imagine those emotions only which thus far we have spoken of, and none of a more tranquil kind, to be taking effect upon feeble or distempered minds, it can be no wonder if reason gives way. In truth, not merely the weak, but the strongest minds might be seen to break down beneath those feelings of anguish and dismay which powerful religious impressions, *of one kind*, unabated, are likely to excite. It can not seem strange that human nature should be convulsed by ungovernable terrors when it wakes, up as in a moment, in presence of the unseen and eternal world, and when it becomes vividly conscious, at once of its own immortality, and of that which renders the thought of immortality appalling—the sense of accumulated guiltiness. The wonder is, rather, that such awakenings do not shatter every bosom within which they take place.

But the same Methodism which produced this agitation carried with it also the proper counteractive motives: or let it rather be said, that it brought with it that Gospel which wounds, only that it may heal. The same human nature which betrays its infirmity when it is borne upon by powerful motives of one kind only, or by unadjusted motives, alternately—as, for instance, by hope and fear, displays—may we not say it—its innate grandeur, and affords a sure indication of its immortal destiny, when, although the forces that act upon it are severally of the highest intensity, these forces are so balanced as to establish themselves in equilibrium, in relation to the intellectual and moral faculties. This balance, or counteraction of motives is, as we know, the spring of tranquil power and of productive energy in the highest order of minds; and to others less distinguished, it secures peace and a fruitful activity.

It may be that, while diverted or distracted amidst the shifting objects and interests of the present life, we do but imperfectly feel how important—how indispensable to our well-being is this equilibrium of motives, especially when these are of a powerful kind. But to those whose habit of mind is meditative and excursive it will often have happened—in a musing hour—to fall into perplexities, when endeavoring to imagine what that condition of the moral faculties, and of the sympathies belonging to this life must be, which shall render a state of undisturbed felicity *possible* in the next, when that shall have been seen and known, the knowledge of which *now* could consist with no tranquillity, much less with felicity. Yet as this knowledge of the alternatives of immortality can not be supposed to undergo erasure from the mind that has once admitted it, we are compelled to imagine that the future "fullness of joy" will arise from a true harmonizing of emotions brought about in some mode bearing analogy to that which, in the present state, secures peace to even the most sensitive Christian mind.

No human mind, probably, in the present state, has entirely succeeded in working its way out from among the perplexities to which we now refer, for they attach to our *position*, as social beings, very imperfectly alive, as we are, to those higher relationships, that are to be unfolded in our after state. Nevertheless, we may with confidence advance a step in saying, negatively, concerning this future harmony of the soul, which is to consist with its happiness, and with its knowledge of that which if now known and contemplated must overthow the firmest mind —that it will not arise from the mere balancing of opposite considerations—so much set down on the one side, outweighed by so much more on the other side—which balance, showing a clear excess of what is favorable and bright, the mind assents, once for all, to the product, and comes to the reasonable conclusion, for itself, to be happy forever! This can not be. It may, indeed, be thus that we consent to reason ourselves into a tranquil acquiesence with our own lot in life, as being on the whole eligible; but it is not thus, or in any such manner, that the deepest elements of our nature are hereafter to be forced into adjustment. The felicity of the good will never be framed out of metaphysic syllogisms, in the manner that has been attempted by the misjudging and insensitive theologians of a scholastic age.

It must be on some other path that spirits, moulded after the fashion of human nature, may hereafter reach a ground of peace and joy. In this state we must always fail to give body and form to that which belongs to another state; yet we may be sure, thus far, that a tranquil happiness which is not founded, either upon an oblivion of what has once been known, or upon grounds of formal calculation, may be the product of the due adjustment of the moral faculties. Whatever may be the intensity of any one class of feelings, it is certain that feelings of another class, being the proper counterpoise of the first, may be brought to bear upon it. The finite spirit—retaining unabated its sensibilities, and having forfeited none of its past experiences—may be imagined to reach its place of rest, when borne upon on all sides by forces which, singly would crush it.

By following upon this path a step or two further, we come in sight of that which we are now in search of—namely, that which was the principal, and the harmonizing element of the Methodistic revival.

Whatever is proper to human nature, inclusive of its most vivid and its most peculiar sensibilities, belonged to HIM who, when he took that nature to himself, as his own, blended it forever with the Infinite Perfections. It is as one Being—finite and Infinite—sensitive as the finite, "ever blessed" as the Infinite—that He liveth who is the one Christ—our God and Saviour; and so is the Representative, and the Head, and the Ruler of the human family. Whatever else, of an adjunctive kind, hitherto unthought of, and unimagined, the future life shall reveal, undoubtedly it shall bring near to the consciousness of every human spirit its own indissoluble relationship to the Divine nature, through Him who is God and Man—bright in eternal attributes; bright also in every grace of a perfect humanity!

Now on any occasion of unusual peril or anxiety, when tumultuous emotions are bearing with distracting force upon an infirm and sensitive nature, if one who is so suffering does but come into the society of a greater mind, known and seen to be at once cognizant of all facts and circumstances, and as much alive as itself to them all, and which yet shows a placid brow, and an eye beaming with hope and love, the mere contiguity of such a superior spirit, with a word of assurance and sympathy, how does it allay the inward tempest, how does it impart hope and comfort! In such an instance—and such belong to the circle of human experience—the reanimated spirit, although it could not have reasoned itself into tranquillity, yet it has caught it, and is now silently partaking of a harmony not its own.

The application of this analogy to our present purpose is not difficult. Although the human mind, in its present condition, must always fail in its endeavor to bring itself into a position such as it may be imagined to occupy in the future state, we may without hesitation affirm from what source must spring that new class of feelings among which the human spirit is to find its equilibrium. These rudiments of joy—a joy not unconscious of contrary impulses, nor oblivious of them, and yet full and secure—must be the product of the soul's contiguity with Him whose own blessedness blends what is peculiar both to the Divine and human natures.

But now how far may a consciousness analogous to this, which we allege as belonging to a future state, be partaken of by those who still tread this low ground of dim perceptions, and of faith? An answer to a question such as this may best be obtained by following the course of an individual mind in its progress onward, from a low toward a higher position. Let us, then, bring before us an instance, of which many, every way similar, might be adduced. An individual history will give the more distinctness to that comparison which we have in view between one condition of a Christian community and another, when no difference as to articles of belief has had place, or would be admitted.

We suppose, then, that we have before us the religious memoirs of one whose advantage it was to be bred and trained in the bosom of an orthodox and evangelic community, and who there received—as without much reflection, so without gainsaying, and with an acquiescent and respectful feeling, the principal articles of the Christian faith, as embodied in the three creeds of the Episcopal Church, or in the Westminster Confession of Faith; or as held and taught by Howe and Matthew Henry. During that high season of fresh life in which an active mind is pushing its way, and breaking for itself a path, hither and thither, among the objects of professional ambition, or of science, or literature, that early indoctrination—or, as it might be called, the catechumen's inherited faith—remains whole and untouched—like a costume dress, which is had out and worn only a few times in the course of years. But a time comes when perhaps the accidental looking into a body of Divinity, or the reading a controversial book, or an incidental regard paid to the history of opinions, brings the gravest questions of Christian theology before the now mature mind. An effective intellectual effort is therefore made, and a degree of serious attention is given to these momentous principles, involving, as they do, not merely the position which is hereafter to be taken in the religious community, but the opinion that should be formed of Christianity itself, as claiming the submission of a well informed and upright mind.

The consequence of this process of inquiry, the biblical and theological, is, we may suppose, the attainment of a belief much in advance of the catechumen's silently accepted creed:—it is a personal possession, the fruit of labor; it is a dogmatic persuasion, on the ground of which a man may hold a serious argument with others, may repeat the creeds with intelligence and feeling; and might even write, and profess his belief before the world.

At those seasons when, whether from any special cause or not, devout emotions are in unusual activity, the mind calls up its now accredited doctrinal belief, and is able, with more or less of feeling, to throw itself upon this ground of religious hope. He who thus believes, thinks, and feels, is undoubtedly in possession of the faith of a Christian man; and such a faith is that of a large proportion of those who statedly occupy pews in churches and chapels, and who never advance beyond it.

Alternations of comfort and discomfort, of confidence and of misgiving, are likely to attach to this state of mind, especially with the ingenuous and thoughtful; and with such there will be an uneasy consciousness of the disproportion between its own habitual emotions, and the doctrines it holds, which will often thus express itself, and such a one will say—"If truths so unutterably vast in their compass, and so momentous, be indeed my creed—if the words I constantly repeat mean what they seem to convey, and I acknowledge it to be so, how shall I give any reason for my own ordinary state of mind, as thereto related? Either there must be something misunderstood in my own mind, when I say I believe such things, or there must yet be something further on in the Christian life, of which, at present, I have had no experience." The consequence of such reflections as these will be, the renewal of serious efforts to redress, if possible, this inward disproportion—this variation of so many degrees between the soul and the creed, and a measure of success may attend these conscientious endeavors; nor ought the *genuineness* of the religious conditions, even if it never advances far beyond this stage of alternating disquiet, and dissatisfaction, and hopefulness, to be questioned—that is to say, if it be not brought into doubt on other grounds.

But at length this Christian man, whose history we uppose ourselves to be following, reaches a new era in his course, and an advance is made which is so marked and decisive, that, whatever he may have believed and felt in times past fades almost from his recollection, as if it were a dream. Not a syllable of his heretofore professed belief has been displaced, or seems to need correction. If required to state in what sense he understands certain passages in the apostolic writings, his reply would be precisely the same in words now as at any former time; he would find it difficult, in fact, to describe, in terms, the revolution which has taken place in his feelings and apprehensions, for it consists in a consciousness to which language gives no utterance—a consciousness of the reality of the First Truth of the Christian system. With this new sense is associated the feeling that it has been granted from above; it has come to him as a bestowment; he perfectly knows that it has not been the product of the laborious workings of his own reason; but that it is a gift—as much so as if he had suddenly found himself endowed with a new sense, as to material objects.

Many religious persons, of thoughtful habit, have come to a conclusion, more or less clearly perceived, to this effect—namely, That inasmuch as the principal fact of Christianity—the union of the Divine and human natures in the person of Christ, and its propitiatory intention has, and can have, no parallel—no instance strictly analogous, and as it includes far more than a finite mind can compass or apprehend, little aid, in the way of explication or illustration, or for obviating objections, ought to be looked for as derivable from the circle of human agencies, or any modes of proceeding known to us on earth. Much has been attempted by theological writers on this ground, and perhaps something useful has been effected: yet it is but little, at the most; and the endeavor has speedily been relinquished by the best ordered minds. The first truths of Christianity are not indeed out of harmony with the human mind; but they are quite beyond its experience, and far beyond its unaided grasp; they are principles which may be symbolized by the things of earth, but not resembled to any of them: they may be announced in words, but can never be laid open by any powers of language; for language has no terms expressive of relationships such as these, between the Infinite and the finite. It is not true that language is so *ambiguous* that it may not run itself around these high truths, definitely, and so as to lodge them securely in a creed: it may do so; but it can never unfold what it so conveys or defines.

A step further may yet be taken. Beyond the confines of that region which language may claim as its domain, the human mind does make excursions, and thus it becomes conscious of a power to admit more than words or phrases may convey: but has this faculty hitherto fully developed itself? Every meditative mind feels that it has not; and hence comes the fervency of that desire which impels such minds to seek and implore the bestowment of light and truth as a free gift from above. Still further than this, it is perceived that that Sovereign Grace whence sprang the redemption of the world, and the deliverance of man from sin and misery, implies (must it not necessarily imply?) a correlative act, in each instance in which this redemption takes effect. If to have devised and achieved his own salvation is a task utterly hopeless on the part of man, so must it surpass his faculties, intellectual and moral, to bring himself individually into communion with this salvation, or indeed to apprehend it: this knowledge of it, not less than the redemption itself, must be a bestowment.

When at length it is bestowed—when what has always been believed on evidence of Scripture is brought home, as a reality, both to the mind and to the feelings, then the hitherto perturbed spirit, which had alternately accepted and mistrusted its first principles, takes them as its own, and is at rest. What was well sustained by argument and evidence is still seen to be so sustained; but now it is known with an assurance such as no intellectual effort could convey.

In theological usage, whatever is involved in the first

truths of Christianity has come to be treated of distinctively, and is argued under a dogmatic form, as constituting so many doctrines. This method may, in relation to its purposes, be good and necessary; but as a matter of consciousness—as a Divine bestowment upon each soul that receives it, it is One Truth—it is the one effulgent mystery, it is the one "great salvation," effected and secured in that ineffable mode which the inspired writings variously affirm.

According to the constitution of their minds, or the discipline they had individually passed through, or the influence of others over them, the leading Methodistic preachers gave prominence to this or that—separately considered—aspect of the one bright truth of the coming of the Eternal Son of the Father into the world for its deliverance. Thus it was that, with some of them, the primary or rudimentary announcement—which is that of the preacher of repentance—namely, a free and full pardon of sins—was the customary theme in the pulpit; and the preacher's characteristic motto-text was of this sort—"In whom we have redemption, even the forgiveness of sins." Another, taking up this primary truth, combined it with bright and enlivening announcements of the unrestricted *intention*, or universal availableness, to all mankind, of this salvation. "Christ"—this is the preacher's text—"is the propitiation for our sins, and not for ours only, but for the sins of the whole world:" or this—"The Father sent the Son to be the Saviour of the WORLD." Another, whose eye is fixed upon the grace and majesty of Him who is "the brightness of the Father's glory, and the express image of His person," enlarges with pathos and copiousness of illustration upon those inexhaustible themes for which the Scriptures afford materials, and which relate to the personal perfections of Him who, as truly man, and truly God, gathers to himself whatever can move the profound and reverential affections of men. To this preacher the tropical language of the Old Testament, when illuminated by the beams of the New, furnishes treasures of impassioned discourse—ever grateful to the ear, and always listened to as if heard for the first time. Or, approaching the same object, as from another side, a preacher takes up the dogmatic and forensic strain, and in a style more severe, and more logical and polemical, asserts the Protestant doctrine of "justification by faith"—faith itself being the gift of God; and conveying to the guilty and convicted sinner a "righteousness" not his own, but "imputed." This preacher, in his style, is textual, categorical, consecutive; and he employs himself much in defending the position which he has assumed against all assailants.

There is, however, yet another style which was characteristic of the Methodistic dispensation, and which, while it may seem to border upon dangers or abuses, has —it must be acknowledged—belonged to those whose souls were of the amplest dimensions—whose habit of thought has been the most rich and ruminative, and whose personal piety has been the most profound and ripe. A preacher of this order takes his choice texts from our Lord's discourses with his disciples, or from those passages in the Pauline Epistles which affirm—plainly or symbolically—Christ's relationship to his people, and his headship to the mystic Church, and which speak of him as the Saviour of those who were given to him of the Father "from before the foundation of the world."

But from whatever side the mystery of human salvation may have been contemplated by the several Methodistic leaders, there was not merely a substantial unanimity among them (wordy differences put out of view) but there was a oneness of feeling, pervading all minds, and which became the characteristic of this company of preachers, and of those who were trained under their influence. This feeling was the very contrary of the undefined and dreamy mysticism of the pietist school, the connection of which with the doctrines of Scripture was slender and precarious; whereas the Methodistic feeling expressed itself in terms decisively Biblical, whether correctly so or not. Nor had it any analogy with that pensive adoration of the meek and suffering Jesus which so beautifully depicts itself in some pre-Lutheran devotional books; for in these books the vital question of the grounds of justification is never well understood. But with the Methodists, notwithstanding Wesley's cautionary retractations, or Fletcher's counter-arguments, the substratum of the pulpit instruction on all hands was a full, free, and sovereignly-bestowed salvation, wrought and obtained for men by the Son of God, and which might now, in this life—even in this very hour—be entered upon, and enjoyed by every one who thereto consented.

A vivid consciousness of this salvation, brought constantly under correction and revision by reference to the Bible, and by an often-renewed appeal to scriptural tests of sincerity, gave a healthy tone to Methodism, for the most part, and long preserved it from subsidence into any of those forms of non-scriptural and sentimental excitement which so often take the place of effective piety. Methodism thus stands contrasted also with that intellectualism to which the genius and eloquence of some few noted preachers and popular writers of more recent times have given currency. Modern congregations, disciplined—under such guidance—in the art and practice of listening to sermons, as amateurs, have drawn preachers, by their plaudits, more and more, into this elaborated manner—the purport of which is to pass Christianity through the refining fires of each successive system of sentimental philosophy that attracts ephemeral attention. Methodism knew of no such tastes, no such refinements, and although it proclaimed the Gospel rudely, often, or under partial aspects, or in objectionable phrases, it was not a sophisticated Christianity that it published: it was that Biblical Christianity which will never cease to be an amazement, a scorn, an insoluble problem to all, of every class, religiously-minded or otherwise, who have not brought themselves to the point of an unconditional abandonment of notions and speculations that are of the "earth—earthy."

During the Methodistic era the popularity of preachers, individually, resulted much less from their personal accomplishments, or their powers as orators, than from their being thoroughly imbued with the doctrine and spirit of the Methodistic company. Whoever it was that thus "preached Christ," was thronged every where, and was listened to as men listen when the message is to them of immeasurably more moment than the style and manner of him who may happen to deliver it. There is a fine line of demarkation which it would be no easy task to trace across the broad field of evangelic pulpit exercises, but on the one side of which the *message* is listened to and thought of; and on the other, the messenger, and his mode and his merits in delivering it. On the one side of this invisible line is the Methodism of the last century:—on the other, what we may hear any where, and every Sunday; and let it be acknowledged that what we may thus hear is, for the most part, sound and commendable—sometimes admirable, and far from being wholly ineffective; but on the Methodistic side, if in these times it were to be heard, there are words of power, in the hearing of which the human spirit, vanquished and trembling, yet full of hope, bows in presence of the Infinite Majesty, who, having taken upon himself the sins of the world, and abolished death, is able, as willing, to deliver from sin and wrath all that come to him, willing thus to be rescued.

THE FOURTH ELEMENT OF METHODISM.

Again we have to affirm, in behalf of the Methodism of the last century, that which, if not peculiar to it, marked it in a manner not to be overlooked or easily misunderstood. Evangelic Philanthropy, considered as a specific class of emotions, or as a habit of the moral nature, differs, in its origin, substance, and form, from all the cognate benevolent affections: nor can it develop itself ever, except in immediate and causal connection with those impressions, and with that vivid consciousness of the Mediatorial scheme which we have named as the third, and the principal element of the Methodistic revival.

As to the benevolent affections, it may almost be said that they have been the creation of Christianity, operating, as it has, in a diffused manner, upon the social system, wherever it has rooted itself among the institutions of countries. Paganism knows little of these emotions, Mohammedanism not much; but the scope and encouragement given to them by Romanism has redeemed it hitherto, and may yet avail to it for much, in times of religious commotion. Yet what we have now in view is something essentially different from that humane impulse which expends itself in the "seven works of mercy," or in any enterprises or labors which spring from the gentler sympathies of our nature, quickened and informed by the precepts and encouragements of the Gospel. Those words of love and power—do they not seem to shine on the page where they stand?—"Then shall the King say unto them on the right hand, inasmuch as ye did it unto these my brethren, ye did it unto me"—what countless treasures of relief have they not opened to the wretched, in the lapse of these eighteen centuries! This stands certain; but it is not our immediate object.

Beyond this, the benevolent affections, when enkindled and enhanced by Christian motives, take a wider range, and prompt Christian men to engage in those enterprises of mercy which have respect more to the religious and moral necessities of their fellows, than to their bodily destitution. Those noble charities of these times which are carrying the Gospel out through the pagan wilderness—these have their rise in motives that are wholly approvable to the Christian law—"thou shalt love thy neighbor as thyself;" for where we lodge Christianity, with its healing influences, and its purifying institutions, in the heart of a pagan country, we do that which embraces the purposes of all works of mercy, spiritual and temporal.

Although that evangelic philanthropy which we have now in view, as a principal element of the early Methodism, entered largely, no doubt, into the motives of those with whom the modern missionary enterprise had its origin, and of many too of those who have gone forth among the heathen, yet, even at the first, and much more since the first season of fervor, and at present, when the work of evangelizing the heathen world has come to be systematized on known principles of social organization—ecclesiastical and educationary—missionary societies rest for their support, and for the zeal that gives effect to their endeavors, upon motives of a somewhat lower order, that is to say, upon those various considerations which Christian benevolence so amply supplies, and for which the degradation and wretchedness of pagan nations afford so much scope.

Motives of this secondary order, intelligible as they are, and warrantable on every ground of reason and piety, are also readily available on those occasions of popular excitation, and of impulsive agitation, which the ordinary working of the evangelic machinery brings before those who are responsible to their constituents for its efficient maintenance. Nevertheless, genuine and well founded as are these more ordinary motives, it must be acknowledged that, to a great extent, if not absolutely and entirely, they are of modern, and of very recent origin: they belong to our lately acquired habit of looking abroad upon the world, geographically, and of considering what, until of late, so seldom entered the thoughts even of the best men—the condition of our brethren of mankind remote from us. These benevolent and frugiferous impulses, stimulating the active faculties, and the affections, and which bring so near to our imaginations, and to our sympathies, the population of a Chinese city, or of an island of the southern hemisphere, are they—in their present form—of much older date than those amazing mechanical inventions of these last times which almost annihilate space and time?

The thoughtful reader of the New Testament can not

have failed to note the fact that, as to this entire class of motives, upon which *mainly* our missionary enterprises rest, as their basis—their reason, and their impulse, exceedingly little exemplification of them—very little of precept, or of rule, is to be gathered from the apostolic writings. Instead of this, which we are so apt to think we shall find in abundance, we meet, on the one hand, with precept, example, and encouragement, applicable to all occasions of *common benevolence*, or of a self-denying regard to the *bodily* wants and sufferings of those around us. On the other hand, and especially in the Pauline epistles, we find an impulse of a far deeper origin, and of more refined quality, and of a less utilitarian aspect, and which employs a dialect that is in the strictest sense peculiar to the Christian system. It is to this impulse that we have now to give attention, for it offers itself to view as a principal element, also, of the early Methodism; it is the spontaneous accompaniment of that vivid evangelic feeling of which we have lately spoken. The elementary expansive principle of Christianity is not natural benevolence, enhanced and spiritualized by religious considerations:—it is a sense, bestowed in an absolute manner from on high upon whoever receives it, of that which is ineffable, and for the conveyance of which language has no terms or powers adequate, but which yet it indicates and affirms, as when we hear of the "unsearchable riches of Christ"—a wealth available beyond the utmost reach of the all-grasping desires of the human mind, and available, as for the individual soul, so for all human spirits. Whoever thus feels, first exults for himself, as rich indeed; yet the consequent feeling follows so closely upon the first, that the two seem one; and it is this second impulse which we assume as THE TRUE MISSIONARY RUDIMENT—the earnest, the burning desire to make known to all men "that which passeth knowledge." It is in the writings of St. Paul, to whom the evangelic mission was specially confided, that we find—and scarcely at all elsewhere in the Apostolic records—this which now we have in view.

That this expansive feeling is a bestowment, specially conferred upon those to whom an unlimited evangelic commission is to be granted, might be gathered from the fact that it barely indicates its presence in the minds of those of the inspired writers whose apostolic function was to be exercised within prescribed boundaries—local or ecclesiastical. The epistle of St. James, which so pointedly enforces Christ's law of beneficence, as related to the present necessities of the poor and helpless,* barely contains a word (one only, applicable by inference) on which we might found our modern evangelizing labors.† No such word occurs in the epistle of St. Jude. In the epistles of St. John there is nothing which, in its direct or obvious import, looks beyond the narrow limits of the Christian inclosure, or at most, which carries us by force beyond that boundary. "The whole world lieth in the wicked one;" but the modern missionary inference from this dark affirmation is not subjoined. The same is true of the two epistles of St. Peter: those of the "dispersion," to whom they were addressed, might think their obligations as Christians fully acquitted so long as they maintained, among themselves, purity of doctrine and of life, gave no occasion to the ungodly to blaspheme, and held themselves ready always, when asked for a reason of their hope, to give it.

It is in the writings of St. Paul, that is to say, within the compass of a few passages in some of his epistles, and in the narrative of his labors, as given by St. Luke, that are found all that presents itself indicative of the existence of that expansive force which, in the apostolic age, did actually carry the Gospel over the entire area of the Roman world, and probably far beyond its limits.

Those who have not given attention especially to the subject, may, in these missionary times, feel a momentary surprise, or even uneasiness, when the fact is first placed before them—that the evangelizing impulse, the motives and considerations which have taken so much hold of the

* James, i. 27.; ii. 15.; and iii. 17.

† James, v. 20.

modern Church, far from occupying a prominent position in the New Testament, are found there very scantily. Nor is this fact our only ground of surprise; for when the few passages bearing upon this subject are examined, they offer to our view a species of motive materially differing from that which is characteristic of the modern evangelizing zeal.

It is only very remotely, or allusively, that the evangelizing work, or its motives, is glanced at in the Epistle to the Hebrews, or in two of the three clerical epistles, or in that to Philemon, or in the Second Epistle to the Thessalonians. Of the passages referred to below, the greater number contain nothing more than an incidental reference to the missionary work;* a few spread open to our inspection the apostolic mind, as related to those labors which carried him around the circuit of the Roman world, and in a retrospect of which he said—"I have fought a good fight, I have finished my course." But what is the complexion of these passages? It is easy to describe them negatively. Although the degraded condition of the heathen world is spoken of in no abated terms, yet this dark subject, brought forward in its connection with a theological argument, is not made use of, or spread out to view, in its details, in any such manner as has become customary with ourselves; that is to say—as furnishing a motive for missionary labors. There is not one word, in the compass of these epistles, that is analogous to the evangelical statistics, and the geographic missionary sketches which are so rife and frequent with ourselves. This "Apostle of the Gentiles" never seems to have computed the "millions of the perishing heathen" that were

* The passages in the Pauline Epistles which, either directly or by remote implication, seem to bear upon the writer's commission as the Apostle of the Gentiles—the Apostolic Missionary—are the following:

ROMANS, i. 5. 14. 16; ix. 24; x. 14.; xi. 13; xv. 9. 16. 1 CORINTHIANS, i. 23; ix. 23; xii. 10. 28; 2 CORINTHIANS, ii. 14; iv. 13; v. 19; x. 16; xii. 10. GALATIANS, i. 16; ii. 7, 8, 9. EPHESIANS, iii. 6, 9, 10; iv. 11, 12; vi. 19. PHILIPPIANS, i. 14. 18. COLOSSIANS, i. 6. 23. 27. 1 THESSALONIANS, i. 8; ii. 2, 16. 2 TIMOTHY, iv. 5.

dwelling on this side of the Danube, or beyond it—on this side the Rhone, or on that; or on the banks of the Rhine. He never, so far as appears, addressed Christian congregations in the incitative style, as if to move them to aid him in accomplishing his work. He speaks of contributions for "poor saints;" but never of collections for propagating the Gospel in heathen lands.

Nor do these epistles exhibit any of those well-founded and warrantable comparisons between Christianity and heathenism, as to the effect of each upon the happiness and civilization of nations, which have become, with ourselves, a staple of missionary eloquence. Nor even, if we look to the deeper sources of evangelic zeal, do we find the apostolic missionary expatiating, as does the modern, upon those saddening subjects which are opened before us by our meditations of the future life, as related to the heathen world. There is nothing in them of this sort; yet it does not follow that *we* are therefore altogether *wrong;* but it does follow that those incalculable revolutions which have carried the human mind so far away from the ground of antiquity, have given rise to modes of thinking for which we shall in vain search the inspired writings, as furnishing either the warrant or the example. It is a fact noticeable indeed that the modern mind—the world-wide philanthropy of these latter days—finds its like of sentiment and expression, and of animation, much rather in the prophetic poetry of the ancient dispensation, than in the writings of evangelists and apostles. The books of Isaiah, David, Daniel, are the modern missionary's treasury of texts, fraught with hope.

Nevertheless the fact returns upon us, that, although it was with views or motives so remotely resembling those which stimulate our modern zeal, the Apostle of the Gentiles did (this fact is out of question) plant the Gospel to an extent throughout the countries then subject to Rome, which finds no parallel in Christian history; or none unless we are willing to bring into comparison with it the preaching of our METHODIST—WHITEFIELD!

But now, if there be ground for any such comparison as this, does it offer to our inspection any analogy as to the prime impulses of the two courses of evangelic labor—the Apostolic and the Methodistic? This is a question, the answer to which would be full of meaning. And here the averment is boldly hazarded that, unless he had, by mere sympathy, caught the feeling, and fallen into the style of those around him, Whitefield, as a platform orator, at a modern missionary meeting, would have felt himself out of his place, and quite unprovided with materials that might mingle homogeneously with the speeches coming before, and coming after, his own. Might it be imagined that Whitefield and St. Paul would together stand apart, on such an occasion—rejoicing indeed as listeners to the Report; but both inclined rather to hear than to speak, and both of them perplexed as much as delighted?

Those who go forth with the Gospel in their hearts, and on their lips, among the impenitent, may fix their eye wholly, or mainly, upon one of these classes of objects; or upon each in turn; as for instance—The missionary may be chiefly intent upon the benevolent design of Christianizing a pagan and imperfectly civilized people, and so of conferring upon them those inestimable secular benefits which the Gospel brings in its train; yet meantime, not unmindful of its bearing upon the future well-being of those who shall cordially embrace it.

Or, the missionary may place before him an object of a more abstract kind, which yet shall not exclude the benevolent considerations just mentioned. His ambition may be inflamed with the hope of extending the boundaries of his Church, and of bringing under her spiritual sway new and splendid conquests—regions now subject to the powers of darkness, over which she may cast forth her line, and where she may erect the symbols of her empire. Such has been the prime impulse, no doubt, of many, if not most of those who have carried Romanism into heathen lands.

Or again—and this is perhaps the feeling which is characteristically that of our modern Protestant Missionaries, combining itself with motives of the kind first named, and more or less with those which we have yet to mention—the missionary may *chiefly* fix his thoughts upon the spiritual condition of the heathen individually, and may direct his endeavors to the one object of effecting the conversion of those, individually, to whom he can by any means gain access. Assuredly this order of feeling and this direction of missionary labors are not reprehensible, nor will they altogether fail of producing their effect.

And yet the eye may take another, and a higher range, and it may fix itself, not exclusively, yet chiefly, upon objects that, as they are far brighter, so do they impart more animation, and prove themselves to be more effective for good. The modern missionary, while perusing the epistles of the "Apostle of the Gentiles," has, as we have said, often entertained a perplexing question on this very ground, and has sought an explanation of the startling fact, that so very small a place in them is occupied by those exciting themes which had so large a part in engaging himself in this arduous work. An allusive word or two—an incidental phrase, which by implication may be made to carry a missionary sense—is all that he finds in these epistles corresponding with those views and impulses that constantly fill his own thoughts.

But is there nothing found in the place of that which he looks for, and does not find? Let the modern missionary gather from the writings of the most successful of missionaries what it is which might auspiciously supplant, in his own mind, much that hitherto has filled it. Does it not seem that the soul of *this* MISSIONARY—successful beyond all example as a preacher of repentance, existed—if one might so speak—in the very blaze of that glory which surrounds the Mediatorial scheme? To none of those considerations which engage so much our own minds, can we imagine him to have been wholly insensible; nevertheless it was to higher themes that he reverted; and it was from a far loftier position that he looked abroad upon the field of his labors. If he thought of the heathen world in its actual condition, he thought much more of Him "who was reconciling the world unto himself," by the Gospel. If he thought of his ministry in preaching this Gospel "among the Gentiles," it was as that ministry was the consequence of the grace which had "revealed" the Son of God "in him"—and had "formed Christ in his heart, the hope of glory." He, no doubt, did think of the spiritual wretchedness and utter destitution of the millions around him, who were "without God, and without hope in the world;" but such meditations (so we must suppose) were incidental only to the settled habit of his mind, which was bright and ardent, and was occupied with nothing less than "the unsearchable riches of Christ." His errand, in traversing sea and land, his impulse, and his ruling reason was, to utter every where the outbursting fullness of his own heart, overfull with a consciousness of the saving grace and power of HIM in whom dwells the "fullness of the Godhead bodily."

Here, then, is a state of mind—a habit of the soul, which, though it does not exclude any of those moving considerations of Christian-like philanthropy, or of common benevolence which have come to take the foremost place among ourselves, is clearly distinguishable from them, and is at once of a more animating kind, is more constant, more elevating, and, in fact, is found to be more effective for securing those very ends which are regarded by such lower reasons.

Now if we take WHITEFIELD as our fittest instance, or sample of the early Methodism, and if we rightly gather from the whole of the extant evidence touching his character and ministry, what his mind and motive was—what the prevailing habit of his soul, what the foremost objects in his view, he will seem to take his position, as an evangelist, in that very class of which St. Paul is the chief, and the brightest exemplar. It was as living himself in the effulgence of the Mediatorial scheme that he went forth to call men to repentance. His motive was not a congeries of reasons and considerations; it was an impulse, spontaneous, irresistible, bright, and fraught with love, hope, and a sure anticipation of abundant success. Whitefield did not measure his powers, as related to the task he undertook; nor could he have drawn discouragement from any estimate formed of them by others, as insufficient for the purpose. Not merely did he look to, ask, and rely upon a power extrinsic to himself; but he so commingled himself with the omnipotence on which he relied, that the thought of his own insufficiency passed out of his view.

It belongs to those evangelizing motives that are (so we think) of a secondary or derived order, to be liable to transmutations, or rather to be themselves always in a transition state. Motives and reasons which are at first in a high degree impulsive, and which express themselves in an impassioned or rhetorical style, pass on, through successive stages of abatement, toward a tranquil condition of utilitarian sobriety. It is not in the nature of motives of *this* order to sustain themselves in their first freshness and potency. Whatever is composite tends, necessarily, to dissolution—its elements combining with other elements around it, in new forms. But it was quite otherwise with Whitefield; and the characteristic of his ministry was, as we have said, its undecayed vitality—its ONENESS of tone, from the first to the last. There is a difference in this respect between Whitefield and Wesley, which the admirers of the latter should not be reluctant to see adverted to: in following the course of his long career, as preacher and chief of a community, one can not fail to notice a gradual progress, or ripening of his views and principles: his fervor, if undiminished, perhaps, almost to the last, yet came under the control of a slowly acquired discretion, and spent itself in modes approvable—if not to the maxims of worldly wisdom, yet to principles which a merely secular intelligence recognizes. More and more, from the middle period of his course, toward its close, his pulpit energies were engaged in repressing ill tendencies, in forefending apprehended mischiefs, and in righting his societies where they were lapsing into doctrinal or practical errors.

Whitefield also gained wisdom from what he saw and suffered; but these wholesome fruits of experience related almost entirely to his personal conduct. He had a nice tact and sense of propriety, and in his later years he held himself exempt from imputations to which, at first, from want of caution, he had laid himself open. But as to his evangelic function, this small wisdom—the wisdom of common life—it touched him not. An ever deepening sense of the richness, freeness, and boundless sufficiency of that Gospel which he preached, held him always to the same path, and made it impossible that he should tread upon a lower level.

It may well be imagined that Whitefield, if brought into the very midst of the modern missionary excitement, and required to put his shoulder to this wheel, would have found that he had forfeited his power, and could barely maintain a position of equality among his colleagues. Not so Wesley, who, with the machinery of our great associations under his control, and with the heathen world now so near at hand as it is, would have thought himself, at length, to have reached the very position he was born to fill, with six hundred millions of pagans at his feet, and a revenue of a million sterling, such as *he* would have made it, at his command! The difference between Wesley and Whitefield, on this ground, is not simply this, that the one was eminently endowed with the governing faculty—the power of disposing and commanding, while the other was a simple soul, distinguished by no such eminent intellectual qualities: it is more than this:—Wesley truly walked in the light of the Gospel; but Whitefield lived in the blaze of it, as it fills the upper heavens.

Whitefield is not thus named as if in disparagement of others of the Methodistic company, among whom some, perhaps, were not at all inferior to him, in this respect. This elementary impulse, which is the exterior and involuntary expression of a deeper feeling, marks the Methodistic era; and it was in various degrees the distinction of this band of men, and it is that which should entitle them to occupy a prominent position in a genuine history of Christianity. On this special ground where do we find their equals—that is to say, where, within the compass of Christian history, shall we find—not eminent and solitary instances—but a company of men, of untainted orthodoxy, clear of sectarian virulence, indifferent to things indifferent, intent only upon the first Truths;—in labors and sufferings equal to the most zealous, and surpassing perhaps all in simplicity of purpose, as embassadors for Christ—entreating men every where, "in Christ's stead, to be reconciled to God."

From out of this elementary evangelic impulse there sprang, after a time, and as its proper consequence, the modern evangelic philanthropy—issuing in the missionary enterprise; but the two, though related as cause and effect, are not to be confounded, nor should they be spoken of as one and the same. A wide unmeasured space had been silently traversed by the Christian community during the few years that elapsed between the subsidence of the Methodistic energy, and the origination of Missionary and Bible Societies. In all those instances of transition, or transmutation, in matters of opinion, feeling, or taste, which mark successive eras in the history of communities, that which is the prominent characteristic of bodies of people, in any one period, passes forward into the next, as the characteristic of *individuals;* or, to state the same general fact in other terms, there are to be found, in every period, individuals who might well be cited as the types of the period that has just gone by. Whenever, therefore, it is affirmed, concerning any definite moral or religious condition, that it has passed away, such an allegation is likely to meet an animated contradiction on the part of those who find it easy to name, among their acquaintances, more than a few eminent men, as instances of the survivance of that which has so been spoken of as obsolete. But such instances are not pertinent when they are thus appealed to. Periods rendered remarkable by the heaving activity and force of certain moral elements, might be resembled to mountain ranges, which, range after range, are found to rise abruptly from their roots on the one side, and to flow down by easy slopes, and to send out many offsets and spurs into the plains on the other side.

It would be resented as a wrong done to the memories of certain venerated men who were the fathers of modern missions, if it were alleged concerning them that the evangelic fervor which moved and sustained them was at all a less simply constituted habit of the mind than that of the first Methodists. We waive, then, any such allegation, if it may seem derogatory to those upon whom it would bear; yet without scruple may it be affirmed that the diffused feeling of the Christian community during the past Missionary era differed greatly, in its elements, and in its composition, from that of the Methodistic period; as again *that* feeling has, since then, passed through transmutations which make it clearly distinguishable from that which at present takes to itself the same dialect, and occupies the same platform.

Allowing all the room for exceptive instances that can fairly be claimed in their behalf, it must be said that, although the product and the consequences of that visitation from on high are on all sides extant, the soul and substance of Methodism have long ago departed, that is to say, when considered as a development of the primary motives of Evangelic Philanthropy.

We have affirmed that the Methodism of the last century was in no theological sense a novelty; yet that it was a manifestation of elementary Christian truths, such as has no parallel:—it was a sense of those truths granted in an extraordinary degree to the principal persons, and through their ministry conveyed to thousands of the people.

It has, moreover, been said that, as this Methodism stands strongly contrasted with the religious condition of all communions at the time when it appeared, so does it stand contrasted (essentially, if not so strongly) with that to which it has since given place throughout the Christian

Community. To some points of this contrast we must return in concluding this volume; but to one special point of it a reference should at once be made, lest a serious misapprehension should suggest itself, and should gain a lodgment in the reader's mind.

Methodism, we say, was not an issuing of new dogmas, but a new feeling toward the existing belief—a sense of things assented to; or, to vary our phrases, it was a VIVID CONSCIOUSNESS of those elementary truths, or rather *facts*, which constitute, in substance, the Christian religion. But if so, then was it not—if we are willing to deduct from it its vehemence, and its peculiar dialect, and to render it liberally into the purer medium of our spiritualized philosophy, was it not, or may it not now be regarded as nearly identical with the system concerning which we are assured by the initiated, that, while it includes every thing in Christianity which ought to be regarded as essentially true, or which can do us any good, holds itself exempt from the unintelligible dogmas, the national symbolisms, the temporary frame-work, and the infantile myths of the apostolic age, and of the (so called) Inspired Writings? "Methodism, you say, was a soul-stirring consciousness of Christian verities. Yes, and our better philosophy, which abhors to assail Christianity, which venerates its founder, and which appropriates its lofty ethics, is also an INTUITION:—it is a *deep*, if not a soul-stirring consciousness of eternal verities. Its jargon deducted, is not then your Methodism the same thing as our Philosophy—better phrased, and better behaved, and every way, therefore, a preferable religion?" We can not grant this;—for instead of being substantially identical, and in *form* only diverse, the two religions stand in vehement contrast, and are forever irreconcilable; and the difference between them is for this reason hopeless of adjustment, because it involves an utter mistake, on the one part or on the other, as to the very structure of the human mind, and its principles of action, intellectual and moral. Before Methodism could be transmuted into the spiritual philosophy of this passing time, proof must be forthcoming, such as shall convince us that our settled belief concerning the mechanism of human nature is wholly wrong.

Christianity assumes, and builds itself upon, this same frame-work—such as we understand it; and if *this* foundation be indeed solid, then the modern philosophy can have none; and inasmuch as we can neither rid ourselves of our belief as to human nature, nor of our conviction concerning Christianity as historically demonstrable, nor cease to see the agreement of the one with the other, we can not but hold the recent philosophy in small esteem.

It is very easy to imagine that just so much of the Christian system—theological or ethical, as this philosophy is willing to recognize, and which it authenticates, as so many portions of universal truth, might have been consigned to writings of remote and unknown origin, the *authority* of which, irrespective entirely of any reference to their authorship, or alleged inspiration, should have resulted, simply, from the accordance of their contents with our innate sense of what is good, true, and beneficial. In this case we should have possessed a religion—whether the gift of Heaven or not, could not be determined—but which, making its appeal to reason and to our moral intuitions, would neither have asked for faith, nor could have demanded submission. Thus it might have been.

But in fact it is not thus that Christianity meets us. Why it does not, is a question to which a reply, under several heads, may be returned; there is, however, one reason why it should not be so, which is both obvious and conclusive, because it involves, as we have just said, a principle of human nature: this principle is recognized and acted upon on all occasions.

A few minds excepted, and those not the most vigorous always, or the best constructed, the human mind does not yield itself to any very powerful impressions, and is not effectively wrought upon, by any reasons or considerations that take their rise wholly within itself, or which are generated by the mere interaction of its own faculties. In the world of mind, not less than in the material world, *force* implies, somewhere, a fixed point of support—a fulcrum, a resistant, or reactive mass—an exterior, or independent force, equivalent to the movement that is required to be produced. It may well be questioned if so much as one human mind has ever been so constituted as to evolve *force* from within itself. Incalculable indeed are the energies of a powerful mind when acting upon, or when getting its spring from that which is exterior to itself, and independent; but apart from such extrinsic point of rest, the movements and the involutions of the human mind are not much better or more productive than a sort of incessant curdling, or endless gyration of elements—coming round upon themselves, with fruitless repetitions.

The active faculties, and the moral impulses (if for argument's sake we allow a few exceptive instances) become productive at the moment when some exterior fact, known to bear upon our well-being, and which, if not palpable, is still accepted as certain, presents itself before us:—then it is that we begin to feel, and to act: then it is that we wake up, and that dreams are dispelled, and that the real world claims us as its own.

Who does not know that this is human nature? How perplexing, then, would it have been if a religion, professing to be effective for curbing the passions, and for ruling the man in the arduous occasions of his course, had itself seemed to be unconscious of this first law of the moral system, and had undertaken its task of training us to virtue and self-denial in contempt of it! It is not so, but the very contrary; and Christianity meets us on the path of passion and selfishness—meets us with its antagonist force, and with its authority—meets us, not as a *philosophy*, but as a FACT; or as a congeries of facts—facts historical, and these attested as any others of the same class may, and should be; and the very secret of its power, when once it has caught the heedless ear, is, as one may say, the *ordinariness* of its apparatus of proof.

Human nature being such as it is, and not such as men

of the closet and dreaming sentimentalists would make it, let the relative forces of a religion of Philosophy and a religion of Facts be brought into comparison in any such way as this:—Let us imagine a congregation to be listening, with charmed attention, to a lecture upon "the Religion of our Moral Intuitions;" or upon ethical abstractions—the purest and the most engaging. But we suppose that, midway in this lecture, there enters some one, known to all, who, in a tranquil and governed voice, and in the briefest and simplest terms, states a fact—new and conclusive in its bearing upon the welfare of all; remote, perhaps, in its consequences, but infallibly certain to touch all present. When this announcement has well fixed itself in the mind of every hearer—shall the lecturer resume the thread of his discourse, and pursue his elaborate reasoning? It is vain for him to attempt it. Every mind before him has wholly broken connection with his own, and it would be a hopeless endeavor to win them back to his influence. The thoughts of all have now come to a centering upon *an extrinsic reality*—upon a fact; and a class of emotions altogether of another kind is getting into play, and is gaining supremacy.

It is precisely thus that Christianity, when it is proclaimed, not as a tissue of azure dreams, but as a fact—when it is set forth as a series of transactions which is now in course, and which hereafter is to reach its conclusion, takes effective hold of the minds of men. Methodism did so proclaim the Gospel, and the people every where were awed by it, and multitudes became "obedient to the faith." And thus it is, we say, that Methodism and the new philosophy, would have nothing in common. Methodism, as its very characteristic, takes up the apostolic *memento*, and thereupon rests its appeal to mankind—"Remember that Jesus Christ, of the seed of David, is raised from the dead, according to my Gospel." The new philosophy, if it does not care to contradict this point of history, holds it as a matter indifferent, and inconsequential.

THE FORM OF (WESLEYAN) METHODISM.

As to its substance, Methodism, Arminian and Calvinistic, may be spoken of as one, although its elements were developed with some diversity under these two modes. But when Methodistic *organization* comes to be considered, then it is solely *Wesleyan* Methodism that can demand any peculiar attention. Already the fact has been alluded to that, as to Whitefield, he never proposed it to himself to bring his converts within the inclosures of an ecclesiastical constitution. Nor was any purpose of this sort carried out by Lady Huntingdon in such manner as might have rendered the "Connection," and its apparatus, and its rules, an object of much curiosity, or likely to yield instruction if brought under analysis. Calvinistic Methodism, after fertilizing the Episcopal Church, on the one hand, and the Dissenting communions on the other, has ceased to attract attention itself, as a communion distinguished from others.

Not so Wesley's Institute, for in this instance the Form—the organization of Methodism offers itself to view as a fact, on every ground deserving of the most attentive examination.

But let a probable misapprehension as to our present purpose in attempting such an analysis be distinctly precluded. Are we then so bold as to entertain the thought of schooling the extant Wesleyan body;—or do we propose to advise "Conference," or to utter judgment in causes now pending between it, and any of its unruly members? Certainly to no such high purposes as these is the reader, in the present instance, to be made a party. What is actually intended comes within those warrantable limits of remark to which all human institutions are confessedly open. METHODISM we have spoken of as that which has long ago accomplished its purpose, and has passed away: to other moods and modes of thinking it has given place; and with its nominal representative—the modern Wesleyan Methodism, we have no more to do, in these pages, than with any other existing religious body.

But the genuine Wesleyan organization—that "Society" which was the product of its founder's mind, claims to be considered as one of the most remarkable experiments in ecclesiastical science that has ever been carried forward. In truth, it stands before us alone, and without a parallel, on the field of Church history, and therefore it may well engage the serious regard of those who, in this day of actual and of projected revolution, or reform, are inquiring concerning the first principles of CHURCH ORGANIZATION. Is it not probable, or almost certain, that, from the contemplation of so noted an experiment, carried on upon so large a scale, much may be learned touching the theory and practice of Christian combination?

If, in fact, a free and unprejudiced criticism of the Wesleyan church system should seem to issue in throwing a shade of doubt upon the perpetuity of the body, in its actual integrity, and present form, the writer must take his place among those who would entertain any such forebodings with extreme reluctance, and would witness the fulfillment of them with a lively and profound regret. One must be strangely insensible toward that which touches the most momentous interests of mankind, and be accustomed to regard the well-being of our fellow-men under the very narrowest aspects, not to be dismayed at the thought of the breaking up, the suspension, or the alienation, of those means of good which, up to this time, have been effective to an incalculable extent toward millions of men. How can a Christian-hearted man take his course, on a Sunday morning, through the streets of a manufacturing town, and not fervently desire the undamaged continuance, and the further extension of Wesleyan Methodism?

Nevertheless, it would be an ill-judging weakness, and a miscalculating caution, that would prohibit the sort of inquiry we have now before us, as if its tendency might be to accelerate a result that is foreseen and deprecated. On the contrary—unless indeed such a supposition should be scouted as utterly presumptuous, it might be allowable to imagine, as possible, that suggestions offered in humility and affection, by one who can be influenced by no sinister motive, may, in some indirect manner, avail for purposes of conservation and renovation toward the Wesleyan body. With very rare, if indeed any exceptions, the institutions, doctrines, and usages of religious bodies have, hitherto, either been set forth, in laudatory terms, by adherents and advocates, or acrimoniously assailed by antagonists; or the weaknesses of such bodies have been maliciously placarded by renegades. May there not be room, then, for the modest intervention of any whose only solicitudes and whose only jealousies relate to that Christianity which is common to all evangelic bodies?

A religious revival or reformation can never be held exempt from the inconvenience and opprobrium attaching to the circumstance of its receiving from the world, or accepting—a NAME. But this disadvantage, whether it be of greater or less amount, is a temporary evil, and may be patiently submitted to until it wears itself away; but the founding of a Church, or communion, is another matter; inasmuch as it is a work intended for perpetuity, and the affixation of A NAME to a Christian Institute can not be regarded in any other light than as a prognostic of its dissolution, at some period not immeasurably remote. Yet among such designations, undesirable as they are—one and all, there may be a choice; and it might be well, and it would show wisdom on the part of a rising community, frankly to take to itself, from the world, a designation given it in scorn, rather than to place, on its own front, as in triumph, the name of its venerated founder. One inclines to think that, in the eye of Heaven, *this* is an indiscretion, if not an offense, which, though venial at the first.

no merits in the body shall avail to perpetuate. It is indeed hard to believe—when thinking of some form of Christianity which we are told is the very purest, and the loftiest, that it should continue forever to be called after the name of its promulgator, whether Luther, Calvin, Barclay, or Wesley.

If Methodism had not so early split itself upon the Arminian and Calvinistic controversy, it is probable, or it may at least be conjectured, that Wesley's Institute might have come down to us exempt from the ominous prefix which is now its designation—in law and usage. There may be reason to think, perhaps, that some oversight in the framing of that institute was such as could not fail to work out its ill-consequence in the course of time; but when Wesley failed to take effective means for forbidding to his friends and successors the gratification of calling themselves and their Church by his name, did he not surely doom it to dissolution? Wesley, if he had sternly enjoined his followers to be content with "Methodism," would have consigned his ashes to an urn with sweeter odors than he did in indulging them with this ill-omened "Wesleyanism."

Once and again the writer has professed his entire faith in Wesley's simplicity of purpose, and his freedom from personal vanity, or ambition: it was from no such vulgar impulse that he bequeathed "*Wesleyan* Methodism" to his people. But, exempt he was not from the autocratic sentiment—from the Founder's self esteem—from that—infatuation—one must call it, which works as an irrepressible energy in the bosom of every man who is born to invent—to originate—to lead the way—to govern—to FOUND. In the view, or in the feeling of the Inventor or Founder, the product of his mind—the ripened fruit of long and painful cogitation—the scheme—the system—the mechanism, which has filled his thoughts, waking and sleeping, from year to year, has become, as a whole, and in each of its parts, even the smallest, identical with his own personal consciousness: to excind any part of this whole is the same thing as to amputate a limb, or to pluck out an eye

The vulgar will persist in taking this strong feeling for vanity or arrogance; but it is not so: it is an illusion to which almost the loftiest and the most vigorous minds have been subject.

It is not difficult on this ground to imagine Wesley's feeling: it seemed to him that his creation—his "Society," would, as to the integrity of its rules, its orders, its doctrines, and its spirit, be more safe under the guardianship of a personal, than under that of an impersonal designation: and it would be so, doubtless, for a time;—but for how long a time? That a feeling of this sort did enter into Wesley's views, and determine his conduct, is not a mere presumption, for it makes itself conspicuous in those injunctions and enactments—variously expressed, as they are, and on different occasions put forth, which, in a tone of almost unparalleled confidence, impose upon his followers—ministers and people, that very form of belief which he has embodied in his own voluminous writings. "My Sermons," "my Exposition," "my Treatises"—such and such. It was not arrogance, not egotism, in the vulgar sense of the word; but it was the yielding to an impulse which a higher wisdom would have taught him to repress, and which a better knowledge of human nature than he seems to have possessed would have shown him could have no other result, after a lapse of time, than to place "The Works of the Reverend John Wesley" on a high shelf, where they will share the fate of Calvin's Institutes at Geneva: the funereal formula is already uttered "dust to dust."

A voluminous writer, or one who, if not voluminous, has appeared before the world frequently, from the middle period of life, to its later years, may well be indulged in so much overweening as to think that the body of opinions maintained in his works, are intrinsically of rather more value and importance than he finds to be attributed to them in the wide world of his heedless readers. A writer may so think, and yet himself be thoroughly superior to the vanity and egotism that attach to inferior minds. Let this be granted; but now, if there be in the structure of a man's mind a particle of the philosophic element—if he be accustomed to indulge in that sort of tranquil meditation which grasps the broadest aspect of things, and which takes account of, and correctly estimates the moral and intellectual forces that are acting around—himself wholly forgotten—such a man, how would he shrink from the astounding presumption of saying to his readers—"There! in the ten or twelve volumes of my works—there look for your belief—whole and lacking nothing. Take and digest what I have written, page by page, line by line, word for word:—you may as well spare yourselves the fruitless trouble of thinking any further, or of going deeper into any subject than I have gone, or of speculating concerning any thing which I have not considered. Take it on my word that, within the compass of my mind you—you—tens of thousands of people—the teachers and the taught, are safe: go beyond that limit, and you will get out of your depth, and be lost."

Wesley did not use any such words as these when addressing his preachers and people; but what he did say embraced the substance of them. His mind might be adduced as a singular instance—when its high energy is considered—of the absolute absence of the *retro-reflective* faculty, or the power and habit of stepping back from one's position, and of measuring its bearings, as related to other objects. What is it that the painter does who, at frequent intervals, and as often as he has exhausted his skill and pencil upon a particular object, recedes to a spectator's distance, and there considers how this last finishing tells in the general effect? Wesley did no such thing. He wrought his picture in mosaics, from side to side of his frame, and nothing could be retouched or considered anew.

Surprising results may be obtained, in any work of art or mechanism, or in any social economy, if only we are willing to pay the cost; that is to say, to compromise every thing else—to sacrifice every thing else—to forget every thing else, for the sake of that one result. It is on this principle that the institutors of monastic orders, and the founders of rigid sects have so often amazed the world by what they have produced, out of the raw material of human nature. Draw the pen, with merciless consistency, through every thing in human nature—its tenderest and most generous affections, its active faculties, its desires, sympathies, hopes, fears—erase all but some one principle, some one passion or tendency; and then bring the entire force of the system, mental and bodily, to a focus—bearing upon that one clear spot; and if you will do this, and will submit to all this damage and destruction, there is nothing that may not be realized, just on this one line:—the man, when he has been thus treated, and thus condensed, goes about as a miracle among others. He who can leap high from a slack rope, and come down upon his palms, and turn over, and regain his erect position, has learned to accomplish this feat at the cost of his entire faculties—bodily and mental:—this is what he can do, and this is all;—he has paid down his whole human nature for this one accomplishment. The parallel to this sort of compromise may be found within the pale of every ascetic community, and something approaching to it within the circle of some noted modern sects; and we must not say that Wesleyanism offers no sample of this sort, if it be not itself altogether an example of it. Jesuitism assuredly is so.

After what has been said in the course of the preceding pages, expressive of the writer's belief concerning the early Methodism, and his reverential idea of Wesley's personal virtues, and of the incalculable good which Wesleyanism has effected, some degree of liberty may be allowed him in speaking of that system of close sectarianism which he bequeathed to the world. It must be granted to be *in costume*, and quite fitting—the garb to the inner man—when religious communities which occupy, as one may say, a few acres only upon the breadth of Christendom, narrow their doors, shut their windows, and manage their interior economy in the most despotic style. Let it be so: but the same indulgence can not so easily be granted to a community, like the Wesleyan, the gates of which stand open night and day, which challenges all passers-by to enter, and which has rebuked other communions, as less catholic than itself. Yet, is it not true, at the present time, and has it not been true from Wesley's time down to this, that a seclusive and repellant style and tone have been the characteristics of the Wesleyan body, as compared with surrounding communities? If it be so then, what we have before us is at once the widest of all sects, as to the area it covers, and its statistics, and the very narrowest as to its temper!

It is quite true that a pent-up force becomes so much the more *a force* by that very means; and the energy of Wesleyanism may, in part, be attributed—no doubt—to its tight lacing. If only you can bring to bear upon the minds of a body of men enough retaining motive, and can induce them to submit themselves to minute rules of personal behavior, to sumptuary restrictions, and to verbal fixities of opinion;—if you can win them to something resembling a jail discipline, if they may be brought to take an Index Expurgatorius as the tether of their intellectual sustenance;—if all this can be effected, scarcely any limits can be set to the effective power which such a machinery may display. It is thus that the Regulars, in their day gone by, have amazed the vulgar world; and thus that Jesuitism has seemed, almost, as if it might achieve its object—the conquest of the human family. It is thus, on a much smaller scale, that fervent sects have filled out their hour; and thus in measure—must we not say it—that Wesleyanism has been outstripping all competitors, now these last hundred years. But so surely as any species of moral force has been generated by means of a moral compromise, or at the cost of the symmetry and beauty of the Christian system—so certainly will that force spend itself, after a time, and leave the materials it had bound together to resolve themselves into their elements.

While we have in view any such instance as this, it is highly necessary to attend to the distinction between a religious institution, and the Christianity which it implicates. The adherents and champions of sects are perpetually deluding themselves on this ground, and are making an idle boast while they attribute to the excellence of their framework—to the wisdom and efficiency of their rules, orders, discipline, that which, in truth, is common to themselves and to all others, retaining and employing an equal amount of the deep energies of the Gospel. What ought indeed to excite our admiration, in contemplating certain religious mechanisms, is that inextinguishable force and vitality of the Christian system, which renders it effective for good, notwithstanding the pressure of almost any burden with which misjudging men may have encumbered it.

Wesleyan Methodism has proved itself hitherto the most efficiently expansive Christian institute which modern times have seen; it must be presumed, therefore, to possess excellence of structure of a very peculiar kind, and which should command the attention of all who make ecclesiastical economics their study. This first unquestionable inference from the facts before us being granted, then it will support another—if such another should force itself upon us—namely, that a scheme which is in itself so effective, working upon and by the aid of the powers of Christianity, has thus far held off from itself the ill consequences of some serious imperfections, which would, long ago, have been fatal to almost any other community.

The eager champion of Wesleyanism would appeal to the broad fact of its unexampled spread and prosperity, in proof of the perfection of the system; but the calm observer, who looks upon it from without, will find, in that alleged excellence, a solution of the otherwise perplexing question—How is it that such and such glaring imperfections have not, long ago, brought the Institution to which they attach to its end?

With a further question, which would involve a calculation of the destinies of the Wesleyan body, we have nothing to do, in these pages; nor shall stay to inquire what number of years may be expected to elapse before the accumulating results of its imperfections shall outweigh its intrinsic forces. Nor, again, shall we prosecute this inquiry—whether the Wesleyan system may admit of such amendments, as, while its integrity is preserved, may extend its duration. Avoiding all such perilous, and perhaps invidious topics, we are to look into this vast and complicated economy for the sole purpose of gathering up from the field of so large an experiment the lessons it may furnish.

Wesleyan Methodism may conveniently be considered under the following heads—namely, as—

I. A Scheme of Evangelic Aggression;

II. A System of Religious Discipline and Instruction, as toward the people;

III. A Hierarchy, or system of spiritual government;

IV. An Establishment, or Body Corporate, related to Civil Law and Equity.

WESLEYAN METHODISM—A SCHEME OF EVANGELIC AGGRESSION.

The advocates of the Wesleyan body may fairly appeal to the candor of other communions in some such manner as this—Our system, they may ask, is it not in itself good as compared with other systems? If you doubt it, see what progress it has made, and what it has done. Reckon the rate of its increase, in Christianized and in heathen lands, within the compass of a century, or little more. If you say it is *Christianity* that has so triumphed, we gladly grant it; but yourselves, as we also gladly grant, have, during the very same course of time—and much longer—professed the same Gospel, and you have faithfully administered it; but yet with no success at all comparable to ours; and while we acknowledge the hand of God in this instance, we must not be forbidden to look to the proximate causes of this difference in the result, and these causes we find in the SYSTEM; that is to say, in those things which distinguish our WESLEYANISM from any previously existing ecclesiastical organization.

The justness of this appeal ought surely to be granted; and if so, then the question presents itself,—What is it in this system which has rendered it, in so eminent a manner, effective for carrying the Gospel out upon new ground? Much of this unexampled success must be attributed to that extraordinary impetus which *Wesleyanism,* at its commencement, received from METHODISM, which was not its own, exclusively; but as this advantage, at starting, was, in the nature of things, temporary, we are still bound to look to the institution itself for the principal reason of the greater and continued success it has commanded.

This success, estimated in the most moderate manner, and after allowance has been made, in the way of abatement, on whatever grounds may seem requisite, ought, as the writer thinks, to be held good in argument—*fact* against *theory*—establishing a great principle of ecclesiastical science, such as this:—That it is always the part and duty of Christian men, put in trust with the Gospel—or, let us so express it, of "any congregation of faithful men in the which the pure word of God is preached, and the Sacraments duly administered," to devise, and to give effect to such methods of procedure as to them, in the conscientious exercise of their reason, shall seem best; and this, as well for maintaining the church which they actually possess, on its ground, as for extending continually the Gospel, near and far, among those who have it not.

This principle, obvious as it is, would seem to need little proving; and in fact it has been tacitly assumed and acted upon, even by those who have rejected it in words. Yet it stands opposed, in the *first* place, to the mystical and spiritualizing theory which aims, if it were possible, to hold the Gospel in a sort of sublimated condition, as an unearthly abstraction. There is always in existence a tendency of this sort; and it is seen more or less to sway the minds even of those who well know that to no such theory can they give indulgence, unless the clearest injunctions of Scripture are to be set at naught. But, on the other hand, the same clear rule of common sense and Christian duty impels us to reject, as an impracticable superstition—a superstition to which hitherto not the most resolute fanaticism has succeeded in giving full effect—the belief that no means or devices intended for securing the maintenance of visible Christianity, or for effecting its spread, can be lawfully employed, other than those which are verbally and specially defined in Holy Scripture. Those who have professed this belief have been ready to cite Biblical warrant for outline and finishing, for foundations and superstructure—for masons' work, and for decoration, of their Church-of-Texts. Amazing have been the refinements of expository sophistry resorted to for the purpose of giving completeness and consistency to the ideal of such a Church; and besides the fierceness of temper, and the bigotry attendant upon this endeavor, it has had the ill effect of training astute minds in the practice of that Rabbinical chicanery by means of which any thing we please may be inferred from any texts given.

This superstition, if not formally renounced, is not now practically regarded by any Christian community;—it is only sighed after by fond theorists, who would fain think themselves entitled to allege the authority of heaven in behalf of all they do and say, as members of a Church.

But if a practical refutation of this groundless doctrine were needed, we should find it most conclusively in the instance of the Wesleyan body. Wesleyanism is a scheme —it is the product of uninspired intelligence; and therefore it has its defects; but notwithstanding these defects, it has been (to use a customary religious phrase) "owned of God," for the good of men, to an extent that has no parallel. Let the facts, as they bear upon the obsolete superstition in question, be broadly and correctly stated. They stand before us thus:

Certain Christian bodies, taking their rise during the Reformation era, or in the following age, adopted, as was very natural, the textual principle, and could be content with nothing but a Church, in all things, conformed to the supposed primitive model: the founders of these Churches indulged themselves to the full in this their ecclesiastical zeal; but what has, in each instance, been the result—taking the lapse of a century into account? The history of such bodies has shown a sure progress from animation to formality and supineness, and a constant recession from the ground at first occupied, to a ground more narrow. Such bodies, left to themselves, and when they have admitted no genial influences of reanimation from foreign sources, have invariably lost, from year to year—their light—their warmth—their area, and their numbers. Is there, then, at this time, any room left for indulging the hope that the world will be widely Christianized by any of those Text-made Churches?

But let us turn to the facts which present themselves on the other side, and we find them in the history of Wesleyan Methodism. Wanting, as it was at its commencement, in almost every adventitious aid, and owing nothing to concomitant political excitements, strong, solely, in its evangelic energy, and in the simple purpose of its promulgators, it possessed itself of a surface outmeasuring far that which, in any properly comparable instance, Christian teachers have brought under their influence, within the same compass of time. And then, after the Methodistic founders had done their work, and when Wesleyanism had come to its place among other communions in England and America, and when it was working its way as abreast of them, after they had received the new life which Methodism itself had diffused through all, still it continued to spread in an increasing ratio, as compared with the rate of its initial advances, and quite beyond the rate of its competitors. In relation to our present purpose, the Wesleyan annual increase must be reckoned to include those who, on several occasions, have broken their connection with Conference; for these offsets have still held to the elements of Wesleyan organization, and are themselves instances confirmatory of our immediate argument.

This organization has, we say, abundantly proved itself to be effective in an extraordinary degree—considered simply as a system of evangelic aggression; that is to say, of aggression upon the irreligion of the world around it; and then, if any are inclined to urge the acknowledged imperfections which attach to this system, or those serious faults of structure that seem now to threaten its perpetuity, as so many countervailing facts which should lower it in our esteem, we make our appeal to those same blemishes and faults in a contrary sense, and we say—This Wesleyanism—notwithstanding its confessedly crude composition, and the misapprehensions and the practical errors with which it has encumbered itself, has yet far outstripped other Church systems, framed in scrupulous conformity to the theory adopted by their founders. Wesley, as founder of a Church, stands liable to some heavy inculpations; and *therefore* it is that, as originator of an evangelic enterprise for extending the Gospel, he may claim the higher praise: looked at in this light, his very faults come in to swell his trophies.

Foremost among the causes to which may be attributed the unexampled success of the Wesleyan body, must be named its UNITY OF INTENTION, or adherence to, and steady pursuit of a great principle. This means something more than a faithful profession of doctrine, or a continuous orthodoxy; for other bodies have had this same merit, and have "held fast the form of sound words" through centuries of prophesying in sackcloth. But these communities, without an exceptive instance, beside their giving less prominence to that effective truth—"salvation through faith," have either derived their organization by tradition from remote times, and have allowed their energies to be shackled by venerated observances; or, what is worse, have, as we have just said, yielded themselves to the will and whim of theoretic Biblists, and have vegetated, or barely breathed, within the bandages of a Church polity according to texts.

No man was more devoutly observant of the authority of Holy Scripture than Wesley; but his understanding was as practical in its tendencies, as his piety was sincere, and he perfectly felt, whether or not he defined that conviction in words, that an Apostolic Church—although right to a pin—which did not subserve its main purpose—the spread of the Gospel, and the conversion of the ungodly, must be regarded as an absurdity and a hinderance to the truth. "What is the chaff to the wheat?" what are wholesome and scriptural usages and orders which leave Christianity to die away within an inclosure? Wesley, not withdrawing his eye for a moment from the great and single purpose of his life, not letting go his hold of his one principle, worked upon such materials as came to his hand, in the spirit of liberty and power. Nothing for mere expediency sake would he have admitted—nothing would he knowingly have done on the assumption that the end sanctifies the means. But so long as no apostolic injunction is violated, and so long as the spirit and intention of apostolic precedents are regarded, a Christian institutor is free (as he he thought) to use the natural ability and sagacity which God has given him, for devising a mechanism which, though it may not give contentment to theorists, shall subserve its high purpose of sustaining and spreading the Gospel. Wesleyan Methodism, therefore, whatever may be its deficiencies, if thought of as a Church system, or how grave soever and ominous its faults as a scheme of government, has yet the great and commanding merit of embodying the evangelic impulse as its one law and reason: it is simple in principle, and with the working of that principle no subordinate purposes are allowed to interfere.

However true it may be that Wesley, as a Founder,

was keenly sensitive as to the integrity of the system he had created, it may be imagined that, if certain material imperfections in that system had been placed before him, in a convincing manner, he would, with an earnest ingenuousness, have set himself to work anew, and either have removed those faults, or have demolished his house, and built it up from the foundation on a better model. Further even than this we might go, and affirm that, at the present moment, Wesley's true successors and best representatives would be the men who—after the experiment of a century, finding Wesley's own Wesleyanism seriously at fault, would—with that grandeur of soul and simplicity of purpose which distinguished him, take in hand the SYSTEM, and mould or remodel it in conformity with the founder's one purpose. How good is the example he has left with his followers on this ground; and even now one may think one hears his voice, echoing in his chapels, and expounding to his people, in its *genuine sense*, those words, so often repeated among them, "Let us mind the same thing;" not meaning thereby a slavish adherence to things as they are, whether fitting or unfitting, but a wise constancy in holding fast a paramount principle, which the lapse of time can not affect, but which can be preserved through the lapse of years in no other way than by new adjustments, introduced from time to time, and always before the hour when they can no longer be resisted.

The unexampled success that has attended the Wesleyan Institute, in winning conquests from the world—and this, notwithstanding its defects, and the meagre style, too often, of its ministrations, furnishes an evidence fraught with instruction, which none but the infatuated will fail to turn to advantage. Actually to effect those changes, or to introduce those subsidiary means which the large experiment before us might seem to warrant, may not be practicable, at any particular moment; nevertheless, it must be desirable to keep the eye upon such items of reform, so that fit occasions for introducing them may not be lost, when they shall occur.

And now, might not that ONE INSTITUTE which holds the affection and approval of the majority of the English people, draw to itself, in an especial manner, those inferential benefits which may be derivable from the Wesleyan experiment? How improbable soever, and undesirable, may be an absorption of Methodism by the Established Church, there are points enough of assimilation between the two bodies to allow of the carrying over whatever may be good in the one, to augment the efficiency of the other. Let leave be granted for affirming that, for the advantage of the Episcopal Church at some time future, there has been carrying forward, during these last hundred years, and on an adjoining field, an experiment precisely of that kind which would best supply hints and suggestions for its own improvement. Wesley, thrust out of the Church in his day, will not, now, or ever, re-enter it with the thousands of his people; but yet he may, at some time not very remote, win the honor of bringing into it the rich fruits of his ecclesiastical sagacity. The Established Church needs—as we have already ventured to say—a place assigned within it for that which we have named as the Second Element of Methodism; and it needs—glaringly so—a scheme of ministrations having an aggressive purpose, in relation to the masses of the people, and on this ground, manifestly, Wesleyan Methodism might read it a lesson.

No ecclesiastical scheme, however wisely put together, will *of itself* avail, either to conserve the Gospel in its purity, or to extend its range; but such a scheme may favor, both its conservation and its propagation; and it has been too often proved to be in the power of an ill-constructed Church polity, as well to deprave doctrine, as to forbid expansion.

Whether it be good and safe, for purposes of government, of discipline, and of financial management, to leave uncontrolled power in the hands of the ministers of religion may well be questioned; and, indeed, it is conceding much to those who would defend such a system, to grant any space at all for a question on that ground. But *this* is not our immediate subject. When purposes of evangelic aggression only are in view, much may be said with reason in behalf of a purely clerical conclave, or deliberative assembly, which shall be exclusive of laymen.

It ought not to be thought that we take low ground, or that we are recommending that which must, in the end, secularize religion, when we pay regard to those secondary principles of action which spring from our common human nature. A church system which utterly refuses to recognize inferior motives will be inefficient and impracticable, except so long as its fervor is at the highest pitch: a church which builds wholly upon such motives is nothing better, at any time, than a worldly polity. We do not build upon any such motives; but we never lose sight of them.

Those arduous, and often perilous labors, by means of which—and on no easier terms, in any state of society, and not less in the heart of Christianized countries than in heathen lands—the Gospel may be carried out and planted upon new ground, imply and demand a very high tone of religious feeling among those who charge themselves with these enterprises. This work of aggression—this dauntless entry upon the royal preserves of Satan, and this continuance in the soldier's course—this endurance of contempt, buffeting, defeat, and "hardness," in many forms of real suffering, and of tormenting annoyance, will never be carried forward by men who have not braced their minds by an habitual recurrence to the ultimate motives of that course of life to which they have devoted themselves. Men—however good, fervent, and benevolent—who listen to gentle whispers, who are wont, as the phrase is, "to think better of it," and who take advice from those that stand at men's elbows ready to endorse the pleadings of an infirm conscience, such will not do the work of which now we are speaking:—in a word, it is a work which demands a high and sustained tone pervading *a select body of men*, and which would almost certainly be lowered or abated by the stated presence, and the official intervention, of laymen. The layman, individually, whose views and temper were such as to place him on a level with the loftiest spirits in a conclave of ministers would, by the very fact of possessing such a mind, cease to be a layman. But when a deliberative assembly is so consti tuted as to include, of right, a certain proportion of lay members, these, in whatever way elected, must be taken as they come, and they can never, as a body, possess a very exalted character; at the best, they will be no better than the best of the people. Some of the more active spirits among these lay deputies will be forward to recommend courses of ministerial enterprise which, if they themselves were ministers, they would never suggest; and in doing so, they will rouse some ministerial counteraction, which will not stop till it has gone too far: the "wise" among the lay brethren will be likely to go over to the same counteractive side; and thus less will be undertaken and done than as if ministers had been left to the promptings of their spontaneous zeal.

Within a purely ministerial conclave, assembling periodically, formally, and *authoritatively*, the ambition (not necessarily unholy) which seeks the welfare and increase, the stability and the augmentation of the INSTITUTE, whence the individual men themselves derive their social and professional existence—their all—will not be wanting. A feeling of this sort is one of the most powerful that are incident to human nature: we gain nothing by depriving it of all space and opportunity; we gain much by giving it a legitimate scope.

An assembly such as we now suppose, and consisting, whether of one, of two, or of three hundred members, will not—unless in times of extreme lifelessness—be wanting in at least a few eminent instances of high energy, practical determination, lofty motive, firm principle; and these will not merely be allowed the influence which is their right—the inalienable right of the gifted—to guide the mass; but they will impart to it their tone, they will diffuse throughout it their feeling, they will animate, by their words and by their looks, the less enterprising; they will defeat the captious, and they will shame the inert. The body will become such as is its inhabitant soul. Far greater things will thus be devised, proposed, enacted, and effected, than any, singly, would have thought of as practicable.

If thus we have secured, within the conclave, the motive power which must spring from the bosoms of a few, we should next see to it that this body of men be such—or be in such a position as that they may best receive, and best transmit, this same impulse, and diffuse it. The Wesleyan Conference, as framed by Wesley himself, was well constituted for *this* purpose. No purely spontaneous and precarious meeting together of individuals will ever exhibit, or has ever exhibited, a sustained energy in carrying out its intentions, or any continuous consistency of plan, from year to year, or any unity of purpose; or has had enough of impetus to overcome those petty oppositions and caprices that swarm about voluntary associations. The members of such a council must feel that their election to it is a distinction, and they should feel, too, that this honor brings with it no trivial responsibilities, and that these, be they what they may, can be foregone on no other condition than that of the loss of status, character, and social existence. Never will great things be effected by a body of men to any of whom, individually, the sort of petitionary question might be put—"Will you not attend our next annual meeting?"—followed by the surmising prayer—"Do, if you can!" It is in no such style as this, we may be perfectly certain, that war can be successfully waged with Satan, and he and his hosts driven in upon their defenses. The individuals of an aggressive evangelic body must all be subject to stern law; they must be accustomed to act and to move by rule and order; and they must go forth singly, full of an effective energy—more than their own—that is to say, the energy of the collective force which sends them out

Human nature, being such as it is, and if we take it in the mass, and exclude from our reckoning some rare and eminent instances—the men from whom arduous services for the public good are expected, must be held exempt from the pressure of private cares—from excessive anxieties, and from all shadow of dependence upon the precarious favor or caprices of individuals, or of small constituencies. When a man is struggling for himself, and for his own, he may be left to meet the difficulties of his position as he can:—not so (a hero now and then excepted, or a martyr) when he is called to suffer and to labor for interests that are not immediately personal. Wesley well understood this; and while calculating his fiscal resources in the most exact manner, and adjusting every claim on the most frugal scale, he lifted from the shoulders of the men who were to be his "helpers" the oppressive burden of their personal cares:—he would have their *help;* and therefore he saved them from the rankling anguish which is daily endured by those who, while serving the Church, are torn with cares for a wife and children. The itinerant preacher, whether single or married—a father, or not, set a firm foot upon the ground he trod: and while frugal, and observant of the Methodistic sumptuary discipline, he was safe, free, cheerful; and he had at command his constitutional stock of courage, unabated: it was not required of him that he should work, travel, preach, govern, while himself subject, every day, to the perennial ague of hopeless poverty.

In considering the efficiency of the Wesleyan system, as to its expansive powers, much ought to be attributed to the position of its ministers, as being, at once, exempted from excessive cares, and yet, as being members of a body, the prosperity and extension of which was not remotely related to their individual welfare. On this ground, and when we consider also the provision made for the superannuated, and the education given to the sons of preachers, it may be affirmed that no body of Christian ministers has stood in a position so favorable as the Wesleyan, for the free and healthful exercise of ministerial energies. Exempt from the law of clerical celibacy, and clear of the degrading influences of that detestable practice, the Wesleyan minister is, on the whole, less exposed to the temptations of ecclesiastical ambition, and is less burdened with the thoughts and cares "of this life" than his brother minister of any other communion.

It may seem obvious to mention the Wesleyan itinerating system as a principal cause of the rapid spread and wide extension of the body; and unquestionably it has been so; and yet this has taken place under conditions which are likely to be lost sight of. If the itinerating ministry of the Wesleyan body be placed by the side of the stagnation, the inertness, the timidity, and the gentle style, that so often have become characteristic of a ministry fixed to a spot, then indeed the advantage will appear to be all on the side of the former. A few individual instances may no doubt be found, and these may be made to serve the purposes of a needy argument, showing what great things a devoted man *may* do, as father of a district, in evangelizing his neighborhood. Such instances, rare always, are of the highest utility when employed as the materials of an instructive and stimulating biography; but they are of no pertinence when lugged into an ecclesiastical discussion.

If experience is to be our guide, there are two modes available, separately, but which are far more effective when brought into combination, in which the Gospel may be extended from any given centres, and may thence be made to embrace the population, until these widening circles meet each other. The first, and most obviously available of these modes is a systematic itinerancy: that is to say, a continuous assault made upon the unchristianized masses of the people, by dauntless yet discreet preachers—preachers who, at risk of life, will gather the people—in the fields, on the highways, in rooms, or wheresoever else they may be encountered; and will there, and thus, waken the fleshly ear by a bold challenge which finds its involuntary response in the depths of every human bosom.

The other of these two modes—and which will be the most effective when it avails itself of the first, is that of a territorial occupation of a country, by an ecclesiastical institute—not indeed asked for by the people, which will never be, but given to them, as it should be given, by an enlightened government: but with this practice and principle our immediate subject does not require us to concern ourselves.

But if an evangelizing itinerancy is to be spoken of, the conditions upon which its efficiency depends should be duly regarded. It seems often to have been imagined that itinerant preaching is mainly useful as affording a preparatory exercise for tyro preachers—a serviceable training and breaking-in, well fitted to the purpose of exhausting a little, and of usefully expending the animal courage and exuberant zeal of young and raw probationers for the ministerial office. "Let these fiery youths," it is said, "go forth for us, and break the ground;—they may perhaps do some harm; but they will do more good; and *we* will follow in due time." Among the errors into which senile indolence may lead men, there can be none, surely, more pernicious, or more awfully delusive, than this;—none that is more conclusively contradicted by the most authoritative of all precedents—that of the apostolic age; or more at variance with the most pertinent of modern instances—that of Methodism. The pattern ITINERANT of primitive Christianity was none other than the loftiest spirit of his age, and the most learned and accomplished man of his nation, and one who lacked nothing that could fit him for this, the most arduous of all services—nothing but a commanding presence. Or did Methodism make England and America its own, to so great an extent as it did, by the sending out of youths—preachers who had more fire than beard? Did the founders of Methodism—did those true heroes and martyrs of the modern Church, did they sit in committee with maps and plans before them, and thence, from their chairs of ease, trumpet the question—"Who will go for us?" It was not so:—these great men—great they were in energy and courage—went themselves:—they never said to others, "go and we will follow you;" but always, "we go:—follow us, and help us."

If the Wesleyanism of this present time be not the Methodism of the last century—a fact concerning which we profess to advance no opinion, as we have no sufficient information—but if it be not such, the reason of the change should be looked for on this very ground, mainly; that is to say, in the substitution of the less accomplished, and the less experienced, and the less commanding ministerial persons, in the place of the PRINCIPALS, where arduous and perilous evangelic enterprises are set on foot.

A growing and a healthy Christian community has, in this respect, no analogy with the animal structure; for in the body the living force must concentrate in the heart and the head, and thence must send its pulsations to the extremities; but within a Church, if it is to thrive and spread itself beyond its limits, the heart and the mind—the life and soul—the very best minds must move forward to the exterior, and plant the advancing stakes of its tabernacle on new ground. No apology shall be pleaded for when the bold affirmation is advanced that, at this moment, a Christian community—holding always a perfect and untainted orthodoxy—that is to say, the doctrine of the two creeds—whatever might be its deficiencies, or its minor faults, if it sent forth its very best men as an itinerant ministry—its seniors—its men of experienced wisdom, its most accomplished and best educated men, and those already possessed of a generally admitted and established reputation—such a Church, *thus* itinerating, and thus manfully confronting the desperate evils that afflict our eyes and ears on every side, and thus giving the irreligious and the unbelieving a proof that those who know most of Christianity are the forwardest to publish it—even at the risk of life, health, and comfort—such a Church would gain upon all competitors by great strides:—in a word, it would spread itself abroad as that Methodism spread which Whitefield, and Wesley, and Coke preached—not by deputy, but personally.

It is altogether in relation to purposes of another kind that the Wesleyan practice, as to its lay and local preachers, finds its reason. Christianity, extended and planted by means of an efficient itinerant ministry, may then (we need not doubt it) be sustained and cherished by these subsidiary and inferior ministrations. And so, in like manner, by the modern expedient of lay-helps—such as city missionaries, Scripture readers, and the like—Christian influences may be made insensibly, and most serviceably, to permeate the godless masses of the people: it is thus that the Gospel may open for itself a thousand noiseless paths, shedding blessings in each; but it is not thus that it will triumph; not thus that it will be honored to overturn the throne of Satan. The *future* Methodism, concerning which the writer intends yet to risk an opinion —that next-coming renovation of the powers of the Gospel, will not—so we believe—take effect upon the world in the hands of any but those who shall stand the foremost as the chiefs and the fathers of the Church, at that happy time.

When *Wesleyanism*, as distinguished from METHODISM, is spoken of as a scheme of Evangelic aggression, its own phase of doctrine ought to be taken into account; for this phase has a meaning, when so regarded, distinct from that which we have already spoken of as belonging to the substance of Methodism.

A field of meditation far-reaching, and difficult to traverse, would be opened before those who might attempt to follow and to exhibit the Divine providential government of the Church universal, as related to the measure of light and truth that is granted to, and possessed by, leading minds in seasons of renovation. No such arduous subject can we venture to touch in the present instance, and we thus allude to it only to introduce what must here be said of Wesleyan doctrine. Was it not then just such an aspect of Christian truth as fitted it for its purpose—namely, that of gathering and of retaining minds of the ruder class? Wesley was not left to adopt, in subtilty and false wisdom, the pernicious principle of *reserve*, in proclaiming the Gospel among the ignorant; but while, in all honesty and simplicity of heart, he wrought out for himself, from Scripture, his own form of doctrine—that doctrine (as we assume, and as the thoughtful reader of the Bible will, we think, be willing to grant) was itself an ill-adjusted Christianity, over which an air of consistency and harmony can be thrown only so long as the eye takes in a few degrees of the broad field of vision. Yet such narrowed aspects of things are well adapted to the quick apprehensions of undisciplined minds, and when forcibly presented to such minds by preachers whose own views are not wider than their style of discourse, and who are most peremptory when least consistent, and the most copious in citations of Scripture when Scripture least befriends them—such aspects, so presented, become effective for the purposes then most important to be secured.

That the barb of the Gospel should well flesh itself in the wild, willful conscience of the rugged populace—that alarms which are indeed too well founded, though not precisely in the preacher's sense, should retain their hold, both of the imagination and the reason *after date*—if one might so speak—and moreover, that that release from guilty fears which the Gospel affords should be thought of as instantly available, and yet as amissible;—these are the conditions, perhaps, of a scheme of doctrine best fitted to the purpose of bringing to the obedience of faith the lost and debauched masses of a Christianized country. Wesley's Christianity was altogether of this sort; and while we see its fitness to its end, we should devoutly acknowledge the presence of a higher wisdom, and of a sovereign rule, which distributes "to every man severally as He wills."

When Wesley went on, so far beyond the necessity of the case, to rivet upon his people forever, and by aid of law, the heterogeneous mass of doctrine comprised in the many volumes of his works, we see him inconsiderately taking a course in which, again, an overruling Providence is to be recognized, as intending an issue which Wesley, while living, would have deprecated with tears, but which we might imagine him *now* to look forward to with complacency. The adaptation of a certain mould of doctrine to the peculiar circumstances and uses of a temporary dispensation can be nothing else than its fitness in relation to what it finds around itself, at the time, and with which it has to contend, more or less directly. Now, while the adaptation of Wesleyan doctrine to the religious and to the irreligious masses of the people of England, a century ago, might easily be shown, under several aspects, that is to say, as related, on the one hand, to the brutish insensibility and profligacy of the many—on the other, to the lifeless Epictetus-Christianity of the Episcopal Church, and again, to the metaphysical sophistications then in vogue among the dissenters—while all this might be shown and sustained by copious proofs, yet will it thence follow that the very same form of doctrine, legally stereotyped as it is in Wesley's writings, and as sustained by the inflexible authority of the Court of Chancery, is now, and at this time—and not to look into futurity—equally well adapted to its intended purposes, as related to the present doctrinal position of surrounding communities? This will not follow; but, on the contrary, the *misfitting* of the twelve volumes to the times current can hardly fail to become more and more obtrusively apparent, and more oppressively inconvenient, at every interval of seven or ten years.

Since Wesley's time vast stores of genuine philological science have been accumulated on the field of biblical exposition—stores ready and available for bringing in that better harmony of sacred truth which shall gladden the coming age. How, then, shall it fare with Wesleyan theology, and with the Poll Deed at the dawn of that time? Even now there is a noiseless progress taking place which, as it advances, must remove the solid earth from beneath whatever was Wesley's own in his system of theology. So far as this relative change has actually taken place, and is going on, Wesleyanism, instead of its being that which the modern preacher may use, as did his predecessor—as an effective engine of assault upon the consciences of men, it is a something felt to be obsolete, and for the preservation of which he must fight a desperate battle.

Let leave be granted for the suggestion that a reconsidered Wesleyanism, which should wholly cease to make itself the antagonist of an obsolete form of Calvinism, might yet restore to the Wesleyan Institute that expansive evangelic force in which once it so far surpassed every other Christian community.

WESLEYAN METHODISM—A SYSTEM OF RELIGIOUS DISCIPLINE AND INSTRUCTION, AS TOWARD THE PEOPLE.

A HEARING has been secured by the Wesleyan preacher; and the people, thus far gained, are not merely willing to listen to him again, but they earnestly desire to do so. Gladly he yields to this desire, and repeatedly addresses them, and he makes good his hold of their consciences and affections, of which he must, by all means, take advantage, for their highest good. But as to himself, his commission requires him to hurry forward to other scenes of labor, and he must provide as he can for the spiritual oversight of the converts he has made: he does so, first, by looking out from among his little company the one who may be naturally gifted in some fair degree, and perhaps also may be a Christian man of older date, and who has already approved himself within some other community, by his knowledge, piety, and consistent behavior: to this Christian man, or to two such if he can find them, the itinerant preacher commends his company of converts: in a word, he does that which, as it appears, St. Paul did under circumstances not essentially dissimilar. This done, he departs, engaging for himself, or for another preacher, to revisit this society after a while, and to renew his labors among them. And who shall say that, thus far, the apostolic practice, as to its substance, and its practical meaning, has not been followed? To Wesley's vigorous and always practically-set mind, this course, notwithstanding his prejudices, fully approved itself; and his energy, and his simplicity of intention, and that faculty of order which in him was so remarkable, quickly brought this practice, which had sprung up under his hand spontaneously, into the form of a well-defined and established institute. At this point Wesleyanism is no longer to be regarded merely as a call to repentance, or a religious movement and revival; but it is a SYSTEM of religious training: it is a social mechanism, sure to be productive of definite and beneficial results, so long as it shall be maintained in vigorous action.

A religious movement and revival, if indeed it be genuine, issuing in unfeigned repentance and faith, must be the work of God, though effected by human agency; but a religious mechanism, or social institute, well contrived, and working according to its own law and rule, is the work of man; yet drawing toward itself, and engaging in its behalf, the blessing of God. METHODISM, as we have assumed, was God's work; and therefore it is worthy of the most devout regard; but Wesleyanism was the work of man, and instead of its being liable, on this account, to a mistrusting, a suspicious, and a cold exceptive approval, it has well shown itself to enjoy abundantly the favor and presence of Him who fails not to prosper the faithful and wisely-directed labors of His servants.

Yet, in so far as Wesleyanism was the work of man, it is open to the freest scrutiny. The system, as to the rudiments of its composition, is conformable to the spirit and intention of the apostolic ministrations; but when we come to follow it into its more elaborate adjustments, our course is less clear, for much that presents itself is of ambiguous tendency:—some of its results offend, not our tastes merely, but our feelings of propriety and consistency; and very much bears upon its face the characteristics of a system of expedients which, though they might be tolerable or warrantable for a time, or at the urgent demand of very unusual circumstances, become intolerable, if extended beyond their immediate limits, as to the occasion, or the time.

Nevertheless, Wesleyan discipline, even if its faults were more serious than they are, has the high merit of having brought in upon the people A SCHEME OF RELIGIOUS DISCIPLINE, IN THE PLACE OF NONE! Frightfully wrong must a form of religious discipline be which one should wish to see quite swept away, leaving *nothing* in its stead! Wesleyanism came in, with its itinerant ministry, its local preachers, its classes, its bands, its trusteeships, and its fiscal organization—it came in, not to supplant any existing system of actual discipline, or of church training, but to establish a culture of some sort, upon the waste howling wilderness of popular irreligion. Where it effected conversions, there it also provided for, and carried forward, the cure of souls. The cure of souls—a very few exceptive cases allowed for—had been wholly neglected, or forgotten, on all hands, at the time of the Methodistic revival. The Episcopal Church, in its several offices, assumes the existence and the efficiency of a universally extended religious training; and it is on the ground of this hypothesis that these offices are susceptible of a good and scriptural interpretation. But as this (supposed) cure of souls—intended to embrace the community, from the first weeks of life, to its close, had fallen into desuetude, and had quite ceased to be a fact, Wesleyanism deserves high praise (apart from its merit as a mission to the irreligious) on this ground, and because it supplied so sad a lack of service on the part of the Church.

As to the several bodies of orthodox dissenters—the religious contemporaries of Methodism, not to speak of the lifelessness which had then fallen upon most of them, the disciplinary principles recognized in these bodies, at that time (in some degree amended since) were founded upon a far too narrow conception of the social intention of the Gospel. The puritanic idea of a Church, although true and right, if we look just to a bright centre spot, where all Christian influences are made to come to a focus, sheds no benign beam of diffusive grace beyond that spot. If you chance to stand a few feet away from that glare, you barely see a glimmer of light, or feel a glow of warmth. Who, at a little distance outside a puritanic Church of the rigid sort, would surmise that he was standing so near to a ministration of—"THE GLORIOUS GOSPEL OF THE BLESSED GOD?" Wesleyanism then, with its more practical and its more widely-based discipline, was a great gain, as compared with the exclusiveness, and the small efficiency of the *then* existing nonconforming communions. If we have deductions to make from this praise, let it first be bestowed in terms so decisive and ample as shall leave abundant margin, even after our severest annotations have found room.

It may easily be granted to Wesley's admirers that he made the best provision which was in any way possible, at that time, for the instruction of his people—a people created, as they were, not by a gradual operation, but evoked almost at a moment. Then, inasmuch as an itinerating ministry was indispensable to that continuous aggressive movement which was the first intention of Methodism, so was it the only condition under which men so imperfectly educated, and so slenderly furnished with biblical knowledge as most of his preachers were, could have discharged the function of religious teachers, with any sort of competency;—especially considering the incessant public services in which they were engaged. Then, in the early times of Methodism, the meagreness which must have attached often to these ministrations, was partly remedied, or their deficiencies supplied, by Wesley's own powerful and effective preaching, and by that of several of his ordained colleagues; and at length, by some of his ordinary preachers, who, in their periodic visitations of the circuits, gave the congregations a better aliment, and carried them forward, each time, a stage or two, in knowledge and feeling.

And beyond this, Wesley would naturally look forward to a time when, in the course of things, his Societies, growing always in Christian proficiency, would become nurseries for the ministry, and would at once create a demand for a higher order of ministrations, and nurture those who should supply it. It ought not to be questioned that these reasonable anticipations (which Wesley, as we suppose, entertained) have been, in a fair degree, realized. Besides, although Wesley seems to have held the several orthodox communions around him in small esteem, and perhaps barely allowed himself to calculate upon any material benefits to accrue to his preachers from the indirect influence which they might thence derive, it can not be imagined that the Wesleyan ministry has in fact so shut out from itself all these beneficial influences, as not to have drawn from them many very decisive advantages. It would be uncandid not to suppose that, since their founder's time, these preachers have caught a tone, and have admitted among themselves a light, and have received an excitement, from exterior sources.

And further than this, it may be granted, that the merely physical influence of frequent change of scene, and the animation that arises from contact with fresh congregational surfaces—if so we may speak, and the opportunity afforded to actively-minded preachers to amend their style, in entering upon a new circuit, and, not the least among these advantages of itinerancy, that knowledge of mankind, which it may impart, all tend to promote the preacher's improvement, to give him a just confidence in himself, to render him fearless of individual countenances, and to fix upon his ministrations a character of force, animation, and freshness. Even if his stores be far less ample than those of others, yet, such as they are, they will be made more available to the hearer; and especially so to the uneducated.

All this allowed and granted, to the full, it must still remain as a theoretic probability that an itinerating ministry will occupy a position several degrees below the level of a located ministry, as to the purposes of religious instruction. Must it be thought an illiberal and unwarranted inference that this theoretic probability has made, and does make itself apparent as an actual fact?

Any one who, endowed with some natural faculty and fluency of utterance, has made the experiment, will have found it far from difficult to acquire the power of continuous and pertinent speaking, upon familiar topics—especially upon religious topics—and so to hold out for a thirty or forty minutes, or more; and if this habit of speaking be well husbanded, and kept always within the safe inclosures of conventional phrases, and of authenticated modes of thinking, this preacher may be always ready to ascend the pulpit—in season, and out of season. His sermon, or his set of discourses, is, in fact, the glib run of the mental associations upon worn tracks—this way or that, as the mind may chance to take its start from a given text.

This sort of mindless facility of speaking proves a sore temptation to many a located minister; and its consequence is to leave many a congregation sitting, from year to year, deep in a quagmire. Better than this, undoubtedly, would be itinerancy:—far better is a frequent shifting of monotonies, than a fixedness of the same. But such an admission will not avail to establish the principle that this shifting system is in itself good; or that it ought to be regarded in any other light than as a necessary expedient, allowed under peculiar circumstances, or (which would be far better, and *indeed* good) as a method, or system, supplementary to a located ministry. Thus used, and put in act—as we have already ventured to say—by the most accomplished and highly reputed ministers of a Church—

by its chiefs and its doctors, every thing that is auspicious might be looked for as its consequence.

This, however, is *not* the Wesleyan itinerancy:—it is not as thus equipped that the Founder sent forth his ship upon its transit of the great deep:—his preachers were, all of them, to be itinerants; and as movement was the law of his own existence—bodily and spiritual, so—this manifestly was his feeling—must perpetual movement be the law and the practice of his Institute: but if so, then must we not accept the double conclusion that Wesleyanism is an economy for a time; and that the Christianity it teaches will always be immature and superficial;—precisely defined—not merely in a horizontal direction, that is to say, as to its bordering upon other systems; but not less sharply shaped *beneath* and *above*, or toward those heights and depths which it is the part of devout meditation to explore?

When, as we have now done, the whole amount of its probable or even possible advantages are freely allowed as the recommendations of an itinerating ministry, liberty may fairly be taken for placing these advantages in contrast with those of a settled or located ministry. We must not be told, to deter us from attempting such a comparison, that these happy and important results of a fixed pastoral residence are far from being uniformly realized: does an itinerant ministry always, or in a larger proportion of instances, reach its own point of ideal perfection?

The permanently located Christian minister, if he be not broken down by over much pastoral labor, and if conscientious in the devotion of his whole energies and time to his high calling, will, in the first place, find leisure—more or less—for perpetually extending, and for *retaining* also, his acquisitions as a biblical expositor, and for availing himself continually of that influx of critical apparatus which, from year to year, is laid at his feet by the unwearied industry of accomplished scholars—German especially. If *this* advantage may now, by some, be set at a low price, the time is coming which will teach the rising ministry a serious lesson, on this ground, and will convince them that any such disparaging opinion of biblical accomplishments involves nothing less than a fatal observance of the present tendencies of opinion.

Grant it that signal industry and an unquenchable thirst of knowledge may enable an *errant* biblical scholar to prosecute his studies; but—man for man, taken alike, has not the resident scholar ,with his own treasures—his Lexicons, and his Commentaries, and his idolized folios, in their own places, on their own shelves, in his little study—the blessed place of his converse with all minds, and with heaven—has not this settled minister and student an advantage which his brother, the like-minded itinerant preacher, will sigh to enjoy?

Yet this is only the beginning, only the preparation—only the apparatus of a full ministerial acquaintedness with those inexhaustible treasures of thought which invite our advance when the Book of God opens before us the portals of eternity! Even if it might be alleged, concerning any passing period of time, that habits of profound meditation are rarely cherished, and that, at any such time, the pulpit does not give evidence leading the reflective hearer to suppose that a soul-deep communion with that which is unseen and eternal has much been sought after, or has actually been enjoyed by preachers, even should it be so, it will remain certain that a life of intense meditation, grounding itself upon an exact biblical scholarship, and observant always of the *written* revelation—that a life of *heart-thoughtfulness*—a life the product and issues of which will impart force and freshness to public services, and will supply nourishment to hungry souls—such a life of industrious biblical rumination can scarcely be possible except under the conditions of a tranquil ministerial fixedness. If ever again the habit of counting the days of the week until Sunday comes, is to grow up in congregations (not a giddy eagerness for the intellectual luxury of a fine sermon), if sermons are to be remembered beyond the moment when the foot reaches the last step at the church doors—if it is to be thus with us, preachers must not be those who shall have it to say, at the close of a weary life of labor, that, in the service of the Gospel, they have traveled half a million of miles!

But the people, if indeed they are to know what that store of blessings is which Christianity holds ready to bestow upon themselves and upon their families, must have near them always, not preachers merely, but pastors; and if the man of incessant journeyings may become a pastor, such as the people need, then also may oaks, in full growth, be had from a nursery ground, and set down before your window. We must have been used to trifle with our own souls, and we must have become regardless of the spiritual welfare of our families, children, and servants, if we have not often desired those influences, for ourselves and for them, which a Christian minister, not a sermon-maker but a pastor, may shed around him. But shall he do this who has been "two years on our station," and who will be gone the next, and who, while he stays, is called upon to dispatch countless public services, and to rid himself well of a thousand formalities of office? This will not be: "Do men gather grapes of thistles?" The vine, laden with ripened clusters, is a plant that loves its own spot, clings to its wonted holdings, sends its fibres throughout its own plot of soil, and may not be torn up, and set elsewhere: the vine draws its sap from the ground it knows, and yields its juices to those who keep it.

What we are now thinking of, as the fruit—the fruit most of all precious—of the pastoral office, when sustained through a course of years by a resident minister, is not the frequency of domiciliary religious visits in the families of his congregation, nor the pointedness, the fervor, the faithfulness of those instructions which this shepherd of his flock may address to assembled families, or to youths in vestry classes; it is not that species of service which may be acquitted in so many hours of each week, and which may be duly entered in the columns of a register; it is not this, but it is that which, beyond every other means of religious influence, and beyond all other means put together, is felt and known to be effective in diffusing a Christian temper, and in securing Christian conduct, within the circle where it is found. It is the exhibition—from year to year, of fervent, consistent piety, in its aspects of wisdom, meekness, self-command, devotedness, in the person of the loved and revered father of his congregation—the man who is greeted on the threshold of every house by the children, and whose hand is seized as a prize by whoever can first win it—the man who is always first thought of in the hour of domestic dismay or anguish—the man whose saddened countenance, when he must administer rebuke, inflicts a pain upon the guilty, the mere thought of which avails for much in the hour of temptation. It is the pastor, an affection for whom has, in the lapse of years, become the characteristic feature of a neighborhood, and the bond of love among those who, otherwise, would not have had one feeling in common.

If it be said, pastors such as this are not found on every side among resident ministers, we grant it; yet some such, in their various degrees of excellence, *are* found, and may always be found within a Church which fixes its ministers in their spheres; but it is not within the range of possibility that Christian eminence *of this species* can be nurtured, or can find its field of exercise under the stern and ungenial conditions of an itinerant ministry.

May we not safely adopt aphorisms such as these? first:—Where there is no itinerancy, there will be no aggression on the irreligious masses—no wide spread of the Gospel: and again, this—Where there are no resident pastors, there will be no Church; no deep-seated Christian love—little diffused reverence—little domestic piety, and much more reliance will be placed upon means of excitement, than upon means of influence: regulations, established orders, conventional usages will take their course; but those impulses and motives which supersede law will scarcely be known.

It is always true, and it is consolatory to think of it as true, that a system which is not essentially vicious, when it is vigorously worked, supplies its own deficiencies, and brings in a remedy, by help of happy anomalies, for its most serious faults. Thus, probably, has it been with Wesleyanism; so that, in fact, though destitute of pastors, it may find an equivalent among its other provisions.

The practice of supplying congregational services by the ministration of gifted laymen—local preachers, may be exempted from the reprehension to which, abstractedly, it stands open—partly by the plea of necessity—partly by the rigidness of the regulations to which it is made subject; and in good measure also by a recollection of the benefits which indirectly flow from it as a means of calling forth those who, on this field of trial, may approve themselves as fit for the ministry.

With the practice of the ancient Church before them, those who profess to be governed by its authority ought to take care in what terms they condemn lay teaching. Under the influence of circumstances essentially similar, the same course has been adopted within the Wesleyan body as was followed by the ancient Church. Whenever a Christian community becomes, as it ought to be always, aggressive toward the irreligious masses around it, two consequences necessarily follow, and require to be provided for:—the first is this, that the preaching of a few able ministers has called into existence many more congregations than they can themselves personally serve; the second is of a kind to aggravate the inconveniences resulting from the first; and it is this, that congregations gathered from the uninstructed masses, and constituted chiefly of those whose religious habits are still unformed, must be dependent upon others always for the aid and guidance they need in spiritual matters. Moreover, as these converts (very few of them) can command at home, even in any degree, the place or time for private devotional exercises, they must be assembled, for worship and instruction, as frequently as possible, and in fact much oftener than can be either necessary or beneficial, in the case of a religiously trained community.

Hence it is that there arises perhaps a threefold demand for ministerial appearances in public; or that, for one congregational service which an established and stationary Church may require—a convert-making Church, in which, after the apostolic model, "believers are added to the Church daily," in such a Church neither its onward progress, nor its permanence, can, in the nature of things, be provided for and secured except by calling forth the gifts, and by allowing and favoring the services of laymen, locally connected with each single congregation. A Church which, in the spirit of rigid or of arrogant adhesion to certain principles and rules, persists in refusing all such aid, and will do what it does only by the means of educated and ordained ministers, must abide by the inevitable consequence—that is to say, it must fail in a main article of Christian duty, and be content to sleep with them that sleep.

To condemn therefore the Wesleyan practice, in this behalf, is to abandon Christianity, as a glad tidings to all people: it may still rest in our keeping, as a subject of luxurious meditation, or as affording the objects and excitements of mediæval devotional services; but it is not apostolic Christianity.

Nevertheless those who know what human nature is, and how much caution is needed when spiritual gifts are to be brought into exercise for the good of others—consistently also with the religious welfare of the individual, such will not need to be told that not merely personal wisdom and discretion are required on the part of those who govern a society, and who direct such services, but more than this—the enforcement of rules and orders carrying with them the weight of a recognized authority. If *all* things done in the Church should be done "decently and in order," so especially should the gifts of the "gifted" be exercised under, and within the limits of well-defined and *absolute* regulations. The *truly* gifted and the right-minded, the zealous and the modest, will rejoice to submit themselves to such restraints which will at once sustain them against their own misgivings and timidity, and defend them against the jostlings of impudent competitors.

It is not our part to inquire how far, at *this* time, Wesleyan Methodism, which stands recommended by so much of system, organization, and RULE, brings this, its own principle, to bear upon its practice, in relation to the lay ministrations which it allows. It is however matter of record (and of recollection with some) that in the Wesleyanism of the time immediately following Wesley's period, and when it was in the main what he had made it, his doctrine concerning instantaneous assurance, and his unwarranted practice of almost demanding or of looking for semi-miraculous interpositions, in answer to prayer, took effect, not very seldom, upon the gifted laity in a manner which can not be thought of without a mingled feeling of terror and disgust. It was well if indeed the regular preachers always observed decorum, and always remembered what is due, of reverence and humility, to the Infinite Majesty;—but as to many of the gifted laity, who charged themselves with the task of praying the converted into a better condition, it will be acknowledged by the candid and intelligent of this communion that, to a very great extent, if not customarily (let us say in times gone by) frightful violences of voice and gesticulation, accompanied by improprieties of language which made the ears tingle, were to be seen and heard in Wesleyan chapels. Where, within the compass of the inspired writings, do we find so much as one syllable which could be appealed to in defense of these extravagances? They must stand, forever, without apology.

But then it will follow that, when Wesleyan Methodism, comes under review, as a scheme of religious discipline, for the people, its original misapprehensions of Christian doctrine, every one of which Wesley riveted by law upon his societies, have not told well upon that practice which, otherwise, would be highly approvable—namely, its lay ministrations. Thus does a theological error—which may seem to be only an innocent abstraction, work its way outward from the region of speculation and of textual exposition, until it comes, fraught with mischief, upon the platform of popular excitement. Justification by faith all orthodox Protestants admit and teach. But, says Wesley, No man is justified who does not know it—know it clearly, certainly, and instantaneously. He who is not sure that he is saved, is still in a state of condemnation; nevertheless from this state he may, at a moment, be delivered; and, for the purpose of obtaining for him this deliverance, the very heavens are to be rent by the boisterous vociferations of prayer!

Thus it is that the inconveniences inseparable from the allowance and employment of lay ministrations, when coming, as one might say, to an intersection upon some incoherent doctrine, have issued in producing the most serious evils. How far the good sense and matured judgment of the Wesleyan ministry may have applied a remedy, in this direction, those who stand outside the Society can not well know; yet we may take comfort in recollecting how much the insensible influence of one religious community upon another avails to mitigate the evils incident to each. Thus, to take the case before us as an instance, it can not be doubted that a corrective influence, real, though silent and unconfessed, derived from surrounding communities, less crude than itself, has, almost from the first, borne upon Wesley's Wesleyanism, and has operated to rectify many of those serious defects to which his unreflective and logical energy gave occasion.

It may be so in the instance we have referred to, namely, the intemperate style fallen into by some lay preachers and leaders: yet is there another principal element of the Wesleyan discipline which, as set on foot by Wesley, has still more urgently called for correction, and has needed every healthful counteraction which it might possibly receive from the better feeling of other Christian communities.

Nothing, in Wesleyanism, has drawn upon itself more reprehension—or, in fact, has been more open to it—than the principles assumed, and the practices established, in its class meetings and bands; but while, on the one hand, the rebukes which this particular institution has met with have often been unmeasured and excessive, and while too much use has been made of some reported instances of impropriety or extravagance, little, if any regard has been paid to the pleas which a disinterested observer may advance in its defense. These pleas, in apology for the weekly meetings in classes, are chiefly two—the first being this, which however no thorough Wesleyan would admit, that the Wesleyan Institute, itself, is not a church; but is rather a system of useful and necessary expedients, brought in, at the first, to supply the wants occasioned by the remissness and the culpable negligence of the existing Christian communities. The second ground of apology, though analogous, is not quite identical, and it is of this sort, namely, that as for the most part those with whom it has had to do, and whom it has rescued from utter irreligion, have come under its treatment with none of that training which an effective church system would have supplied, it could adopt, toward these converts from heathenism, none other than extreme measures, adapted to the ruggedness of the material upon which it had to work. When therefore, on this ground, Wesleyanism is blamed, or when it is blamed by members of the older communions, such condemnation as may be called for can not ask to be listened to unless it is prefaced by expressions of unfeigned compunction in the recollection of the ecclesiastical sins and supineness of ourselves, and of our fathers, of generations back. Is it so that class meetings are of very ambiguous tendency?—Grant it;—but let it be remembered that an utter neglect of the masses of the people is of no ambiguous tendency; for it is a pure and certain evil—without relief, and admitting of no plea of extenuation. Far better must it be to assemble in classes those whom we, and others, have left banded together in sin, than so to leave them any longer, even although much of what might be heard in the class meeting would offend our fastidiousness, or be liable to some just reprehension. Easy is it for us, with our nice notions, and our unacquaintedness with the manners and habits of the lower classes, to think much of the improprieties of religionists, and little or nothing of the miseries and degradation, the ferocity and the utter ruin of the unreclaimed multitude! A humane and Christian-like temper will prompt the earnest wish that Wesleyan Methodism may go on in its course and prosper, notwithstanding its heaviest faults of system or practice, and even if they could be proved to be heavier than they are.

Such faults have perhaps already, in great measure, met their correction; or whether they have or not, a reference to them, made in the spirit of love, should not be considered as offensive.

The evils of the class-meeting system have been made a frequent theme with those who have assailed Wesleyanism: they seem to be summed up under two or three articles; but the actual mischiefs resulting from them are probably much less than theoretically they would seem likely to produce; and be they what they may, they must be accounted smaller evils by far than those of which Methodism has been the cure.

If the class of persons is considered who, for the most part, are brought together in these weekly conclaves, what is most needed for them—besides those devotional exercises which tend to keep fervent piety alive—is a course of sound instruction, catechetical and didactic, embracing the doctrines and duties of Christianity;—that is to say, instruction brought home to each mind, and brought down to the level of each understanding, in a manner which can scarcely be effected from the pulpit. That which the class-meeting urgently needs is, a competent Bible-class teacher. But how slenderly are even the best trained congregations furnished with teachers so qualified! how few are those, even whose religious advantages are at the highest pitch, who can intelligently and judiciously expound Holy Scripture! How then should Wesleyan congregations, newly gathered and undisciplined, find among themselves any such teachers? It will not be: it is impossible. They may, however, and ordinarily they will be able to select a sufficient number of fervently-minded and well-reputed persons, raised a few degrees above their brethren or sisters in experience, and possessing a faculty available for giving direction to an hour's religious conversation: and how much better it is that this hour should be so spent, than spent as otherwise it would be!

Nevertheless, a religious meeting, thus constituted, and thus directed, will not merely fail of accomplishing what ought to be its purposes; but it can scarcely fail to give that wrong—because *retorted*—direction to the religious affections whence spring most of the disorders and irregularities that rob the Gospel of its honors. So it would be under such a system, taken at the best; but Wesley's logical sophisms, when he brought scriptural precepts to bear, in a forced sense, upon human nature, have had the effect of sadly aggravating these evils. What could he imagine would be the consequence of instructing his class-leaders to demand of each member an unreserved exposure of a week's sins and temptations? What is it that could be the product of such disgorgements when each was solemnly enjoined, with a remorseless disregard of delicacy, of reserve, of diffidence, to pour forth, before all, the moral ills of the past seven days? May there not be some ground for the alleged comparative harmlessness of auricular confession? The gross-minded and the shameless will be prompted by egotism and by a bad ambition to discharge the week's accumulations of their bosoms very copiously; but it is certain that the sensitive, whose consciences are the most alive to feelings of healthful compunction in the recollection of sin, will not, until the system itself has spoiled them, be able to bring themselves up to any such pitch of ingenuousness; those who should be silent, will be loquacious; those who might speak, will violate their best feelings if they do.

It is not easy to imagine how it can be otherwise, so long as Wesley's instructions are literally complied with;

but it is probable that that good sense and better feeling which so often comes in to exclude the practical absurdities attaching to a theory, have availed, and do constantly avail for good in this instance of the class-meeting confessional.

But—so far as these unedifying outpourings of ill-conditioned bosoms may still take place in a class-meeting, one can not but be dismayed in thinking of what must be the moral consequence which, in a course of time, will be produced upon the imagination and the religious sentiments of those whose fate it is to listen to the same! Again we must profess the hopeful belief that such ill consequences are (one knows not precisely how) reduced always, or generally, to a minimum. Yet is it exceedingly difficult to imagine that a weekly listening to the revelations of the class-meeting can have otherwise than a very corrupting influence upon young and uncontaminated minds.

Let it, however, be granted that the natural discretion and better feeling of class-leaders do avail, in most instances, for excluding what would be of ill tendency toward any who may be present; but even then a misdirection is being given to religious feelings, which is so much the more prejudicial, because all the parties concerned—alike the teachers and the taught, believe it to be wholly good. Already, in these pages, this subject has been referred to; but the importance attaching to it demands a further remark, inasmuch as *Wesleyanism* has reduced to system that which *Methodism* had cherished, and which, so long as it continued to be quite spontaneous and incidental, would be far less hurtful than when it came to be cut, and fitted, and timed, according to statute. The spiritual life, the true life of the soul toward God, will never yield itself to the rigid will of the legislator: formality and hypocrisy may thus be dealt with; but not truth—not the depth of genuine religious feeling.

It is that extensive convert-making from among the utterly irreligious, and which was the glory and the true praise of the early Methodism, that has set Wesleyanism wrong, on this ground. How different an aspect would our Christianity wear, if developed by the means of an effective apostolic Church—a Church embracing all homes, and all souls there, and carrying out the benign intention of the Gospel, toward all born within its circle!

The contracted theological views of some parties, and the perpetuated mediæval errors so fondly clung to by others, have, in their antagonism, shrouded from the eyes of all very much of that bright beam and that life-giving glory, the distant glimmerings of which make glad the meditative reader of the inspired books. The Gospel, wherever it is dispensed, claims for a rescue all human souls, in the name of "God our Saviour." We demur about this claim, and we put it under conditions, and we make it liable to exceptions; and while we are thus grudging its amplitude, we actually fail to give effect to its beneficent import in those instances in which our line of duty is clearly chalked out for us.

Christian families, trained within a Church which should well understand its commission in the world, and should be alive to its duties, and mistrustful, never, of the grace, the power, and the faithfulness of God, such families, so trained, would send forth from their nurture-bosoms, for catechetical instruction, their junior members—the "members of Christ—the children of God—the inheritors of the kingdom of heaven"—those to whom the customary hour's talking in a "class-meeting" would be strangely unsuitable. But this is a subject too deep and wide for this place. When we have affirmed, once and again, in these pages, that Wesley did not construct a Church—a main part of what we mean finds its interpretation at this point:—Methodism was a proclamation of the Gospel, lasting its season, and doing its work:—*Wesleyan* Methodism was an economy well adapted to the purpose of sustaining that aggressive evangelic movement after the impulse in which it originated should have subsided. But when it comes to be considered as a permanent system of religious discipline, as toward the people, it presents itself under an aspect far too special, and, one might say, too well adapted to the rude masses with which chiefly it has been conversant, to be entitled to the praise implied, if we were to call it a Church. If the rejoinder should come in the form of an animated question—" Where then is *your* Church?" this is a question to which we are not bound, in this place, to supply an answer.

WESLEYAN METHODISM, CONSIDERED AS A HIERARCHY, OR SCHEME OF SPIRITUAL GOVERNMENT.

WESLEY'S rightful claim to our esteem as a Christian ruler, and our admiration of his ability as the founder of a great community, would not surely be enhanced by any attempt to allege, in his behalf, that, while contemplating one species of organization, and while having in his view a certain well-defined purpose, what he had devised for effecting that purpose has, in fact, proved, itself to be the very best possible—if he had intended to bring about something, not only wholly different, but of a contrary tendency! As if a mechanical contriver had constructed, as he thought, a power-loom which, with all its movements and frame-work unchanged, was found to perform, without fault, the part of a printing press—or any thing else!

The evidence is copious and various which attests the fact that Wesley, in instituting his Society—which he thought of only as an evangelizing supplement to the Established Church—entertained no thought, intention, or wish to construct a Church;—that is to say, to frame a spiritual polity, which should stand by itself—should comprise all powers requisite for a complete ecclesiastical organization, and which (especially) should embrace within its provisions that necessary balance of powers, clerical and lay, apart from which the choice must always lie between hierarchical despotism, or democratic despotism;—that is to say, between an unabated spiritual supremacy or impracticable and ungovernable popular caprice.

It has become usual to say much of Wesley's rare sagacity; and this praise may well be allowed him, if we think of that bright intuition which, as by a flash, discerns the true bearings of things present, and which, in the same instant, adapts itself to the shifting circumstances of the hour or day, and works its purposes onward from day to day, with high success, by aid, and under the luminous guidance of this ready wisdom and skill. In *this* sense the Founder of Wesleyan Methodism, or, let us rather say, its chief and ruler, was pre-eminently sagacious.

But there is another usual sense of the same word, in which it conveys a loftier idea, namely, that of a far-reaching and, one might say, a *prophetic* forethought of the distant issues of movements and of tendencies now in course of development, and which takes its measures in due time, provides for probable results, and includes, in what it now does, some well-calculated adaptations to remote products. Sagacity, in this more enlarged sense, we can not think was Wesley's distinction. If indeed we thought him to be sagacious in this sense, as one who looked far and wide into the future, we must, of sheer necessity, abate very much from the reverence with which we are used to regard him, as a thoroughly ingenuous and simple-minded Christian man. If indeed, which we think obviously was not the fact—Wesley was endowed with a far-reaching sagacity, and if indeed, from the very first, he discerned—as an ambitious spiritual hierarch would have discerned—what must be the issue of the movement he had originated, and if he saw, in the distance, what Wesleyan Methodism would come to mean, and what position it would occupy, and what the successors of his lay preachers and his "Helpers" would be, at the moment of the centenary celebration of the founding of the Society, if indeed it was thus with him, then what interpretation will there remain for us to put upon his professed and long-adhered-to reluctance to allow to his preachers and helpers, and to his societies, those functions and that independent liberty of action which they—ministers and people, were, from year to year, so importunately asking to be granted them? This reluctance might indeed be very *politic*, and it might be that which a far-seeing sagacity would dictate to a chief in Wesley's position; but if *politic* in this sense, then it was not *ingenuous;* his reluctance, though real as to the *inner* motive which prompted it, was unreal, nay, it was absolutely *false* as to its declared motive: it was a hollow pretext—it was a trick and a disguise.

Of no trickery or paltry conduct was John Wesley capable; of no such falseness, or of *any* falseness was he ever guilty. But then, if not—these are the consequences of our so thinking, namely—he was not gifted with a long-sighted sagacity; and then it will be certain that, when he spoke of his institute as a "Society," or collection of societies, and when he declared that he did not intend it to be a Church, his meaning was—that, as it was not, so it could never become, a Church; and then further, if we regard him, as we may, as a skillful builder, and as being (in the sense we have reserved for him) a sagacious contriver or social mechanist, then will it follow that the organization which he left to his followers must show fault, and must work ill, and must strain itself in its joints, and must be liable to frequent shocks and jars, when it comes to be put in play for purposes nor merely *unlike* those for effecting which it was constructed, but altogether of an opposite tendency.

When Wesley gathered his helpers, and his preachers, and his colleagues around him, that he might confer with them, and obtain the benefit, if any, of their advice, he honestly intended *precisely* what he spoke of, and therefore he did not intend something wholly different—something of vastly greater dimensions, and of incalculably greater difficulty—namely, the bringing together the elements of a permanent spiritual government. Thus it is that we save Wesley's Christian reputation, which is dear to the hearts of all Christians; but then we save it at the cost of Wesleyan Methodism, if it assumes to speak and act in the character of a Church.

Two very serious ill consequences have resulted from the anomalous position which the Wesleyan ministerial body has (involuntarily) come to occupy in the course of events;—the first is their standing perpetually in an attitude of antagonism, or self-defense toward their people;—the second, following as the consequence of this, has been that their writers and apologists have, by the urgent necessities of this their accidental position, been driven to adopt, and resolutely to maintain, a ground of clerical pretension which should be left in the hands of ultramontane Romanists, and which has an almost grotesque appearance when it is assumed by Wesleyan ministers.

How do these pretensions (when urged on this side the line between Protestantism and Romanism) sound as compared with the spirit and meaning of the apostolic writings?

Disclaiming, as we do utterly, the doctrine that a Church may be educed in its specific orders from texts, we hold ourselves the more free to draw broadly from the manifest *intention* of the apostolic writings those great principles which can never be lost sight of by the framers of ecclesiastical constitutions, without immediate damage, involving also the eventual breaking up of what they so construct. Putting out of view the nugatory arguments of those who have set about to expound Scripture under the high pressure of some sectarian necessity—putting all such flimsy perversities out of the way, then manifestly does it appear to have been the intention of the inspired men who gave visible existence to Christianity, and under whose guidance it became *a social organization*, to set apart, for its service, a class of men—variously gifted, and exercising, accordingly, very different functions—who should devote themselves *wholly* to these services; who, exceptive and peculiar circumstances not preventing, should alienate themselves from all secular callings—should give themselves, without distraction, to the work of the ministry—meditative and active, and, in a word, should live *for* the Gospel and live *by* it

Clear is the correlative duty of those—the people—who are benefited by these services, to see to it that the laborer, "who is worthy of his hire," receives it. In what mode these duties are to be rendered, and under what conditions, it is the part of Christian men to determine, in the exercise of their best discretion.

Equally clear is the duty of the people—the instructed and the "ministered unto"—to yield obedience in spiritual matters to those of the ministering body whose function it is to govern;—the limits of such obedience being easily ascertained, resulting as they do from the *nature* of the relationship itself, from its obvious *intention*, and from the quality of those motives which are characteristic of the Gospel. Can we think that a servile submission to priestly arrogance is embraced within the meaning of this precept—"Obey them that have the rule over you in the Lord?"—how should it be so, when these very rulers are forbidden to demean themselves in a lordly manner, and when, on the contrary, they are enjoined to be examples to the flock of meekness, gentleness, long-suffering humility?

Yet these are not the only Church principles, which obviously present themselves to the ingenuous reader of the New Testament. Such a reader, without putting his finger upon single texts, will have seen and felt, and will be ready to acknowledge (let the inference be what it may) that the doctrine which makes the clergy every thing in the Church, and the people nothing—or nothing but its raw material—that this doctrine is not of CHRIST; and then, when he looks through the vista of history, and sees in what manner this pride-born doctrine has worked, and what have been its fruits, he will scarcely hesitate to say—it is of Satan.

The precept "to obey," where is it found, and in the midst of what matter is it embedded? These very injunctions, upon which the despotic hierarch insists, and which he expounds with a richness and an unction as if the very substance of God's message to man were therein summarily comprehended, these injunctions, do they not find their places in the very midst of theological arguments, and of biblical commentaries of that very kind which the hierarch tells the people *they* have nothing to do with, and which *they* can never understand? But these injunctions to "obey," take their place also in letters disciplinary, addressed to "all the faithful brethren in Christ Jesus." These faithful brethren—even the mass of Christian people—the "congregation of faithful men," are instructed in what manner, and according to what principles, they should carry forward those measures of Church organization *which are essentially of a spiritual kind*, and which—we might have thought, belonged, as of office, to the ministerial class. That the people—call them the laity—should exercise a control, direct and absolute, over that which *they themselves have created*—namely, the palpable and visible property of the community—is a principle too obvious and unquestionable to be formally asserted, as if it needed INSPIRATION to advance or sustain it. But beyond this clear rule of natural right, the people are, throughout the apostolic epistles, so addressed, and they are so instructed, and they are so cautioned, as to imply, undoubtedly, that they have (or should have) an organic existence, in a spiritual sense, in the Church. Ingenuously reading the apostolical epistles we recognize—not with reluctance indeed, but with a deep-felt and devout satisfaction—as therein seeing the "mind of CHRIST," that the Christian Laity are not merely to be *in* the Church, nor merely of it, but that they, with their ministers, are IT.

When we follow the course of events to which Wesley, from year to year, and with so much address and tact conformed himself, it is quite easy to see how, and under what influences, he was led, so to construct his Society, and so to organize its legislature, and its judicial, and its administrative council as in fact nullifies, nay, puts contempt upon, the very first principle of a true Church organization. Wesleyan conquests from the world are the materials which, from year to year, are to be wrought upon by Conference. But does a social structure, such as this, meet our idea of what a Christian Church should be?

The problem—how to give its due place to the popular influence within a Church, so as to promote, not to impede, the ministerial functions, has been variously solved, or has been attempted to be solved, by the several communions that have come into existence since the Reformation. These we must not, in this place, particularly specify; but shall only refer, in an incidental manner, to those two or three instances which, as they stood always in Wesley's view, must have offered themselves to his acceptance, as available, in whole or in part, as precedents, if in fact he had intended any such thing as to construct an ecclesiastical polity—a design which manifestly did not engage his thoughts; for if it had, who can doubt that he would have taken the English Episcopacy as his model; not excluding its essential principle, as it stands distinguished from Romanism—namely, the supremacy, or constitutional control, exercised by the State—as representative of the laity?

Within those churches that were of puritanic origin—Independents, or Congregationalists (*English*, not American; for these latter have in fact taken up the useful elements of the Presbyterian scheme) the popular influence, according to the theory of this system, is supreme, and uncontrolled; nor have instances ever been wanting in which this theory and the practice thence resulting have, for the humiliation of the ministry, been nearly coincident. But more often, the democratic principle, happily, has so been overlaid by a legitimate ministerial influence, as that in the working of the congregational machine the theory has been thrown into the place of a faded emblazonment of honors long since obsolete. The Christian Pastor—such as he should be—has so ruled in the hearts of his people as to find it an easy thing to govern and guide them—the "Principles of Independency" notwithstanding. It has been the less skillful, or the less pastor-hearted, minister—often a not less estimable man—or less able preacher, who has suffered as the victim of demo cratic supremacy.

But besides that happy counteraction which has thus come in to moderate the popular power in congregational societies, the very principle of these bodies has supplied a reactive influence, preventing what must otherwise have come about. Notwithstanding the centralizing tendency of some provincial associations, or of more comprehensive combinations—precarious, inconstant, and powerless, as they are, the congregational bodies have always shown a dispersive, rather than a cumulative or concentrative tendency. With these bodies it has always seemed a more *natural* or easy operation to split than to join—to fly asunder, than to band together—unless indeed at moments of high political excitement, for the carrying some special purpose, or for defending their rights as citizens and Christians.

Thus it has been that the laity of these communions—or their representatives, the body of deacons—has not come into the habit, and has not possessed itself of the organization requisite for any effective purposes of combined popular action. The dissenting laity at large does not congregate; popular supremacy does indeed exert itself in many small circles, not in the happiest manner; but nowhere has it become a formidable power, presenting a broad frontage which might breed alarm.

But whatever may have been the conditions of the democratic element in the nonconforming communions, it does not appear that Wesley knew much (probably little or nothing) of their constitution, or of their actual state; nor indeed would his prejudices, as a Churchman, have favored his giving due attention to what might so well have engaged it, in the structure and working of the Independent churches. From Moravianism he borrowed what might seem available, on points of discipline; but this body was too special in its intention to allow of a transfer of its structural principles to his own more widely-based society.

Yet of Presbyterianism, Continental and Scottish, he was not ignorant; nor could he have forgotten it. It was not possible that, while his own institute was growing under his eye and hand, he could have failed to recollect that, in the Presbyterian Churches, a well-considered and a scripturally sustained combination of the clerical and lay elements was open to his imitation: here, full in his view, was a carefully equipoised ecclesiastical structure, which, although wanting, as it would be in his opinion, as to the episcopal function, yet claims a respectful regard on the ground of the jealous care it takes, as well of ministerial honors, as of popular rights.

Why then did not Wesley take pattern—in some way—from so applicable an example as this?—why did he borrow nothing from the Presbyterian model? This question admits of but one answer, which is this—that, in framing his Society, and in investing Conference with its absolution, and in putting into the sovereign hands of his superintendents the irresponsible power to bind and to loose on earth, he no more intended to construct a Church than he intended to frame a new British Constitution. All those mischiefs and perils which, since his time, have ensued within the body, seem comprehended in the one practical error of those who have attempted to work a complicated machinery for a purpose almost the very contrary of that which the contriver himself had in view.

It may be alleged that, as to Presbyterianism, Wesley was not intimately acquainted with it; or, if acquainted with it, that his Episcopalian prejudices would be likely to prevent his availing himself of any aid from that quarter. What have we then to say, when we recollect that, with the constitution and the working of the Established Church he was thoroughly conversant—that he cordially approved this constitution, and that the very characteristic of this Church, and the point of its contrast with Romanism (or, let us here say, Popery) is this very principle of lay influence, lay control, lay appeal, lay supremacy, in spiritual matters? If Congregationalism admits the influence, and works by the means of the Church at large, the members and their officers—if Presbyterianism also thus rests upon the broad basis of a mixed government, clerical and lay, the Established Episcopal Church does so much more. The constitutional rendering of the phrase "Church and King" is in fact King and Church; and this interpretation is carried out, from the throne, to those extreme instances in which a layman demands, and makes good, against the purely spiritual will of the parish priest, his rights as a member of the national Church.

The system of patronage (whether good or evil in itself) and the position of the episcopal order in the State, as barons of the empire, and their place among the lay lords, in concurrence with whom, and not without their consent, they can carry any ecclesiastical measure—and the absolute authority of Parliament, Commons as well as Lords, in Church affairs; and that power which is quite separable from the constitutional function of the Crown as one with Parliament—namely, the royal supremacy—the headship of the Church; all these provisions for giving operation to lay influence, and for securing a peremptory lay control in matters both spiritual and ecclesiastical, are, whatever opinion may be entertained as to some of them, in fact so many notable instances of the prominence intended to be given to the popular element in the structure and working of the Established Church. Besides, and beyond all this, it is upon the Established Church—it is upon its bishops and clergy, and in a proportion immeasurably greater than in any other instance—that the mighty influences of public opinion are perpetually bearing. The surrounding religious communities attract public attention very rarely, or only in some feeble and incidental manner. A religious dissenting body must have stepped quite out of the course of its ordinary routine, and must have made itself strangely remarkable, before it can draw toward itself the eye, or waken the ear, of the great and busy world. Not so with the clergy of the Established Church, who, one and all, higher and lower, the primate and the country parson and curate, stand daily and weekly, as one might say, liable to a citation to answer for their behavior before the periodic press. The daily, the weekly, the monthly, the quarterly press makes, for its court, a TERM of the year round, and constitutes itself at once a bench of magistrates, a court of appeal, a star chamber, and a "holy office," to which all clerical persons are instantly amenable.

It does not appear that Wesley disapproved of the constitution of the Established Church in this behalf, or that he formally asserted, in contravention of it, the ultramontane doctrine of absolute spiritual despotism. Is it not, therefore, manifest that, when he constituted his Society on a principle which is at variance with that of every Protestant Church, and which is in harmony with nothing but the loftiest and most arrogant pretensions of the Romish hierarchy, that, when he did this, he did it because he was constructing a supplementary Society, not rearing a Church? Nor, indeed, could he have undertaken any such task with the materials that came then, or at any after time, under his hand. What was the Wesleyan laity, such as he saw it around him? A laity, competent to perform its functions to good purpose within a church organization, must have been religiously trained, and it must have grown up in the knowledge and practice of those social religious virtues which tend to bring about a due adjustment of forces between zeal and wisdom, or prudence. An efficient laity grows up by the side, and under the teaching, of an efficient pastorate. Preachers who are not pastors will never see around them elders, deacons, and people, able and willing to work with them in carrying forward those various means of good to which Christianity may, and will, give effect.

Wesley, we say, had not at his command, while he was laboring to bring his Society into order, either the ministerial or the lay materials by means of which he could have organized a Church, even if he had proposed and wished so to do. But it is manifest that he did neither wish nor intend any thing of the sort. Nevertheless, if he had possessed that sort of sagacity which, in love to his memory, we do not attribute to him, he would have seen, as the inevitable consequence of the vast machinery he had set in movement, that Wesleyan Methodism would, at no very remote period, come into a position for which he had made no proper provision; that is to say, it would become a Church, wanting the necessary elements of church organization.

To what extent this serious, if not fatal, deficiency in the Wesleyan community may since have been supplied, or how far the evils resulting from it have been remedied by the several concessions granted to the people by the Conference, of late years, it is not our purpose to inquire; nor do we ask, whether some thorough and effective modification of the system—such as might give reasonable contentment to the popular feeling—might yet be practicable. Yet it may be permitted to the writer to say that which many, who are not of the Society, would, no doubt, join him in professing—that a Wesleyan Reform, spontaneously effected, and not brought about by violence, and which should reanimate the body—should restore harmony within it, and enable it, as of old, to move outward and aggressively upon the impiety that surrouuds us, would deserve to be hailed as an event in the highest degree auspicious.

Little as Wesley could have imagined such a course of things as likely to arise from the constitution he gave to his Conference, there has in fact resulted from it this singular state of things—namely, that, in respect of the position of the ministers toward the people, which is that of irresponsible "lords of God's heritage," the professedly Christian world is thus parted:—on the one side stand all Protestant Churches, episcopal and non-episcopal, Wesleyanism excepted; on the other side, stands the Church of Rome—with its sympathizing adherents—the malcontents of the English Church, and—the Wesleyan Conference! This position, maintained *alone* by a Protestant body, must be regarded as false in principle, and as in an extreme degree ominous.

WESLEYANISM, A CORPORATION OR ESTABLISHMENT.

There is a problem which hitherto has received no solution, involving those conditions under which, with the least damage to the spirituality of the Christian system, and with the most advantage to it, as an instrument of good to mankind, it may come to an adjustment among the various social interests wherewith it connects itself, and may take its bearing upon the palpable matter of this world's elements. In regard to this problem it may assuredly be said that those who have devoted to it the most thought, and whose temper of mind is the most tranquil, will be the last to exult over those, not of their own Church, whom they see to be sorely perplexed in contending with the untoward influences that arise perpetually from this source.

At the moment when Christianity connects itself, as it must do, with the things of this world, and when it becomes a visible institution, holding property in stone, and timber, and plots of ground, and having to deal with funds, stipends, trusteeships, pews, taxation; and, in a word, with Law, how best may it constitute itself, in all these uncongenial relationships, securing its high intention with the least detriment to itself?

The Church of Rome has always dealt with this problem in a summary manner; that is to say, after claiming all things on earth, as well as in Heaven, as its own, in the most absolute sense, it then finds little difficulty in granting out of these, its comprehensive stores, such morsels of sustenance or of privilege as it may be good for its laity to receive and use. The Romish Church is a wise, not an indulgent, mother, who feeds her babes, whether they be kings, nobles, or peasants, with her spoon-meat, in such quantities as may suit their feeble stomachs. But it is not thus that modern nations and Protestant people can be treated.

Those who occupy Protestant ground, and who think, speak, and act on behalf of Protestant communions, should better understand their own principles, and should be more considerate than to do what has been so common, namely, to hush the evils, the abuses, and the perplexities, that beset their own ecclesiastical scheme, while, with blast of trumpet, they blazon the scandals and the overthrows that are occurring around them. In this course there is as little of philosophic breadth of mind, as of Christian temper. Some most desirable reforms would cease to be hopeless if the contrary practice were adopted—namely, if the wise and honest of all communions, agreeing to put to silence their own noisy fanatics—were, each communion for itself, fairly to render account of those ascertained evils which might be considered as characteristic of each, and, in attempting a remedy, to take up whatever seemed to be better contrived in other communions. Is it then utterly chimerical to imagine, as a fact, the prevalence of so much common sense as this?—alas if it be so, then the most despicable passions shall have a sway allowed them on sacred ground, which is forbidden them upon the field of this world's affairs!

Protestant communions, one toward another, as they stand related—in common, to the Church of Rome, or let us say, the Papacy—should feel as do constitutional and representative governments, as related to the unmixed despotisms of Russia or Naples. How urgent and formidable are the embarrassments inseparable from the working of even the best-adjusted representative polity! —and how near at hand and efficacious is the one remedy! —let us of the West invite the Emperor of all the Russias to take upon himself the administration of the perplexed affairs of Europe, and the heaving billows instantly are calmed—the winds are down—silence and order reign through the world! But are we prepared to invite this tranquillity, at this cost? A like remedy is available to the Protestant world, if only it will return to its obedience to Rome.

The alternative—that is to say, the cost at which liberty, political or religious, is to be had and maintained—is the having to contend perpetually with the difficulties that arise in the working of institutions which in themselves are always compromises between theory and practice, and which go on, one knows not how, from year to year, working by and through, and in spite of, their unadjusted antagonisms: inconsistent always they are; nevertheless they yield to us—to us Protestants—the priceless benefits of life, political and religious—life and liberty, in comparison with which the false advantages of despotism are not more to be desired than are the silence and the putrefaction of a sepulchre.

Every one of our religious communions is, in fact and law, an ESTABLISHMENT; and as such it is liable to those entanglements, and is open to those abuses which attach, in the very nature of things, to *religious* interests, when they come to be legally associated with *secular* interests. The difference between one mode of establishing a religious community and another mode, is substantially this, that, while an incomplete establishment holds itself exempt from some abuses, it secures this immunity by means of a proportionate degree of inefficiency and limitation: whereas a complete establishment—a thorough Church-and-State system, open as it is, and must be, to many and great abuses, occupies that only position whence, in ample measure, the highest purposes of visible Christianity can be secured.

Much that may claim to be considered when, as now, Wesleyan Methodism is spoken of as an *establishment*, or an institution giving organic action to visible Christianity, might, with nearly equal propriety, have been treated of under one or other of the preceding heads; for in fact the distribution of subjects, in this instance, can not be perfectly logical, or be very clearly defined. Regarded either as a system of discipline for the people or as an establishment, Wesley's institute has a high merit on this ground—that SOCIAL ORGANIZATION so thoroughly pervades it and is its very soul, and is carried out from its centre to its extremities, taking hold of, assimilating, and employing absolutely every individual who is enrolled on its lists. On this ground no church or society has gone so far, or can be brought into comparison with it; and to this very cause—that is to say, to the *thoroughness,* if so we might say—of the Wesleyan organization—must be attributed, in great measure, the unexampled rapidity of its spread, and, until of late, the tenacity of its hold where once it has taken possession of a field of labor.

In other communions, if organization has been elaborate and complete, as with the Society of Friends, it has been much more upon the seclusive, than upon an expansive principle, and the causes of the stagnant condition of the body are conspicuous. But in the Wesleyan community organization has always had one intention, namely, systematic *labor*—a labor sustained by systematic excitements, and having an expansive purpose as its object. Its stated and very frequent gatherings, whether for purposes of worship, public or select, or for the transaction of its routine business, combine always the two elements—that is to say, excitement, or excitation rather, and the apportionment and the reporting of the work allotted to each. No Wesleyan Methodist (where the *system* has had its free course) falls out of notice, or is suffered to lapse into forgetfulness, or is left as an inert fragment, not partaking of the momentum of the mass. An organization which touches every one, and brings every one into his place, and exacts from every one his contribution, spiritual and secular—an organization which is comprehensive in the most absolute sense as to *persons, gifts, talents, and worldly means,* is that which has secured for Wesleyan Methodism—until of late, its foremost place among the Protestant communities of England and America, and which has given to its labors among the heathen a proportionately greater amount of success than has attended the equally zealous endeavors of other bodies, perhaps of several such bodies reckoned together.

It must be, of course, with an explanation appended, that one should affirm Wesleyan Methodism not to be a *voluntary* society; for undoubtedly no compulsion draws you into it, and none prevents your secession. Yet there is another, a deeper, and a far more pertinent sense of the term VOLUNTARY, in which sense it could not well be applied to this religious association. Saving the civil liberty not to enter it, and the same liberty to depart at pleasure, every thing *within* the Wesleyan inclosure is strictly compulsory, or is the very opposite of voluntary. No place, no indulgence will it allow (we are speaking of Wesleyanism, such as the Founder made and left it), no place for "doing as you please," or for doing nothing, or for giving nothing, or for rendering no account of yourself, or for kicking against constituted authorities, or for putting contempt upon regulations. No place has it for, no license does it grant to, the willfulness, the individual whims or preferences, the laxity, the precariousness, the indifference, the dronish incapacity, and the inertness that belong to, and that flourish under the soft maternal wings of voluntary Churches. Stand off from Wesleyan Methodism—if you please; but if you touch it, if you enter your name upon its lists, you are voluntary no longer; or not until you secede.

The great modern experiment that has been exhibited by Wesleyan Methodism, might be held quite sufficient for establishing the principle that *a working force*, or social religious power, must be the result of organization, so carried out into detail, and so applied to the total religious behavior of each member of the body, as shall thoroughly discharge from the mass whatever is properly spontaneous, or which has its rise in, and draws its impulse from, the bosom of the individual. If individually you must retain entire your spontaneousness and your personal liberty, you must forego the animating consciousness of being a member of a spreading and powerful community. If, in the fullest sense you will and must be free, you should be content to walk in and out of church or chapel, on Sunday, to pay for a sitting, and to greet your minister with a courteous distance-making smile, as often as you chance to encounter him on your path; but you must eschew ORGANIZATION, whence, and whence alone, springs power; and power, in all instances, costs the liberty of the individual.

A well rounded territorial occupation of the soil on which it enters, has, from the first, been the characteristic of Wesleyan Methodism, and, doubtless, a main cause of its successes, especially as compared with its sister Methodism—the Calvinistic, which has been sporadic only, or topical. Every elastic fluid—say the chemists—is a vacuum to every other, and this principle holds good, to some extent, in the social system. In a country where perfect toleration is law, religious bodies, keeping themselves exempt from the arrogance and the treachery of Rome, and from sectarian encroachments, one upon another, may frame themselves, harmlessly and usefully, on the assumption of a plenary territorial occupancy of the land. Two, three, or more of such elastic bodies may, without any offensive interference one with another, thus stretch their line over counties and provinces; and may become, each according to its ability, geographically integral. It is true that geographical designations, associated with whatever is great in the history of a country, seem to draw with them a grotesque inconsistency when we chance to hear them linked with the small doings of obscure bodies; but it is not so when the topical and territorial designation is well borne out by courses of arduous and successful labor, and when tens of thousands of the people swell the muster-roll of provinces. It is energy and success, exempt from suspicion of a treasonable ambition, that redeem territorial titles from contempt.

On the one hand, without itinerancy there will be no evangelic expansion; and, on the other, without territorial occupation there can be no permanency, and no entireness of the Christian influence, as related especially to the rural districts of a country. Paganism—using the word in its original meaning—yields to nothing but a territorial and a parochial church-system, carried out and maintained, as a public service, and which, in the most absolute sense, must be irrespective of the expressed or the anticipated wishes and contributions of those for whose benefit it is effected.

Wesleyanism has, in a good degree, worked upon this two-fold principle, and thus, to so great an extent has it dispelled the paganism, if not of the rural districts of England, yet of its towns and cities; and it has done so where, during the lapse of one, two, or three centuries, the Gospel, in the keeping of less enterprising bodies, has lain embedded, as rough diamonds do, in masses which they neither illuminate nor adorn.

Thus far then, by its effective organization, by its spirit of order, by its machine-like adjustments, and its planting itself territorially upon the length and breadth of the land, Wesleyan Methodism, considered as an establishment of visible Christianity, has been excelled by no religious institute of ancient or modern times; or at least it has not been surpassed by any as to efficiency, and the moral force or power which has been generated within it. Why then should it not continue to spread itself, and to prosper as at first? It may or it might yet do so, and Christian men must wish it, until they see its place supplied by other means; but whence arises the foreboding which indicates a different issue?

If it were alleged that some Wesleyan practices—objectionable always, are constantly becoming more so; or are found to be less and less in harmony with the spirit of the times, we should reply that—in this and other instances, the system will, doubtless, learn to adapt itself to the progress of society, and will know how to assimilate its usages to the growth, or to the shiftings of the religious mind around it. Such imperfections, therefore, do not necessarily involve Methodism in any serious risk, as to the permanence of the body: it can never be that a great and useful institution, administered by intelligent men, should dissolve from causes such as these.

But Wesleyan theology, is it not much at fault? Can it be thought possible that the ill-digested and antagonistic mass—the heterogeneous congeries of religious opinions spread over the pages of the Founder's writings, should stand intact another century, and should continue to command the assent of an *educated* body of ministers, through the term of the present, and the next generation? This it might be hard to believe; and yet if difficulties of another sort did not meet us on this ground, there would be room to suppose that a wise and silently effected consignment of Wesley's theological writings to a respectful oblivion, would leave room for the advancement of the Wesleyan ministry at once in religious intelligence, and in scriptural consistency.

Or, might we not advance a step further, and suppose that the instinct of self-preservation, prompted by the ominous indications of popular feeling, not to mention religious motives of a higher order, would bring about, sooner or later, and before it be too late, such a reconstruction of Wesleyanism, as a hierarchy, as might at once give reasonable contentment to the laity, and bring the body clean over from its present false position upon ultramontane ground, and place it, where it should stand, in contiguity with other Protestant communions? But here we are peremptorily told, that no such reformatory movement, even although seen to be indispensable to the preservation of the Society, is, in the very nature of things possible! The very idea of change should therefore be dismissed as chimerical. The Wesleyan laity petitions—the Wesleyan ministry (let us suppose it) would gladly yield itself to be constituted anew, for its own sake, even; but itself, and the people, and the Court of Chancery, and Parliament, are in this unparalleled instance alike powerless! We assent then to this lamentable decision; and, ceasing to indulge fruitless regrets, turn for a moment to consider the instructive fact that a mind, such as that of John Wesley, should thus, while intending to secure the permanence of his Institute, so far have misapprehended the constant and inevitable tendency of human affairs as to have rendered its continuance, every year, more and more difficult and precarious, from the moment of his death, up to the present time.

A vast property in chapels and other effects had been created by the Methodistic movement, as governed by Wesley; and it had become imperatively necessary to bring it fairly out from among the shoals and the sunken reefs where then it floated at hazard, and to lodge it securely, for the purposes intended, upon the terra firma of law. In a word, Wesleyanism was to become, as every form of visible Christianity always must—an Establishment—an endowed institution, and a holder of lands, goods, and revenues, subjected to conditions such as should be intelligible in courts of justice, and such as should entitle it to the benefits of a readily available civil protection.

The problem then to be resolved was one of a class which would be complicated and difficult even if the purposes and interests that are to be legally secured were all purely secular and homogeneous; but when these purposes and these beneficiary interests involve things so heterogeneous as are palpable properties, civil rights, and religious principles, opinions, usages, and modes of feeling, the difficulties inherent in the subject assume the most formidable aspect. It may be safely affirmed that no question of social and legal adjustment is more perplexing than this.

In no instance, hitherto, have circumstances been altogether favorable for dealing with this problem on any abstract principle, whether religious or legal. Churches and communities have done the best they could, or what seemed to them the best, in ridding themselves of urgent perplexities, rather than in satisfying their better convictions. Protestant Churches, at the best, are reparations of ruins: they are not normal structures; and so it is that, in looking into them from without, occasion is never lacking to those who seek it, for making up heavy indictments on the score of those abuses and disorders that may be attributed to the intrinsic faults of the system. On this field narrow minds, inflamed by a sectarian temper, find it easy to fill their catalogue of scandals.

The best imaginable church establishment, as it can be nothing better than a compromise, effected among and between irreconcilable interests, the choice before us, in any instance, will be of this sort—namely, we may take to ourselves a scheme embracing the greatest objects, and likely to secure extensive practical benefits, yet liable—in the nature of things—the world being such as it is—to abuses and perversions. Or, on the other hand, timidly contenting ourselves with the *minimum* of efficiency, the smallest compass of resulting advantages, we may exclude, not entirely, but to some extent, the liability to abuse and perversion. Somewhere between these extremes every Protestant Church hitherto has taken up its position.

In making his choice, on this ground, Wesley's temperament signally displays itself. The decisively practical tendency of his mind, his energy, courage, and promptitude, at once impelled him to aim at the most extensive results, and to embrace and secure, at all risks, the high benefits which his burning zeal taught him to desire and pursue. He was not the man to please himself with a faultless ideal—so faultless, that it could be made to work only on the most diminutive scale—a Church in a corner—or a machine, exquisite in contrivance, but never to be turned to any good account. But in thus boldly devising his system, the high tone of his mind, its lofty moral aspirings, his abhorrence of laxities, and his intolerance of perfunctory remissness, led him to adopt a complicated disciplinatory system—remedial and preventative, by means of which, as he thought—and, on the whole, his anticipations have not been falsified—the problem would be solved, and a religious machinery constructed which, while it embraced the widest purposes, should hold itself exempt from abuses; that is to say, that it would be at once *efficient* and *pure*.

The unexampled successes of Wesleyan Methodism,

during its first fifty years, afford ample evidence of its Founder's sagacity, and, one might say, genius, on this peculiar ground. The difficult problem of a religious Institute, broadly based, and in the highest degree efficient for its purposes, and at the same time in a great degree exempt from disorders and abuses, was so far solved. That was done which no founder of an institution hitherto had done; but it was in fact done by aid of the silent energy of his own personal influence—an influence never surpassed, perhaps never equaled, by any human being who has individually swayed the minds of his fellows. Wesley was well conscious of this influence; but he would not allow himself to give it a definite expression, as a force or element, making up the sum of Wesleyan effective power; and therefore he did not, or it does not appear that he did, distinctly consider how this same mechanism was to work when *that* single energy should fail. The Wesleyan system, at the moment when it came to work on its own proper forces, showed what had been the miscalculation of its contriver, as to futurity. The few years of Wesley's decrepitude gave indications of troubles to come, and almost at the moment of his death those troubles broke out which, at intervals, have convulsed the Society during the course of fifty years, which have thrown off several large secessions, and which perpetually threaten its utter dissolution.

Wesley's function, through the later years of his life, whatever else it might embrace, was mainly that of Mediator between his people and the irresponsible body of ministers which he had called into existence. This mediatorship, so natural in its origin, and so efficacious always, as he found it, for the preservation or restoration of peace and order, seems to have blinded from his view the ill-boding fact that his people and their ministers—the governing body—the *legal* hundred, did not stand related, the one to the other, in any CONSTITUTIONAL manner, whether for better or worse: clergy and laity were forces having absolutely no *structural* relationship the one to the other.

A *vital* or spiritual relationship did, or might, subsist between them; that is to say, the people did, and might long continue to love and venerate their ministers; and these might continue well to deserve their affectionate esteem. The people might be always willing implicitly to obey, and the ministers might so exercise an uncontrolled despotic power as should give no occasion of complaint, and generate no impatience. That a relationship so fearfully precarious as this should actually have availed so long, and so far as it has, to conserve Wesleyan Methodism, speaks much in behalf of the merits and temper of the governing body; but more in behalf of the Christian feeling of the governed; and strikingly does it illustrate that excellence of Christianity itself which avails to carry ill-contrived human systems through the roughest waters.

Nothing in the compass of literature can be at once more sharply logical, or more thoroughly unphilosophical than are Wesley's reasonings, in support of ministerial absolutism, and in enforcing the duty of popular submissiveness. With a heart that would have grieved to injure any man in the smallest matter, he upheld a Church theory on the ground of which heretics, in troops, might consistently be burned. This misunderstanding of the first principles of Apostolic Christianity came, in his mind, to an awkward misadjustment with his determination not to construct a Church, but a Society only; and so it was—strange medley of incongruities! that he left in the hands of a body of *preachers*, whom he would not consent to think of as *Clergy*, a power as irresponsible and absolute as that which the most despotic hierarchy has ever challenged as its right, by ordinance of Heaven!

These anomalies might, however, have worked themselves insensibly into some sort of accordance, if Wesleyanism, as a purely religious institute, could have held itself remote from those embarrassments that attend always, and unavoidably, the legal settlement of properties and revenues, held and enjoyed for religious purposes. In his mode of adjusting these legal relationships, Wesley—not from motives of personal ambition—no stain of which attached to his moral nature—not from vanity or egotism but at the impulse of the Founder's prepossession—the Inventor's plenitude of feeling, concerning *his own* IDEA, took that course which brings with it the maximum of embarrassment and difficulty; that is to say, he lodged the Wesleyan property, the dues of the ministers, and the rights of his people, upon the irresponsible will of a self-perpetuated body of ministerial persons, and these ruled, and overruled, by a voluminous and heterogeneous mass of polemical writings!

Whether or not a religious society be endowed with revenues drawn from *other* sources, its plots of ground, and the structures thereupon erected, its places of worship, its ministerial residences, its school houses, and the like, especially when held by those whose holding is a fee simple, constitute a property, and give rise to claims of which the State, in its courts of law and equity, must of necessity be cognizant, and of which it must be—as of all other rights, claims, and properties—the guardian, or TRUSTEE GENERAL.

Such trusteeship the State may exercise immediately, by its own officers; or mediately, that is, as the ulterior authority or court of appeal, when disagreements arise between private trustees and the parties claiming to be beneficially interested in the property so devised, and when called upon by either party to protect its invaded or disputed rights.

The several elements of the matter in hand, when a religious body seeks to make the State legally cognizant of its corporate existence, and to place itself and its property within the precincts of legal protection, are these four:—*First.* That which may be called the *final cause*, or ulterior intention of the corporation, holding or managing the property in question: thus the care and cure of the indigent sick is the *final cause* of an hospital, as it is the ulterior destination of the revenues that may have been created for its support. The three other matters are means, drawing their rule and reason *wholly* from their fitness to subserve and to secure the final purpose of the institution, or, as we say, the "Charity." The *first* of these three *means* is the nomination of trustees, in whom is vested the legal property, and the determination of their powers and responsibilities as such. The *second* embraces the rights, claims, duties, and responsibilities of those to whom is to be confided, from time to time, the actual performance of the work implied in giving effect to the said Charity, so as that its benefits shall indeed, and in full measure, reach the persons whose welfare is in view. In the instance of an hospital, the persons contemplated under this head are the visiting governors, the physicians, the surgeons, with their assistants, the nurses, porters, and other servants of the house. The *third* of these instrumental matters are those conditions and restrictions, those rules, customs, *costumes*, and orders, if any, in conformity with which the beneficent intention of the Charity is to be carried out, and its revenues administered. Thus, for example, it may be determined by the founders of such an institution—an hospital, let us suppose—that the physicians and surgeons elected to fill its lucrative appointments, shall for ever be such as will bind themselves to practice medicine and surgery according to the principles laid down in the writings of Hippocrates, or of Galen, or of Hunter, or any other. The founder, or founders, may furthermore insist upon compliance with a hundred minute regulations, as to hours, liveries, expenditure, diet, and what not. It must be granted that no principle of natural justice is infringed upon when a munificent THOMAS GUY thus devotes a princely fortune to a purpose so good, and when he uses his undoubted right as benefactor, in tying down trustees, governors, physicians, surgeons, nurses, and patients too, by even a complicated tissue of regulations, whether these laws be wise or unwise.

Some obscurity might, however, seem to be thrown over this case of conscience (as to the founder's right ot prospective legislation) if, in fact, the property devised, instead of its being, in the simplest sense, his own, had, by his exertions and influence, been accumulated in the mode of contributions from his friends, or the public at large, the intention of such donations being stated and understood on all sides. In that case, indeed, if no stipulations, *formal* or *virtual*, had accompanied these contributions, the founder must be held free to legislate as he might have done in relation to his own.

Now, in fact, it is in this last-named instance that we find the nearest case of analogy that can be found at all, illustrative of the course taken by Wesley in lodging his Society, side by side, with other legally constituted charitable corporations. It is in this light—and in no other, that the "Deed of Declaration," and the regular Trust Deeds of the Chapels, and the "Minutes at large," and those passages in his writings which are usually appealed to in this argument, can so be read as to seem consistent with any admitted and general principles of law, or of abstract justice. Wesleyan Methodism, with its properties, its chapels, its residences, its body of ministers, its officers, of all grades, is, or constitutes, an hospital, dispensing—and it well and usefully dispenses—spiritual remedies, and affording spiritual curative attendance to the people;—these having been persuaded to accept such benefits, if not freely or gratuitously rendered, yet rendered on terms fair and advantageous, on the whole, to the recipients.

All is intelligible, if the Wesleyan institute be looked at in this light, that is to say, as a widely-extended spiritual "Charity." Nothing is intelligible, nothing in the social and political structure of this scheme consists with the admitted principles of social justice;—by no ingenuity, by no refinements of interpretation, can Wesleyanism be brought into harmony with the unquestionable rudiments of the apostolic-church system, if we are resolved to consider and to defend it, as if it were intended to be a Church, or an equipoised association of Christian men, ministers and people.

A few terms, and names substituted, and then the "Deed of Declaration," enrolled in Chancery, and signed and sealed by John Wesley in 1784, will read well as the Will of the founder of an hospital or dispensary, or of any similar institution, intended to afford needed benefits to whoever, in all time future, might be willing to accept them, on the conditions named. Wesleyanism, thus considered, offers to the eye nothing that is despotic, nothing reprehensible, nothing which should, or, indeed, which could, give rise to a turbulent resistance on the part of the recipients of this eleemosynary good. The only ground of exception that could be taken against so noble a charity would be of this sort—to return to our analogy—"It is a pity that a body of physicians and surgeons should, at this time of day, and when medical science has been so much advanced, be compelled to practice according to Hippocrates!"

If it would not seem trifling with what is so serious, one might be tempted to transcribe the Deed of Declaration entire, making therein no other changes than the leaving blanks for the names of the parties, and substituting, for the recurrent phrase "to preach and expound God's holy word"—this—to practice physic and surgery, and to dispense medicines. In this case, the "Thomas Guy" is our "Rev. John Wesley"—the annual "Conference" is an annual meeting of life governors and directors, these having the power, uncontrolled, to fill up vacancies in their number, and to expel obnoxious individuals. The only difference being this, that these same governors and directors, accountable to none for their collective conduct, stand *also* in the position of the physicians and surgeons of the hospital; and thus they have charged themselves with the blended responsibilities of those who appoint to certain functions, and of those who discharge such functions!

In this declaratory document, which may be regarded as the Magna Charta of Wesleyanism, which was prepared with the utmost care, and which embodies the Founder's mind and principles, as matured at a late period of his public life, namely, more than forty years after the origin of the Society—in this document not one word meets the eye of a reader who, uninstructed in Wesleyan lore, but well conversant with the apostolic writings, and not ignorant of Church history, looks into it, not doubting that he shall therein find a formal recognition of the rights and claims of the Christian laity. No such recognition—no saving allusion to the mass—the people, to those to whom the apostolic epistles are immediately addressed—"the saints and faithful brethren in Christ Jesus," is therein discoverable!

Hopeless then must be the endeavor to expound the Wesleyan establishment on any principle that is purely and properly religious, or that is distinctively *Christian.* It is a charitable foundation, supported, in part by "voluntary contributions;" but governed, absolutely, by a close corporation, perpetuating itself by its own acts *from within.* Thus considered, we ought neither to wonder, nor to complain, if the "patients" or people find no place in the charter.

It does not appear that the idea had at any time presented itself to Wesley, when thinking of his society—of a christianized body—a congregation of faithful men, instructed, religiously intelligent, and competent to take the place, and to discharge the functions that are implied and supposed in the apostolic writings, as belonging to the PEOPLE, the body of the Faithful. We may understand how it was that this idea—this church aspect of the Christian system, did not force itself upon his thoughts. But even if it had, his principles, in relation to government, civil and ecclesiastical, were, in a high degree, autocratic, if not despotic. If he had come into the place of certain noted hierarchs of past ages, his course would have been theirs. With a fervent and paternal love he loved "his people;" but the notion of a Christian laity, as something more than the patients of an hospital, or the recipients of "relief," he does not seem to have entertained, and therefore he made no provision for the *constitutional* government of the Society in perpetuity.

Nevertheless he was not blind to what would, and must be, the course of things after his death. This is certain: on frequent occasions he said—"the people obey me, and will do so while I live; but they will not obey (Conference?) after I am gone." What, then, we may fairly ask —what was Wesley's expectation, when he allowed him self—and surely he must have done so—to forecast the future? Can we imagine that a man such as he would be content to go to the grave with that formula of intense egotism upon his lips—after me the Deluge! Nothing would be more dishonoring to his memory than any such supposition. Could he tranquilly have sunk into decrepitude, believing that a wide anarchy would overthrow and dissipate the work of his life, within a few years, or even months, after his decease? this must not be believed.

Yet he foresaw that the "people called Methodists," would, as soon as he was well gone, resent and resist the irresponsible government of a self-electing corporation of ministers. He knew that the anomalous constitution which he had *legalized*, as well as put in action, was of a sort which could not be made to work on its own forces. What then was to happen? Would he complacently reconcile himself to the thought that "Conference," adhering to the *letter* of this constitution, and actuated by those powerful motives, so deep-seated in human nature, which have always impelled the holders of absolute power to hold it on, at all risks—that his successors, thus influenced, and thus acting, would go on to defend and maintain their supremacy against the impetus of popular feeling; and that they would be able, in fact, to hold out in their citadel through successive seasons of turbulence and agitation. A forecasting of events, such as this, should be reluctantly entertained, for it does not well consist with Wesley's claim upon our reverence, as a wise and simple-hearted Christian ruler.

There is one other supposition for which there may be room, and which saves his reputation in this respect; although events have not been such as to bear it out, or make it appear worthy of a mind so highly gifted.

Wesley—let us for a moment imagine it, might thus have forecast the history of his people, and he might have said:—"I have had to do with babes; but these infants are becoming, and will become, men: then, as Christian men, they will acquire at once a mature discretion, and the consciousness of it. To treat them in perpetuity, as children, will be not merely unwise, but wholly impracticable. My successors—the legal Conference Hundred, will not fail to know and feel this: they will understand—and will understand in good time, or before it be too late, that, as they do not wield the secular arm or sword, and as they stand in fact upon the ground of a voluntary association, their common interests, their duty as Christian men, as well as every motive of prudence and piety, will prompt them, at an early time after my decease, to invite the people, by their delegates, or otherwise, to consider, and to reconsider the Wesleyan Constitution—to form it anew by mutual concessions, made in the spirit of love, upon a broader basis; and, in a word, they will, no doubt, find the means of safely transmuting this temporary Wesleyan Methodism into a Protestant Communion, or Church. My preachers will doubtless take this course; and certainly they will take it rather than risk their own existence, and the perpetuity of the Society itself, by a pertinacious adherence to that which has so little congruity, either with human nature, or with the temper and usages of the Anglo-Saxon race, or with the principles of Apostolic Christianity."

Let it be imagined and believed that Wesley thus thought, and that he died with this, perhaps, undefined prospect before his eyes. How far, or whether in a timely and effective manner, or otherwise, the concessions that have been made by Conference to the people—the Wesleyan laity, from time to time, have filled out the measure of reasonable popular demands, we do not affect to know, nor are called upon to inquire or consider.

If Wesleyan Methodism be regarded—and it is in this

light alone that, in these pages, it is regarded, as an instance, unparalleled—as to the breadth and the success of the experiment, available for the guidance of those who make ecclesiastical polity the subject of their thoughts, and who would reduce it to a scientific form, then, and before any inference should be drawn from the facts it presents, we should set off from it, when inquiring concerning the causes of its wide and rapid spread, the impulse—incalculable, which it received at its commencement from that METHODISM out of which it sprung. No such inchoative force can we at any time reckon upon, as if it were at our command, or as if it would necessarily be evolved from those means of any sort, which human wisdom and zeal may bring into operation. As part and parcel of the Methodistic impulse, giving its early triumphant course to the Wesleyan movement, must be reckoned also, that which sprang from the extraordinary personal influence of Wesley himself, and this was as great as any man, known to history, has ever exerted.

These several forces reckoned off, so far as such an elimination may be practicable, then what we have before us in Wesleyanism—is an instance, more conclusive and more ample than any elsewhere found, of what may be done by aid of ORGANIZATION, whether the actual structure within which it takes place be the best possible, or not. In following this scheme into its details (and not now to refer to the absolute principle on which it rests) there may seem room for better adjustments in various instances; but, better or worse, this thorough organization, what will it not effect? Had the Wesleyan Institute, from the first, embraced those elements of Christian combination which in fact it overlooked and rejected, it may seem a not chimerical supposition that, in the course of its first century, it would well-nigh have drawn around itself the Christianity of the British people. Had it indeed been a Church, and had its theology been large and tolerable, the surrounding Protestant communions might all have undergone a process of absorption into itself.

But then, if it be so, the question comes—Are all these complicated movements—and is this supplementary invasion of the social system, and is this wheel within wheel, and this incessant whirl of the religious power-loom, and this interaction, and this counteraction of authorities, and this anxious balancing of forces—is this over-organized Christianity abstractedly good; or does it not actually produce, as one would be inclined to suppose, a mechanical pietism? or even if not, *is it necessary?* Might not the entire benefits of social Christianity be secured, at a cheaper rate? or, more properly speaking, might not the same advantages be obtained in a mode that is less conventional, less arbitrary, less formal, and in a style more in harmony with that unobtrusive and genial domestic habit and temper which, in a peculiar manner, is the characteristic of the English mind, when best ordered and best cultured?

If an answer, in a summary style, were demanded to this previous question, it might safely be given in the form of a peremptory negative. Wesleyan hyper-organization, whatever good may have sprung from it, or may yet spring from it, is *not* necessary to the full development of the energies of the Gospel. Further than this we go, and say, that, when the genuine and intrinsic forces of Christianity shall be brought to bear—in conformity with Apostolic Church principles, upon the social system, and, when the ample import of "salvation in Christ" shall be carried home from churches to families, no such artificial and complicated mechanism as that of Wesleyanism will have any place left it, or will be called for.

And besides, Wesleyan Methodism, rapidly and widely as it has spread, has drawn a limit around itself which though, at the first, it might be nothing more than a chalk mark upon the ground, will become a barrier impassable, when Christianity shall work itself clear of all similar entanglements, as undoubtedly it will.

How stands the case? Wesleyan Methodism, as a legally recognized establishment, is known to the State, and is protected by it, in this manner:—Its chapels and other chattels are held in trust, for, and under the control of the "Conference of the people called Methodists;" and these chapels are to be entered upon, used, and enjoyed by the members of that corporation, and by those, forever, whom they may appoint; and these ministers, thus entitled to use the property of which the trustees are legally seized, are themselves bound by one condition only; but it is a condition which was ill-imagined at the first, and the intolerable oppression of which must be sensibly enhanced by every instance of progress in intelligence and scriptural understanding that may be going on around it. The Conference Preachers themselves, and those whom they appoint, and the body of local preachers, are to teach that doctrine, "and no other," which is set forth in the first four volumes of the Rev. John Wesley's Sermons, and in his Notes on the New Testament! It is the part and duty of Wesleyan trustees to hold the preachers, tightly, to the letter of some dozen volumes of heterogeneous and polemical theology! undesirable duty—impracticable obligation!

But we return to the preliminary paragraph of this section. We have said that the constitution of visible Christianity, as an Institute working upon, and among, other institutions, and so as not to forego or damage its own peculiar and anomalous prerogatives, offers a problem of the very highest difficulty—a problem which hitherto has not been solved, with any notable success, by any Church or religious community. Thoughtful, well-informed, and ingenuous Christian men perfectly know this; and they acknowledge it, and while they admit it as a fact, in relation to the Church to which they may have attached themselves, they can not but hear, with disapproval, the noisy exultations in which interested and sectarian speakers and writers indulge themselves, when occasion gives publicity to those abuses or embarrassments that are incident, peculiarly, to this or that Christian body. Quite of another sort are the feelings indulged by, and the reflections excited in, better ordered minds on such occasions.

As to Wesleyan Methodism, in its actual relationship, on the one hand to the masses of the people, and on the other to surrounding religious communions, and to the Established Church, such minds—or, let us say, large-hearted Christian men, accustomed to weigh the wheat against the chaff, would fervently rejoice to see Wesleyan Methodism righting itself internally ;—that is to say, finding, and availing itself of, some happy expedients by aid which it should surmount or remove its structural difficulties, and should return in power to its original place, and its proper function, among other bodies, as the foremost evangelizing force, brought to bear anew, and in the spirit of its illustrious Founder, upon the impiety of the millions around us.

METHODISM OF THE FUTURE.

We leave Wesleyanism, and return for a moment to Methodism.

Concerning the Methodism of the last century, we have assumed that it was indeed a dispensation from Heaven. But when it is thus considered, this inference is involved, namely, that this recent renovation of the powers of the Gospel must stand related, as well to the future as to the past: in other words, that it must be held to take a position in that series of events, through the medium of which Christianity has, from the apostolic age onward, continued to work its way forward toward its destined issue—the subjugation of the human family, and the universality of a pure religion.

Inscrutable always are the reasons of the Divine Government; nevertheless, the evidences of the fact of such a scheme of government, having its marked stages, and its sequences, linking each conspicuous period of religious revival with the one preceding it, and then with the next—the evidences, we say, of such an ordered sequence of events force themselves upon the notice of the meditative reader of (what is called) Church history. Yet, although illustrations of this alleged causal connection of events might easily be adduced, yet to carry them clear of all plausible exceptions, and to construct, by means of them, a well-compacted and impregnable argument, would be difficult. So arduous a task, who shall attempt it?

A purpose far less venturous we have now before us, and, therefore, we shut off from our view that wider prospect which would claim to be contemplated if the intention were—to bring Methodism to its place in the general history of Christianity.

It must suffice here to say, that, if the wide-spread revival of evangelic piety which followed the itinerant ministry of Whitefield, and Wesley, and their companions, be regarded as "from Heaven" (and this belief will, at this time, be rejected by few religiously-minded persons), and, if this Methodism be thought of, as it should, as a following up of that recovery of true theology and of a pure worship, which it was the work of the Reformation to bring about, then will it be inevitable, or it will come upon us as an irresistible impulse, to look onward from the now extinct Methodism, to its destined sequence, or to that which we have here ventured to designate, beforehand, as the Methodism of the coming time. If the hand of God should be acknowledged in that work which Whitefield and Wesley effected, can we think that that hand has been withdrawn from the sphere of human affairs? or are those high purposes which then were moved forward, rescinded or broken? Shall the Reformation of the sixteenth century, and the Methodism of the eighteenth, and the missionary impulse which followed hard upon it, shall these movements onward toward an issue proportionate, shall they stop short, and be looked back upon, ages hence, as a dawn that was followed by no day?

We otherwise think. But even if Christian men might incline to abstain from all forecastings of the future, they would not be suffered, in quietness, so to do, by those on every side, who, adducing in triumphant tones, and with apparent reason, as the grounds of *their* anticipations, the actual and indisputable course of events, and the tendencies of opinion in the educated classes throughout the civilized world, are challenging the Christian community to look well to that which is coming, and to interpret, as they do, the signs of the times. We may not then, even if we would, refuse to consider that which is impending in the times that are now next us, and near at hand.

The Romanist—naming *him*, for convenience sake, as the truest representative of all who, Romanists or not, hold substantially the same principles—the Romanist believes, and in so believing he is justified by a great amount and variety of evidence, that the religious instinct of mankind, so far as it assumes the form of a definite creed, and so far as it conforms itself to an external worship, is now fast gathering itself around the one visible source of authentic belief, and which is also the centre of spiritual government, and which enjoins the one form of worship acceptable to Heaven. The Romanist believes—and this his persuasion has, at least, its semblance of reason, that, yet a little while, and the eyes of all men shall be seen to turn toward the chair of the Prince of the Apostles; at least, so it shall be with all who profess any sort of dogmatic faith, and who adhere to the usages of a visible worship. This belief, recommended as it is by its simplicity of expression, is strong also on the ground of its antiquity, and of its wide diffusion, and of the apparent tendency of devout minds.

On the other side, again for convenience sake, and for brevity, we name the PANTHEIST of the present time as the representative of that various mass of undefined opinion which has existed always as the counter-belief, though not the real antagonist, of Romanism. It is this Pantheism and this Romanism which, from the earliest periods known to history, have, under different names, shared between them, in shifting forms, the empire of the human family; the one shaping itself always in counter-conformity to the other; and the two, like binary celestial masses, revolving round a common centre, are found to be necessary, the one to the other:—annihilate either, and the other would fly off from its orbit, and be lost in infinite space. Each, silently conscious of its dependent relationship to the other, has been tolerant of the other; and thus it is that, while Romanism, under cover of mysticism, reserves a place for Pantheism, Pantheism has been used to say, and is now saying aloud, "Inasmuch as the mass of mankind—the herd, high and low, must and will have a dogmatic belief of some sort, and must have an ostentatious worship, Romanism supplies both in a mode that is well adapted to satisfy the instincts, and to meet the prejudices of the unthinking many."

But the Pantheist, resting his calculations of the future at this time, upon the observed tendencies of modern science, in all its branches and amid its amazing developments, of late, and seeing also toward what end social and political institutions are moving, announces it as a fact, well-nigh accomplished, or as now evolving itself rapidly, that the entire body of instructed and intelligent men, throughout the civilized world, and leaving, by peaceable connivance, the Romanist to take to its bosom the uninstructed and the unintelligent—that this thinking class is now preparing itself for its near approaching time of triumph—its millennium—when it may ingenuously profess its rejection of every dogma, and its independence of every authority in matters of thought, and its tranquil contempt of all forms of worship alike. The Pantheist, in support of this, his confident anticipation, appeals to the admitted fact that, already all, or nearly all, educated men, from end to end of Continental Europe, those of the Anglo-Saxon race alone excepted, if they have not yet declared themselves on his side, are held back from doing so only by motives of conventional propriety, or of policy.

Now the question between the Romanist, on the one hand, and the Pantheist, on the other, and those who hold to the religion of the Bible, on the third part, would not relate to the *fact*, which is obvious and notorious, of the present prevalence of both Romanism and Pantheism, or of the probable future triumph of both; but only as to the extent, or the amount, and the *value* of that exception, which both must admit to exist—namely, the firmly-held Christian belief of multitudes within the circle of Protestantism. The overweening feeling of the Romanist impels him, indeed, to set down, as of little account, Protestantism, in its several forms;—he swells and boasts himself too much. The Pantheist, ever vague in his mode of thinking, and prone to beguile himself among baseless speculations, apart from evidence, and regardless of facts, professes not to know, or knowing, not to care, whether, at this moment, the Christian exception, or "remnant" of faith," be larger or smaller: the world, or the world of mind, is, or it will speedily become, his own undisputed property, and he can be patient a few days or years, until that which is inevitable has actually come about.

Rather than enter upon an ambiguous controversy, as to facts which in themselves are not to be precisely defined, or ascertained, as between himself and the Romanist, or the Pantheist, the Christian, or he who holds to articles of belief, as authentically taught in Holy Scripture, and to a worship thence gathered, will do well (for himself, and as a means of reaching a tranquil position) to grant, for an hour at least, to both his antagonists, that the facts *are* as *they* severally profess them to be, and that the anticipations which spring from these facts are not chimerical. Let it be so then, that our prospect of the future—the immediate future—is to be constituted by blending, in some manner, the predictions of the Romanist with those of the Pantheist! This prospect, then, is that which we have to do with. Of what interpretation is it susceptible? This is our question.

Many of those who are on the side of Christian faith, will loudly protest against any such admission as this, even though it be introduced only in a hypothetic form; for they will peremptorily deny that it rests upon any solid grounds; and, in contradiction and refutation of it, they will make an appeal triumphantly to facts of a very different order, indicating and proving, beyond doubt, the actual hold which Christian truth has secured for itself in the world, and the constantly augmenting efficacy of its principles, as "mighty, through God, for casting down imaginations," and for bringing into captivity every thing that opposes its beneficent influence.

All this we do not deny, nor would we abate any thing of the warmth of that persuasion which impels Christian-hearted men to anticipate, as near, an order of events the very reverse of that to which we have here given a conjectural place.

Be it so. Still we return to those facts, on the other side, that are not to be denied, namely, that, to some extent, and an extent unusual, if not absolutely unexampled, both Romanism and a mystic philosophy, which is essentially pantheistic, are winning the favor, and are securing for themselves the adherence of multitudes around us; and that thus they are making their advances, as well in the upper, as in the lower classes of the community. So much as this is not disputable; for the facts obtrude themselves upon us every day, and are seen in all societies; and they are admitted and reported in tones, either of uneasiness and alarm, or of triumph.

What is it then, that is indeed going on, and of what sort is that preparation which, by *such means* as these, is now in progress, for bringing about that which we here assume to be "at the doors," or not indefinitely remote; namely, a time of renovation and refreshment, and which, by accommodation, we have ventured to speak of as THE METHODISM OF THE TIME COMING?

To answer this question in a word, we say, that, by these very means—by the aid of Romanism on the one hand, and of Pantheism on the other—the Christianity of the apostolic writings is throwing off, and is getting itself clear of, every thing which hitherto, through the medium of a diffused profession, and of a conventional religiousness, it has come to be entangled with, but which is not its own, and with which it has no true alliance. Christianity is, as we believe, shaking off from its surface the encrustations of recent times: it is parting company with the multitude that of late has pressed about it, and thronged it, and is drawing itself off to the desert, for converse with those who are not offended with it, as it is.

Well fitted are these two agents for the purpose they are subserving: fitted for it they are, separately and conjointly. It is the Romanist, and none so well as he, who can draw off from the wide field of English Christian profession the many, whether rude or refined, that have listlessly trodden its inclosures. It is the Pantheist of this time, who has just now learned how to take into his use the language of a spiritualism which he has borrowed (as to its dialect) from the Scriptures, it is he, and none so well as he, who can beckon away from all Christian congregations, one by one, the youth, the intelligence, the ambitious and the stirring thoughtfulness they may contain.

A customary, and now, perhaps, an exhausted topic, with Protestant writers (and a very legitimate ground of argument doubtless) has been the adaptation of Romanism —or, if we were to use more comprehensive phrases, we should say—sensuous Ritualism, to engage and charm imaginative, sensitive, and meditative minds; not now to speak of its all-prevailing influence with the thoughtless multitude, as a gross superstition and a polytheistic apparatus. This Ritualism, in a word—and if we now think of it only in its more refined form, such as it assumes when it has to recommend itself to the notions and habits of a Protestant country—it is this Ritualism, with its attendant mysticism, which offers to devoutly-disposed and cultured minds that which the craving of such most earnestly seeks for, namely, a subjective religion, all the elements of which are found within the circle of human nature itself, and are always at its command, independently of that grace and illumination which is felt to be, not from itself, nor at its command, but which must be looked for, and obtained, from above. The devoutly-disposed mind *must* have its religion; and it *may* have it at first hand, by the aid of a worship like that of Romanism.

Ritualism, subjectively considered, is the soul's own product; and it is therefore clung to, and rested in, with a deep-felt complacency. Some of the purest minds have been content to stop short in this homogeneous and wild growth of human nature. Then, according to the temperament of individuals, it readily coalesces, on the one hand, with the themes of a lofty and abstruse meditation, or on the other, and in minds of a more vulgar cast, with polytheistic admixtures, and with the semi-sensual gratifications that are supplied by music, painting, architecture, and the various branches of the decorative arts. It is in this endless variety of combination that we now, and in every circle, meet with the ecclesiastical artistic feeling, so worked up with the devout, that much more than an ordinary skill is required in those who would attempt to separate these ingredients. A time ago, which some of us remember, the tastes of the same class of minds among the opulent, sought their gratification in what might be called the sublime in upholstery, and in the cognate devices of the arabesque and the grotesque—carved, sculptured, or painted. We have now the *symbolic* for the *grotesque;* we have saints in the place of satyrs, cherubs for dolphins, implements of martyrdom for the paraphernalia of chivalry; and all to meet the whims, and to exhaust the purses, of the very same order of persons, fired by a new enthusiasm, or an enthusiasm that has been newly raked out of the deposits of the middle ages.

But there is something much deeper than this in the now spreading eagerness of the Ritualistic temper. A mere fashion, or "rage," as it is called, for ecclesiastical performances, and for the sumptuous accompaniments of such exhibitions, would wear itself out in a season or two; and that which, in its elements and its impulses, is indeed of the world, would presently sicken of the gloom and chill of churches, and would return to its proper haunts—to saloons, theatres, galleries, and the like. The now prevalent Ritualism means more than a fashion, for it is a deep working impulse; it is AN INFATUATION. What, then, do we mean by this word, as thus applied?

A perfectly distinct answer to this question it is not easy to give; but a sufficient answer may be supplied by the means of an illustration, more or less exact and pertinent. One enters, let us suppose, upon some infected region, over which a miasma—not to be seen, or felt, or to be shown and proved to be present by any human means—is reigning, as vicegerent of Death. All countenances speak of this invisible power, and man and beast stoop and fade before it. Though unseen, it does not leave the casual visitor to doubt the reality of its sway; for an uneasiness not to be shaken off, but which is the prognostic of worse, warns him to retreat, and to make his escape while he may.

If we turn then to the world of mind and opinion, and ask what it is which we should thus speak of as an epidemic infatuation, we answer, it is an influence which is found to be spreading from mind to mind, to be taking to itself families and districts, to be enchaining even some of the intellectually robust, and which, nevertheless, when one would apply to it any known mode of rational treatment, or if one would seek to submit it, in the form of propositions, to logical analysis—if one would endeavor to confront it with evidence, historical or biblical; or, in a word, to deal with it on any principle of which reason is cognizant or which authentic piety can bow to—this impression—this inappreciable, but all providing feeling, eludes all such means of detention:—while one grasps it—it is gone. As well bring argument to bear upon the flashing of the arctic Aurora, as upon this ruling tendency of the minds around us.

An infatuation, taking a religious form, is thus seen to draw to itself, and to bind in its threads, first the young, the amiable, and the sensitive among women; and then the sensitive, and the less masculine among men:—then follow those who, worldly as they may be in habit and temper, must have a religion, with its Sunday observances; and this need must be supplied by that which is not so inane as that it could not dissipate *ennui;* and it must be in good repute, and must be easy in its conditions. By aid of its ever varying recommendations, ritual Pietism engages minds that are very differently constituted; but, in so engaging them, it wholly abstracts them from that which is strictly Christian. No form of worldliness or frivolity is more absolutely remote from the Christianity of the apostolic writings, than is the Ritualism, which now draws the crowd.

Thus it is then on *this* side—the religious side—that Christianity is, by the means of the Ritualistic infatuation, setting itself clear of that which it is not of itself, and is retiring to a distance beyond the broad margin of that religiousness wherewith, for a while past, it has been intimately blended.

A separation of another sort is, however, necessary to complete this same disjunctive process. The GOSPEL must wholly cut itself off from the fond philosophy of the present time; and it is doing so by the aid of an infatuation of another, and of a more refined species, namely, the philosophic or pantheistic. So long as science, mathematical and physical, stood opposed to a species of faith which itself was vague, undogmatical, and tolerant of all differences, men devoted to science, and who themselves had no religious feeling, found it easy to allow, or to connive at, a religion that never obtruded itself, and that gave no one any annoyance. But in times such as these, when a very decisive orthodoxy has taken the place of the toothless Christianity of the last century, and when the only alternative presenting itself to the choice of educated men is, either to yield assent to a creed peremptory in every clause or to reject Christianity altogether—at such a time, a reaction inevitably takes place, and in its course it forces upon the non-religious scientific mind a more determinate form of unbelief than otherwise it would have chosen. Philosophic non-religion thus becomes articulate infidelity; and we now hear it uttering itself in various tones, and propounding philosophic creeds, all of them resolving themselves into a system which, in substance, is Pantheism.

This Pantheism, more or less emotional or imaginative in the ingredients with which it combines, is at present the belief of many of the best constructed minds of the scientific class. Nothing else can well be looked for at a time when a formal orthodoxy, having little vitality, and which clothes itself in the costume of the now prevalent Ritualism, is that which educated men must take to and profess, if they are to become religious in a Christian sense:—while it is so,

Pantheism, under some form, will be the religion of the great majority of this class. It is scarcely possible that any other species of antagonism than this should obtain in a community within which a severe and exact philosophy—abstract and inductive, holds its ground, on the one hand, and on the other a dogmatic belief is professed and pronounced with unwonted animation, and in alliance, too, with so much of formality in worship.

Then this same pantheism which is silently, and one might say *defensively*, rather than obtrusively, held by scientific and well disciplined minds, dilutes itself in descending among those of inferior quality; and, as thus brought down, it is now pouring itself forth from the press, in styles adapted to all tastes;—sometimes elaborately spiritualized, sometimes in forms that are rich and imaginative; often as allied to some species of pseudo-scientific quackery; and very often in combination with political fanaticism, such as that of Socialism. So it is, that if the higher or more abstruse philosophy is too strong for you, you may be served with the same drug, dilute in a deluge of vapidity.

We have said that these two discriminative agents, Ritualism and Pantheism, which are so effectively subserving their destined purpose of ridding Christianity of its admixtures, apart, do also work to the same end as related the one to the other. This incidental connection of the two has made itself conspicuous, of late, in some notable instances. Ritualism retains its hold, with difficulty, of active and *progressive* minds: such take to it in a moment, as a solace, or a taste; but they soon weary themselves *in* and *with it:* they turn aside with impatience from a path that, as they find, runs an endless circuit, and brings them ever and again round to the same spot. Ritualism, therefore, is continually losing itself or melting away into Pantheism; and so it is that the world is often challenged to listen to the moanings of those who, with strong religious instincts in their bosoms, have sickened of "Cults," and have fallen back, disconsolate, upon the philosophy which they had already once rejected as a lifeless abstraction! Those who escape the meshes of Ritualism are taken up by that net the property of which is to *hold* whatever it touches.

The one or the other of these two absorbing influences, or infatuations, as we have ventured to call them, is now meeting us in every circle, and is dividing families; and the victims, too often, are the well trained—the intelligent, the amiable. Those whose own Christian belief is deep and immovable, seeing these things, are filled with sorrow and alarm, or even dismay; and such persons—parents often—look around for help, and are impelled to call loudly upon Christian teachers and writers to come forward with dissuasives, with sermons, tracts, or conversations, such as shall avail to stay the evil in its course: but by such means it will not, in many instances be stayed. To a limited extent, and only for an hour or a day, does reasoning, even though it be the most conclusive, take effect upon those who have once surrendered themselves to either of these fascinations, each of which finds its way, with ease, into the deepest recesses of human nature. Always is it possible to pass from the domination of the one influence, and to come under the sway of the other; and this shifting of the mastery of the bosom may, as it seems, be often repeated; or otherwise, relief may be had by a surrender of the soul and body to worldly impulses, and to sensual seductions. Thus may a tyranny which is intellectual be shaken off, by selling the body and soul to a tyranny that is earthly.

In various modes are these spreading illusions of the time resisted and repelled on the part of those who represent and profess Biblical Christianity. Sometimes, and not seldom, by vehement if not virulent invectives; or if not so, by the angry outbursts of an undigested zeal which denounces its antagonist—Romanism ("Popery") or Infidelity—in language that, while it exhausts the vocabulary of contemptuous wrath, falls like the clatter of hail upon a slated roof. How little is this loud barking at the gate heeded by the wily fox who has already entered, from behind, the inclosure, where he has found what he was in search of, and is glutted with his prey!

Men of a more governed temper, and of better training, employ themselves in their studies commendably, and, perhaps, usefully, in redressing the staple argument, or the round of arguments, long ago admitted to be conclusive, and which, in fact, stand unrefuted, and by means of which it may be shown, entirely to the satisfaction of all dispassionate and reason-loving persons—*first*, that the pretensions of Rome are utterly unfounded—that its distinguishing doctrines and rites are innovations, the rise and history of which are no way obscure, and that the entire system is as corrupt and cruel as it is anti-christian; or, turning toward our adversary on the left hand, arguments that are good and sufficient, and more than sufficient, may be brought to bear, as well upon Christianity, to authenticate its claims, as upon Pantheism, to expose the inconclusiveness of its reasonings, and to show the vague and nugatory character of its speculations.

Now these several modes of tranquil argumentation can not be thought to have lost any of their intrinsic value; and therefore, they may well be set out afresh, from year to year, as valid and impregnable defenses. This advocacy of the truth does, in fact, avail with those who might, perhaps, have been retained within the inclosures of Christian belief without its aid, or by the use of other means of suasion. But as to those whose lips have but once touched Circe's cup, the authentic argument which is customarily employed in defense of Biblical Christianity, as against either Romanism or Atheism, takes effect in instances that are as rare as the rarest of natural phenomena. We feel—or those feel it who thus labor to stay the spreading evil—that what we have to do with is not an error that may be corrected, but an infatuation, out-lying far beyond the range of reason.

The experience, or the mortifying consciousness of this impotency of argument to drive back the silent encroachments of the two great delusions of these times, has led, on the part (chiefly) of young, ardent, and ambitious writers and preachers, to an attempt the most unwise, the actual product of which has been only to re-act upon their own minds, and to loosen their hold of their professed principles, as well as to enfeeble their influence as religious teachers. Such preachers and writers have said—or it appears that they must so have reasoned with themselves—"We find that our Christian argument takes little effect upon the mass of men; and none at all upon those who, in an active sense, stand opposed to us. Nor ought we much to wonder that it should be so, for this style of reasoning, which had its rise in dark times, stands in no true relationship toward the human mind in its present advanced condition; it is thoroughly obsolete; nor ought it to be required of the educated men of these enlightened times to listen to that which is so stale. Besides, not only are the arguments we have been using out of date, but the Christianity which we have inherited from our ancestors (good men indeed !) is itself superannuated. The Gospel has been misunderstood, as every thing else came to be misunderstood, during the middle ages. Then the theology that was unadvisedly compacted at the time of the Reformation was a conglomerate of logical, metaphysical, polemical, and political truths and errors—an inextricably entangled mass. The work, therefore, that is *now* to be done, and which is to be done by us, the rising ministry, is (with all due reverence for the text of Holy Scripture) to reconsider every thing—to pass our creeds through the refining fires of the modern philosophy—to render the substance of theology into the intelligible terms of the modern philosophy ;—in a word, what we have to do is, to put forth for the acceptance of the enlightened times on which we have fallen—a Philosophy of Salvation. To encourage our endeavors on this ground, we may assume it as certain, that there is nothing in Christianity, when truly understood, which may not be made perfectly intelligible to all reasonable men. Mystery is a phantom of times gone by;—it was itself born of superstition, and it becomes the parent of more. We will show men that their prejudices against Christianity have all been founded upon misapprehensions, the blame of which rests upon ourselves and our predecessors more than upon those who entertain them."

Thus, in substance, have some reasoned with themselves, and on such grounds have they addressed themselves to the labor—a labor how vain!—of engineering a road, upon an easy slope, up the steeps of Paradise, from the levels of Disbelief; and so that the table land of Heaven may henceforth be laid open to the feet of all men.

While time and toil are thus, or in similar enterprises, expended to little purpose—that is to say, in relation to the middle classes, and to those who frequent churches and chapels—to arrest the spread of dangerous opinions, it is found, it is felt, it is confessed, on all sides, that Christianity has nearly lost its hold of the masses around us; or that if nothing has been lost, because never possessed, little or nothing has lately been gained on the broad field of the popular mind. It is true that *a proportion* of the laboring classes, in towns, and through the country, is still held in hand by each of the Protestant communions, and which, with its score or two, fills, as one might say, the interstices of congregations; or—to use a phrase which in itself is of ill sound—there are, in all places of worship, there are occupants of the "free sittings;"—alas! that any sittings should be not free where the Gospel in its purity is proclaimed.

But even if churches were every where built, and if the "sittings" in them were all free, the question presents itself, would that ministration of the Gospel which now we have at our command, would it avail to recall the thousands of the people? A mere possibility of so happy a consequence is, no doubt, enough amply to warrant all costs and labors requisite for trying the experiment. Yet, hitherto, the course of things has been different. Congregations have called for churches (buildings), not churches for congregations: the sepulchral voice of an empty church does not fall well on the popular ear.

Let leave be granted for affirming that, to gather the thousands of the people—the tens of thousands that now loiter away their Sundays within sound of the church chime, there must be brought to bear upon them an effective ITINERANCY:—the multitude that is gone astray must be followed, and must be pursued into their fastnesses of ignorance and profligacy by apostolic men—that is to say, by none other than the best men of whom the Church—the Christian body at large—might make her boast. This recovery of the lost will be no task for ordinary spirits. Yet this is not all; for a *Doctrine*, as well as an *Agency*, is now called for; and we wait, not merely for the men who shall preach it, but for that which they must carry with them, namely, A NEW METHODISM.

There is a tendency, we have said, in the two now prevalent illusions, which have become characteristic of these last days—there is in them a tendency to open the ground for the coming in of this re-animated Gospel—this METHODISM OF THE FUTURE. When it does come, although it will come "from above," yet will it come in the track of ordinary causes, and these, even now, are speaking of its approach.

There never fails to take place somewhere, a reaction, proportioned, more or less exactly, to whatever influences are in active operation around us. If, indeed, as many seem to think—if this now prevalent ritual formality on the one hand, and if the modern atheistic philosophy on the other, should go on to spread as an inundation, encircling a constantly diminished company of those who cordially affect the Christianity of the Bible, then would there be reason to look for the gathering of an intense feeling within the bosoms of a few, among whom would spring up this renovating spirit—presently bursting its way outward, and moving with power through the masses of the people. Of what sort then will be this reactive impulse, and what will be its grounds? We venture thus to predict concerning it, abstaining from speculations that would unwarrantably meddle with incidental circumstances, and fixing our thoughts upon that which is of the very substance of a religious revival, in harmony always with the *written* Revelation.

Granting as possible, yet by no means assuming it as certain, that those now prevalent departures from the faith which so much alarm Christian men, shall severally, and in combination, spread still further, thus narrowing the space that is occupied by the Christian community, and at the same time undermining this ground, and reducing the faith of many to a wavering acquiescence, and to a passive Sunday habit—should it be so, then, within some two or three minds—minds of power and compass—there will arise a stern questioning of themselves, in this manner:—"What is it that we do believe, or profess to believe, and on what grounds? or how is it that we are henceforward to maintain our position, few as we are, against the world?" There will follow from such an inquest—not the renewal of a fruitless and interminable controversy with the hundred-headed errors that are on all sides triumphant; but a straight-forward pursuit of truth, on its own ground—the Scriptures—and such a pursuit of it—a pursuit in such a mood of intense earnestness as does not fail of success. At such a time, and in the instance of these Christian men—the originators of the future Methodism—there would be a fulfilment and an illustration of the words—"the kingdom of heaven suffereth violence, and the violent take it by force."

These fresh minds, applying the unsophisticated energy of their understandings to the problem before them, will reach ground which they will know to be immovable:—this will be the course so far as the faculty of reason, unassisted, may go. But thence these minds will be carried onward by a Sovereign Energy, consentaneous with the natural powers, yet far outstripping their limits. They will convince themselves, while using diligently all proper implements of criticism and exposition, that Holy Scripture has, in the main, been truly understood from the first; and then they will awake to a sense of what it is which this, their now proven faith, imports.

The Methodists of the time past took up *their* theology as they found it ready for their use, in the confessions and articles of the several Protestant Churches—among which the points of difference are immaterial. But their successors, of the time future, will take to themselves the same theology, under conditions of mingled advantage and difficulty, as thus.—It will be an advantage for them that the grounds of religious belief, as derived from the canonical writings, have, in the lapse of this half century, been swept quite clear of that mass of nugatory exceptive criticism which once encumbered it. By the boundless industry of scholars—Christian and non-christian, the flimsy stuff wherewith the Socinianism of Priestley's time clothed itself, has been well disposed of, and it will trouble theology no more. The question *now* is—not what the apostles believed and taught; but only this—The apostolic belief, conspicuously certain as it is (historically and critically regarded) should it be *our* belief, because it was theirs?

Now in dealing with this residuary question (if indeed there be any difficulty attaching to it) we of this time are, and the Christian men of the future time will still more decisively be, aided, though unwillingly, by our adversary Romanism. Let us imagine that the wide world, or the Church, so called, and the world, has—a protesting few excepted—surrendered itself to this universal spiritual authority, and that its flagrant superstitions and its tyrannies are bowed to, and obeyed, on all sides. Then it must be that those who shall continue to loathe these idolatries, and to resent this despotism, will find themselves driven in upon the only position where a stand may by any means be made, namely the authority of Scripture, this being held as absolute, and not to be abated by admixture with any other pretended sources of belief. It will thus be, as by an urgent necessity, and as the only means of resisting the abominations and the cruelties of a triumphant superstition, that the few whom we are supposing to stand steadfast in their faith, will make good their footing on the only practicable ground; and when they are thus, and there established, the question, as between themselves and their *infidel* antagonists, will have been superseded. This question, on *that* side, might seem to be less easily determinable; but, as toward the Romish superstition, all is peremptory and clearly defined. At such a time there will not remain an inch of space whereon the foot may rest, between these two positions; that is to say, unless, in the most peremptory manner, and to the exclusion of all reserves or evasions, the sense of Scripture, ascertained and interpreted on a true principle, be resolutely adhered to there is nothing gross or abominable in the superstitions of Southern Europe that must not be submitted to. The tyranny of the Romish system will not be remiss in forcing its idolatries upon those who yield themselves, at all, to its pretensions; and there will be no other means of resisting those pretensions, but a resolute adherence to Holy Scripture. Hitherto it has always been easy to hold Romanism at bay, and the Bible too; but this liberty will be gone when Romanism and Ritualism shall have gained the ascendant, and together shall fill the world.

Thus, by the compulsion of these two forces, coming in on either hand, and driven to betake themselves to the authority, and to shelter themselves in the plain sense of Scripture, those who shall put in movement the future Methodism, and whom we suppose to be, not the zealous ἀγράμματοι and the ἰδιῶται of less remarkable eras, but well taught biblical scholars, will feel, as we of this time do not feel, the necessity, *first*, of defining, with unambiguous explicitness, what it is they mean, when they speak of the apostolic writings as "given by inspiration of God," and then of laying down, and of invariably adhering to, certain principles of interpretation.

As to the *first* of these preliminary labors, it is not merely in itself a work of peculiar difficulty, but it involves the breaking up of so many inveterate superstitions, and the dissipation of so many cherished illusions, that we may be sure it will never be attempted, or, if attempted, never carried through, in easy tranquil times, like the present;—it is a work which will be forcibly effected by strong arms in some season of anguish and anxiety, and when those who set about it shall feel that they are wresting immortality and its hopes from the grasp of two lawless adversaries.

As to the *second*, it will flow out naturally from the first, and it will bear an analogy to the revolution that was effected in physical science by the promulgation of the Baconian philosophy, and in accordance with that analogy it will effect the final expulsion of metaphysical schemes of Christian doctrine; in the room of which will come the fearless THEOLOGY OF INTERPRETATION—offering to the eye, as it must, many of those breaks and "faults"—those inferences—irreconcilable the one with the other, which, while they torment the theorist and the logician, open the fields of immortality before ingenuous spirits—and which are, and must ever be, the characteristics of a theology that is fragmentary and disjointed, for this very reason—that it exhibits portions of eternal truths, to finite minds.

The movers of the future Methodism will indeed hold in their hands the same Bible which we hold; but then it will be to them, as one might say, a new Revelation;—not because it will bring into the creed any new article, or expunge any; but inasmuch as it gives to each an immeasurable expansion, and enriches each with a treasure of hitherto unthought-of meaning.

Such a renovated creed these preachers will find the need of in making good their first assault upon the consciences of men, which lately have undergone a sophistication that quite turns aside the shafts of the modern preacher. The Methodists of the past time (as we have said) found the consciences of men greatly benumbed, indeed, or paralyzed, by sensuality and earthly passions; yet not generally recusant of the preacher's appeal. Not so the masses of men at this time; for the wide currency that has been given to various schemes of physical metaphysics has, in a positive sense, *perverted* the moral consciousness of multitudes, and has furnished the minds that have been thus perverted with the plausible sophisms of a spurious philosophy—a miserable quackery, by aid of which men persuade themselves, and each other, that sin is not *sin*, but misfortune.

A popular ministration of Christianity, which should lay anew a solid foundation on this ground, and which should thence move forward to awaken the fears of men as guilty, could not fail to convulse the social system; and especially as there would follow close upon it a more distinct and impressive interpretation of those passages that are affirmatory of future punishment. The past Methodism took to itself the belief which it found; but the coming Methodism must derive its belief *anew* from Scripture, by bringing to bear upon this difficult subject a reformed principle of biblical interpretation.

The urgent necessity that will be felt by the preachers of the future time for making good every step of their ground, when they come, in the present state of opinion, to assail the consciences of men—infatuated more than stupefied, must lead to consequences that are little apprehended. When once this weighty question of the after life has been opened, and when it shall have come into the hands of well-informed biblical interpreters, a controversy will ensue, in the progress of which it will be discovered that, with unobservant eyes, we and our predecessors have so been walking up and down, and running hither and thither, among dim notices and indications of the future destinies of the human family, as to have failed to gather up or to regard much that has lain upon the pages of the Bible, open and free to our use. Those who, through a course of years, have been used to read the Scriptures unshackled by systems, and bound to no conventional modes of belief, such readers must have felt an impatience in waiting—not for the arrival of a new revelation from Heaven, but of an ample and unfettered interpretation of that which has been so long in our hands.

Thus the future Methodism, as we assume, will feel the need of, and will acquire for itself, under pressure of the most urgent motives, an incontrovertible exposition of the Scripture doctrine concerning the future administration of justice; but then it will not make this acquisition as if it could be held as an insulated dogma; for whatever is further ascertained, on this ground, will come to stand in its true relationship to much beside, which, in the course of the same argument, will have started to view, as the genuine sense of the inspired books. The doctrine of future punishment, as a belief drawn from Scripture, and so drawn as to dissipate prevalent illusions, and to spread on all sides a salutary and effective alarm—such a belief will take its place in the midst of an expanded prospect of the compass and intention of the Christian system.

The past Methodism was far from being a message of wrath, proclaimed by men of fierce and fanatical tempers:—it was a message of joy, hope, and love; and it made its conquests as such, notwithstanding those bold and unmeasured denunciations against sin which it so often uttered. And so it will be with the future Methodism; and although it will rest itself upon a distinct and laboriously obtained belief concerning the "wrath to come"—a belief such as will heave the human mind with a deep convulsive dread, yet, and notwithstanding this preliminary, the renovation which we look for will come in as the splendor of day comes in the tropics—it will be a sudden brightness that makes all things glad!

Who is so bold as not to draw back trembling, although the prospect be bright, when he approaches a meditation such as this, and ventures to inquire what that feeling shall be, and what that condition of the Church shall be, when, in its simplicity of expression, and in the incomprehensible vastness of its import, the First Truth of the Christian system shall present itself to the minds of men—not as a verbal proposition, but as a reality? Those wordy mists wherewith controversies, long continued and often repeated, enshroud religious principles, will have passed away; and the darkness of misbelief, which sheds a gloom beyond its own limits, will have gone off to the distance as a cloud. Preachers, well understanding that science, though good and genuine in itself, can contribute absolutely nothing toward the interpretation of truths eternal, and feeling well that human eloquence has little or nothing of its own to add to the impressiveness of those truths, shall allow them to be offered in the strictly rendered terms of Scripture, to the reason and to the consciences of men.

But although philosophy can never succeed in its attempts to expound salvation, nor eloquence do much to recommend it, human nature from its depths responds to it; and in the hearing of it wakes up to a new existence, which is felt to be, indeed, its destiny. What is it that is meant when it is said that "God created man in his own image," and that "in the image of God created he man?" Of this eternal alliance man has long ceased to be distinctly conscious, albeit the struggling of his insatiate desires gives him notice of it as a mystery of his being: but now, in the hearing of this truth, that God has not forgotten that which man has ceased to know or regard, he listens as to that which, although it be new, is not strange; in hearing it he returns to his destined position, and, while pride is utterly humbled, he rejoices to be "made partaker of the divine nature," in Christ, who is God and man —Head of the human family, and its Almighty Deliverer.

The anticipations that are now most often uttered, when a bright future is the theme of the preacher's discourse, have this complexion—namely, That, by a blessing granted much more copiously than heretofore to the various means of religious instruction and influence, as at present employed;—and by the diffusion of Bibles, and the building of churches, and the carrying out of plans of popular education, and the like commendable labors, Christian communities will at length be christianized indeed; and that thence, and by such means, the pagan world will slowly or speedily be converted. There are also those (zealous theorists) who, in looking forward to better times, in a religious sense, fix their eye, with a restless eagerness, upon the downfall of this or that false system, the existence of which they think is now the one and principal hinderance, standing in the way of Christianity. "If popery were in the dust, and if all state religions were trampled on—then would the Gospel take its triumphant course!"

But if, in any such modes as these, or in the track of *this* order of causes, the Gospel is anew to take hold of the masses of men, in a powerful manner, then will a renovation, thus coming about, be indeed an anomalous event; for it will have no sort of correspondence with any preceding instance of religious advancement. In every instance that offers itself as bearing upon such a question, truth and piety have first retired, and have been lost to the view of the world in the bosoms of a silent "seven thousand"—known only to the Searcher of hearts, and not even to each other, or to the world. Such has been ever the state of things in the hour preceding the dawn of day. The return of truth and piety has been a bright and sudden visitation from on high, as in the thickest gloom of night, and in the course of this visitation elementary principles have broken away from their entanglements with secondary truths, and have stood revealed in their simple majesty before the eyes of men. Thus it was that, in a time of wide-spread death, the Gospel brought in the Reformation, not the Reformation the Gospel. And thus, too, at a time not less death-like, did the same Gospel carry Methodism over half the world; and thus, as we venture to think, shall these first truths, at a moment when the two now prevalent delusions have reached their destined limits, burst through all restraint, and claim for Christianity anew, its own position as the source of all good, and the only ground of hope for man. Those influences (legitimate as they are) to which Christian people are looking, as the proper causes of the expected triumph of the Gospel, will follow as its consequence; and they will so be brought into operation, on a vastly extended scale, as shall give a new aspect to every country wherein they shall be allowed freely to take effect.

And which are those countries? If we are to adhere to the rule of analogy, the next coming religious renovation, when the Gospel shall again, and in its power, its majesty, and its ineffable mystery, come home to the minds of men—this approaching visitation will take its course *restrictively*, as among professedly Christian nations, and then (not according to any assignable rule) shall it spread over, or make inroads upon, the non-Christian wastes of the world. Christianity, at the first, went wherever a preparation had been made for its reception by the scattering and settlement of the Jewish race, and by the pre-existent diffusion of the Scriptures of the Old Testament, in the Greek language. Within *these* limits the Gospel seated itself, and there it held its position with more or less of continuity; and beyond the same limits it was, indeed, carried forth, and it won its triumphs; but soon it lost its hold; soon it retreated, and disappeared, leaving only some scattered and scarcely appreciable fragments on its spots, to denote the course it had taken.

The Reformation also yielded itself to a restrictive influence; or, as we might call it, a law of limitation, and it did so in a manner still more marked. It broke, as a sudden glare, over the entire surface of Europe; and it entered and convulsed every one of the countries then representing the Roman empire; but as to most of them, it convulsed them only for a moment, and soon was driven out and extinguished. As a permanent religious renovation, scarcely did it extend itself over the space occupied by the several families of the Teutonic race; and within even these limits, its occupation of its original surface has been precarious, giving way perpetually, as well to the returning influence of Romanism, as to the more fatal spread of a feebly-christianized infidelity. In any true and *religious* sense, does the work of the Reformers survive any where, but among the English people? It is among the English, and these only, that an unambiguous creed—orthodox and evangelic—the faith that was recovered by the Reformers, is boldly professed, and is sustained concurrently, by independent communions.

The Methodism of the last century swept over nearly the same surface, and gave animation to those communions only which still held the creed of the Reformation. Upon *this* surface the renovation which was brought about by Methodism has well maintained itself in its several transmuted forms, such as a revived church feeling, a diffused evangelic profession; and then the missionary zeal, and then those many modes of Christian benevolence which pursue their objects by means of voluntary organizations.

In the British Islands, and in the colonies, every where, and in the States of America—that is to say, wherever the English language is spoken, and nowhere else—there are to be found individuals many, and communities, by and among whom a new ministration of the Gospel, in its power and purity, would be hailed with profound emotion, would be welcomed, and listened to, and obeyed. So far as calculable probabilities might be allowed to find place in relation to so high a subject, there are two events which would seem in an equal degree amazing and unlikely, and they are these, namely—That a renovated Christianity should not be listened to, and joyfully accepted, by the religious communities of the English race;—or, That it should be so listened to by any of those cultured nations of continental Europe, which have long since thrown Christianity out of their serious regard, and have learned to think and speak of it as a religion which, though better than some, is now effectively obsolete.

Assuredly it is with no leaning toward a puritanic interpretation of the Fourth Commandment (which was a Jewish, or rather a Rabbinical, and not a Christian rendering of it), but under the sure guidance of a moral experiment which has been carried forward on the largest scale, and under all imaginable varieties of circumstance, that we may thus conclude, that, where the SUNDAY retains, in unabated force, its sacredness, as well in the feelings of a community, as in their habitudes and usages, there will be found—not scattered individuals merely, but masses of the people, ready to accept, and eager to listen to, the Gospel, once again proclaimed in its grandeur, simplicity, and power.

A throwing off of the Sunday feeling, and an easy contempt of religious usages, such as has become the well-nigh universal characteristic of the continental nations, may consist, and it does consist, with the tolerated presence of small clusters of Christian men, still clinging, as they may, to a serious religious belief, and adhering to religious forms; but in such countries, a new METHODISM, if, indeed, it shall visit them at all, will provoke, in one mode, or in another, its new MARTYRDOMS. The Gospel, if it takes its course through such lands, will run this way and that, over the surface, as a torrent of fire.

It may well be imagined, and it might almost be predicted that, at such a time, when Christianity in its purity shall break in (if ever it does so break in) upon the national impiety of France, Spain, (Germany), Austria, Italy, Russia, the ecclesiastical authorities, whatever may be their mind, or their readiness to do their office as of old, will be spared the necessity of grasping the sword and brand in defense of the Church; for it will then be seen (so we may predict) that the soul of Decius, of Galerius, of Diocletian, may find a lodgment in the bosom of the modern atheist, more thoroughly to its taste than was that of an Innocent III., or a Bonner.

But whatever may be thought of the actual religious condition of the people, or of the tendency of opinion in England, or elsewhere, throughout the world, where the English have created for themselves a home, it is still true that those feelings are cherished, and those usages are adhered to, by the mass of the people—certainly by a majority of the middle classes, which hold them in readiness always for the reception of a revived Christianity. There is a marked difference between ourselves and every other branch of the civilized commonwealth—the nations of continental Europe—in this respect, that *they* are looking about with a vague anxiety, in this direction and in that, hoping for social ameliorations to be effected by some process of political regeneration: *we*—that is to say—the observers of Sunday, and the holders of the Bible, though not indifferent to political improvement, yet deeply feel that no alleged improvement can be in itself desirable, or be permanently good, which does not spring out of Christianity directly, or at least receive its sanction.

The religious convictions of many around us may have been loosened or impaired; yet not so injured, as that the renovation of them would not be joyfully welcomed, even as a man exults in the restoration of sight or hearing. Multitudes are there on all sides, to whom, although they have gone out of the way, a return to Christian belief and Christian usages would involve no strange or incongruous revolution of mind; but only a repentant acquiescence in principles too long forgotten, or misunderstood. Multitudes also are there, who, although their present religious condition is, in their own estimation of it, ambiguous, yet stand prepared to listen to a boldly-proclaimed Gospel with gladness and animation: they are the constant frequenters of public worship—to its forms and observances they yield themselves, not reluctantly, nor yet cordially, but wishing that the service they take part in was borne out in their bosoms by a less evanescent feeling. Churches are filled by those to whom the first wakening sounds of another Whitefield's voice would be hailed as bringing "glad tidings of great joy."

When, as now, we think of such a renovation, we include in this idea of the future no new or supplementary revelation—no new creed—not the rising of a new sect, but only this, that there should be brought to bear upon human nature the full energy of Eternal Truth, by means of the existing ministrations of the Gospel. A difficulty inseparable from the subject, and consequent upon its very nature, attends us whenever the course of religious movements is spoken of, which, while they stand connected always with visible causes, with human agency, and with known motives, have also a higher cause, namely the Sovereign Will of Him from whom all good comes, and of whose counsels man knows nothing.

Thus, in this present instance, it might be easy, or not extremely difficult, so to forecast the present tendency of opinions, in England at least, as might warrant the belief that a powerful religious reaction is near at hand. But here we should be checked by considerations of another kind; for a mere *reaction*, arising from the return of calculable influences, is not what we desire, or what we now need. Puritanism was, to a great extent, a reaction only; and so, too, was that profligacy and impiety which broke over the land when Puritanism met its political overthrow. But the Methodism that soon followed was no reaction, which might have been foreseen; for it rose without visible causation; it came from above; it found its lodgment in the bosoms of two or three—the chosen instruments of Heaven;—and as was its commencement, such its progress.

Shall not then the now looked for and needed renovation come in upon us in a like sovereign manner? We do not expect unearthly visitants to descend, and to become the preachers of the Gospel; for those who shall speak as did Whitefield and Wesley, will be men such as they were, compassed with those infirmities that are inseparable from humanity. But they will not be the men whom *we*, of this or that Church, should have singled out;—far otherwise: perhaps they will not be of "our" Church at all; and the course they will pursue, and the means they will adopt for making full proof of their ministry, will be of a kind that shall sorely grate upon the tastes, and shock the cherished convictions of many. On the one hand they will be reviled because they are seen to render what will be thought an unwarrantable homage to constituted authorities, and because they refuse to lead the onslaught upon this and that "corrupt system." On the other side, not improbably, the irregularities which such a ministry necessarily involves, will deprive them of all favor in high places.

Every season of religious renovation comes upon the men of that time as a winnowing. He who comes at such times, comes with "his fan in his hand," and he ceases not in his work until he has "thoroughly purged his floor." That is to say, as often as first principles are presented to the minds of men with power and freshness, this presentation acts discriminately upon all who are placed within its influence. The evangelists do not leave us to surmise that this dispersive effect attended the preaching of Christ, on all occasions, for they affirm it repeatedly. The arrogant, the fanatical, the self-opinionated, and the worldly-minded were "offended at him," and these four sorts of gainsayers make themselves conspicuous in each returning season of religious refreshment. *Small truths*, or secondary principles, may be promulgated in loud tones, and with extreme vehemence, and yet the world will bear with it; but great truths, when they are proclaimed by those who feel them to be such, are never listened to without producing an effect of one kind, or of another. Human nature, touched to the quick, kindles at the first hearing of them, rouses itself to resistance, and then either yields itself, or resents, as an insult and an injury, the preacher's challenge.

But while, in this manner, a new proclamation of the Gospel acts upon the multitude as a process of discrimination, it finds always a small number whom it beckons forward, to follow gladly, rather than challenges to choose their part; and these are those who long have been looking for, and expecting, this visitation which now makes them glad.

We have thus spoken of the Methodism of the past age, and of that which we presume to be future, so far as these, or any such like refreshments of Christian piety, make themselves visible on this side the unseen world, and so far as they may furnish the subjects, and supply the materials of religious history. Yet the very same order of events stands in relationship—although it be occult—to that invisible community; nor do these recurrent seasons of animation fail to give some dim indications of this remote connection. With due caution, this subject may be glanced at for a moment.

The pomp and circumstance of ecclesiastical affairs—the rise and fall of hierarchies—the springing up of new opinions—the alternate loss and recovery of Christian doctrine—and the part played by the leading Churchmen of each age, together with the witness-bearing and the sufferings of martyrs—these things attract the eye, and engage the ear, and we are prone, while contemplating the ever-shifting scene, to think that the entire movement—the compass of religious history, is before us. Yet we can not so think if, in a more religious mood, and with the inspired writings in our hands, we look onward and beyond this range of proximate objects, and penetrate the mist that rests between us and those things among which Faith ruminates.

When religious history is thus contemplated, as from a higher position, and when it is seen apart from its mundane glare, and its accidents, and when we stand at such a distance from the noisy arena as to hear nothing of its agitations, then does there come forth, if dimly, yet not unsubstantially, an order of events obeying a law of the spiritual economy, such as this, namely—that there is going forward, through the lapse of ages, a periodic gathering of human spirits, in multitudes—in crowds—for replenishing that kingdom which is under the hand of the "Shepherd and Bishop of Souls." He, the Redeemer of the world, as he is the "First-born of the Dead," is the Sovereign of that realm of ransomed spirits. During the running out of this present economy it is among, and over, this company, which "no man can number," that his shield and sceptre are extended.

No age has been so dark—no time so corrupt in doctrine, or in manners, as not to have sent forward from Earth to Hades a tide, albeit a slackened tide, of souls, ransomed from the ills of earth: but at moments—and as with a sudden swell—it is as if the portals of Paradise were thrown wide open, and as if the plains of that region were to be made glad with the arrival of hosts of spirits, safe housed, and as if, from time to time, fresh proof were to be given to the expectant inhabiters of that realm, who are "the prisoners of hope," that the scheme of human salvation is still in full progress on earth, and that the promised gathering—the harvest—shall not fail to be brought home in its season.

NOTES.

THE materials or documents wherein the history of Methodism is to be found, are not recondite: for the most part they are readily accessible to every one, and, in fact, the succession of writers who, whether with a friendly or a hostile feeling, have put this history together, each in his own manner, have, for these various purposes, brought forward almost every thing that is the most pertinent in this mass of evidence. Nevertheless, it would not be difficult (and would not have been so to the present writer) to cull some fresh passages from the same sources; and he might, moreover, have brought forward a few unpublished letters, which were kindly offered to his inspection by some who are possessed of such treasures. But inasmuch as it has not entered into his plan to compile biographies, nor to attempt to do again what has already (in a literary sense) been well done, he has refrained from availing himself, to any great extent, of these materials, at least in giving them a place in this volume.

It seems, however, desirable, and indeed it is incumbent upon a writer who takes a position differing from that occupied by others, to adduce evidence in support of opinions that are likely to be called in question. A few pages, therefore, of this volume will be devoted to the purpose of bringing together, chiefly from Wesley's Journal, and from the Minutes of Conference, passages that may serve to illustrate, and to sustain, the averments and the opinions which the writer thinks warrantable and correct.

As to METHODISM at large—the facts relating to its rise and progress have long since become the staple of religious history, and they are such as need little or no attestation. It is solely, or chiefly, on points touching Wesley's mind and intention, as the founder of Wesleyanism, that it seemed desirable to adduce evidence. The reader who is little acquainted with Wesleyan affairs might be unprepared to admit some allegations which the following passages incontestably establish. As to those readers to whom these sources of information have always been familiar, the production of a few paragraphs, as it could add nothing to *their* knowledge, so would it fail to affect their long-ago adopted opinions.

NOTE to pages 31 and 43, *et seq.*

When Wesley's credulity, or his tendency to listen to the supernatural, is affirmed (and it can not be denied), justice demands that instances should be adduced, showing that he did—if not always, yet sometimes—hold and profess a suspended opinion, and content himself with a simple statement of facts—or of what he believed to be facts—followed by a conjectural solution, only, of the perplexing circumstances of the case before him.

The following narrative occurs in Wesley's Journal, June 1st, 1764:—"About seven, Mr. B. was occasionally mentioning what had lately occurred in the next parish. I thought it worth a further inquiry, and therefore ordered our horses to be brought immediately. Mr. B. guided us to Mr. Ogilvie's house, the minister of the parish, who informed us that a strange disorder had appeared in his parish between thirty and forty years ago, but that nothing of the kind had been known there since, till some time in September last. A boy was then taken ill, and so continues still. In the end of January, or beginning of February, many other children were taken, chiefly girls, and a few grown persons. They begin with an involuntary shaking of their hands and feet. Then their lips are convulsed; next their tongue, which seems to cleave to the roof of the mouth. Then the eyes are set, staring terribly; and the whole face variously distorted. Presently they start up, and jump ten, fifteen, or twenty times together, straight upward, two, three, or more feet from the ground. Then they start forward, and run with amazing swiftness, two, three, or five hundred yards. Frequently they run up, like a cat, to the top of a house, and jump on the ridge of it, as on the ground. But wherever they are, they never fall or miss their footing at all. After they have run and jumped for some time, they drop down as dead. When they come to themselves, they usually tell when and where they shall be taken again; frequently how often, and where they shall jump; and to what places they shall run. I asked, 'Are any of them near?' He said, 'Yes, at those houses.' We walked thither without delay: one of them was four years and a half old; the other about eighteen. The child we found had had three or four fits that day, running and jumping like the rest; and, in particular, leaping many times from a high table without the least hurt. The young woman was the only person of them all who used to keep her senses during the fit. In answer to many questions, she said, 'I first feel a pain in my left foot, then in my head. Then my hands and feet shake, and I can't speak; and quickly I begin to jump or run.' While we were talking, she cried out, O! I have a pain in my foot—it is in my hand. It is here, at the bending of my arm. Oh! my head! my head! my head!' Immediately her arms were stretched out, and were as an iron bar. I could not bend one of her fingers; and her body was bent backward, the lower part remaining quite erect, while her back formed exactly a half circle, her head hanging even with her hips. I was going to catch her, but one said, 'Sir, you may let her alone, for they never fall.' But I defy all mankind to account for her not falling, when the trunk of her body hung in that manner.

"In many circumstances this case goes far beyond the famous one mentioned by Boerhaave, particularly in that, their telling before when and how they shall be taken again. Whoever can account for this, on natural principles, has my free leave: I can not. I therefore believe, if this be in part a natural distemper, there is something preternatural too. Yet, supposing this, I can easily conceive Satan will so disguise his part therein, that we can not precisely determine which part of the disorder is natural, and which preternatural."

This mode of dealing with facts so strange is not far from being sober and safe. It does not appear that these cases were in any way connected with religious feelings. The instances much resemble some that have of late years been obtruded upon public attention by the professors of the mesmeric art. Wesley's testimony concerning facts of his own knowledge ought always to be received implicitly (as, for example, such as the following), and then candor will demand that a man who not very infrequently witnessed what no philosophy can explain, may be pardoned if he sometimes accepts, too readily, the stories related to him by others. His journal of January 13, 1743, has this entry:—

"Rode to Stratford-upon-Avon. I had scarce sat down before I was informed Mrs. K., a middle-aged woman, of Shattery, half a mile from Stratford, had been for many weeks last past in a way which nobody could understand. That she had sent for a minister; but, almost as soon as he came, began roaring in so strange a manner, her tongue at the same time hanging out of her mouth, and her face being distorted in the most terrible form, that he cried out, 'It is the devil, doubtless;—it is the devil;' and immediately went away.

"I suppose this was some unphilosophical minister; else he would have said,—'Stark mad! send her to Bedlam.' I asked, 'What good do you think I can do?' One answered, 'I can not tell.' But Mrs. K. (I just relate what was spoken to me, without passing any judgment upon it) 'earnestly desired that you might come, if you were any where near, saying she had seen you in a dream; and should know you immediately. But the devil said—those were her own expressions—I will tear thy throat out before he comes. But afterward she said—his words were—if he does come I will let thee be quiet;—and thou shalt be as if nothing ailed thee, till he is gone away.' A very odd kind of madness this! I walked over about noon; but when we came to the house, desired all those who came with me to stay below; one showing me the way, I went up straight to her room. As soon as I came to the bedside, she fixed her eyes, and said—'You are Mr. Wesley. I am very well now, I thank God. Nothing ails me, only I am weak!' I called them up, and I began to sing—

Jesu! thou hast bid us pray;
Pray always, and not faint;
With the word, a power convey,
To utter our complaint.

"After singing a verse or two, we kneeled down to prayer. I had but just begun—my eyes being shut—when I felt as if I had been plunged into cold water; and immediately there was such a roar, that my voice was quite drowned, though I spoke as loud as I usually do to three or four thousand people. However, I prayed on. She was then reared up in the bed; her whole body moving at once, without bending one joint or limb, just as if it were one piece of stone. Immediately after it was writhed into all kinds of postures; the same horrid yell continuing still. But we left her not till all the symptoms ceased, and she was, for the present at least, rejoicing and praising God."

Wesley's deliberately expressed opinion as to the source of the outcries of converts (referred to pp. 43, *et seq.*) should be brought forward in fairness.

"*March* 12th, 1743.—I concluded my second course of visiting, in which I inquired particularly into two things; first, the caso of those who had almost every night, the last week, cried out aloud during the preaching; secondly, the number of those who were separated from us, and the reason and occasion of it.

"As to the former, I found, first, that all of them, I think not one excepted, were persons in perfect health, had not been subject to fits of any kind, till they were thus affected. Secondly, that this had come upon every one of them in a moment, without any previous notice, while they were either hearing the word of God, or thinking on what they had heard. Thirdly, that in that moment they dropped down, lost all their strength, and were seized with violent pain. This they expressed in different manners. Some said they felt just as if a sword was running through them: others that a great weight lay upon them, as if it would squeeze them into the earth. Some said they were quite choked, so that they could not breathe: others, that it was as if their heart—as if their inside—as if their whole body was tearing all in pieces. These symptoms I can no more impute to any natural cause, than to the spirit of God. I can make no doubt that it was Satan tearing them as they were *coming to Christ;* and hence proceeded those grievous cries, whereby he might design both to discredit the work of God and to affright fearful people from hearing that Word whereby their souls might be saved. I found, fourthly, that their minds had been as variously affected as their bodies. Of this some could give scarce any account at all, which also I impute to that wise Spirit, purposely stunning and confounding as many as he could, that they might not be able to bewray his devices. Others gave a very clear and particular account, from the beginning to the end. The word of God pierced their souls, and convinced them of inward as well as outward sin. They saw and felt the wrath of God abiding on them, and were afraid of his judgments. And here the accuser came with great power, telling them there was no hope; they were lost forever. The pains of body then seized them in a moment, and extorted those loud and bitter cries."

The judgment Wesley formed upon cases of this kind was followed by a practical conclusion, therewith well consisting, as thus:

Sunday, 13*th*. I went in the morning in order to speak severally with the members of the society at Tanfield. From the terrible instances I met with here, and indeed in all parts of England, I am more and more convinced, that the devil himself desires nothing more than this, that the people of any place should be half awakened, and then left to themselves to fall asleep again. Therefore I determined, by the grace of God, not to strike one stroke in any place where I can not follow the blow."

To whatever cause or causes we may please to attribute the violence and noise so often attending conversions under Wesley's preaching, *he* must not be much blamed for giving credit to them as genuine, when they were so very often occurring in his presence, and were issuing in a favorable manner.

"At Weaver's Hall seven or eight persons were constrained to roar aloud, while the sword of the Spirit was dividing asunder their souls and spirits, and joints and marrow. But they were all relieved upon prayer, and sang praises unto our God, and unto the Lamb that liveth for ever and ever.—*Journal, August,* 1739.

Whitefield, though much less inclined than Wesley to view these demonstrations favorably, yielded, in some degree, to the force of instances occurring in the course of his own ministry.

"In the afternoon I was with Mr. Whitefield, just come from London, with whom I went to Baptist Mills, where he preached concerning the Holy Ghost, which all who believe are to receive; not without a just, though severe, censure, of those who preach *as if* there were no Holy Ghost. *Saturday,* 7th, I had an opportunity to talk with him of those outward signs which had so often accompanied the inward work of God. I found his objections were chiefly grounded on gross misrepresentations of matter of fact. But the next day he had an opportunity of informing himself better. For no sooner had he begun (in the application of his sermon) to invite all sinners to believe in Christ, than four persons sunk down close to him, almost in the same moment. One of them lay without either sense or motion; a second trembled exceedingly; the third had strong convulsions all over his body, but made no noise unless by groans; the fourth, equally convulsed, called upon God, with strong cries and tears. From this time, I trust, we shall all suffer God to carry on his own work in the way that pleases Him."—*Journal, July,* 1739.

Yes; but the previous question might well have been asked—Do these animal paroxysms constitute any part whatever of "the work of God?" Before the affirmative can be granted, it must be shown that the ministry of Christ, or of the apostles, was attended by any such frightful seizures. This can never be done. Nevertheless it would be easy to fill pages with extracts from Wesley's Journal, conclusively proving and exhibiting the soundness of his judgment, on several occasions, in dealing with the disorders that attended the Methodistic movement. Some reference, at least, to such instances of discretion may seem to be called for, in justice, as corrective of any statements of a contrary import which may have met the reader's eye. Such an instance occurs in the Journal of the date *October* 29th, 1762, which, although too long to cite (it occupies four pages), the writer would not be thought to have overlooked.

NOTE to pages 32 and 86.

KINGSWOOD SCHOOL. There is nothing pleasing, but quite the contrary, in what Wesley reports of the religious movements that at times took place among the boys at Kingswood. That these promising commencements (so he thought them) produced exceedingly little good, he candidly and frequently acknowledges. "The children are not religious: they have not the power, and barely the form of religion." *Minutes of Conference*, 1783. "Nor did they even make as much progress in learning as other boys; neither do they improve in learning better than at other schools: no, nor yet so well." This failure—to him a source of bitter disappointment, he attributes to the neglect of the masters in enforcing his rules:—and what were these rules, or the spirit of them? He says, "they"—the boys—"ought never to play, but they do, every day: yea in the school." What wonder children should play in school, who are forbidden to play out of it? Wesley had no consciousness toward human nature, except in certain of its aspects. With a better understanding of human nature, his excellent good sense would no doubt have secured, in this instance, a fair measure of success; but it did not: the school continued to be to him a perplexity, and a vexation, through a long course of time. There is an entry in his Journal, dated nearly thirty years earlier than the preceding Minute of Conference—namely, August 24th, 1754, which may properly be compared with the one above given.

"I endeavored once more to bring Kingswood School into order. Surely the importance of this design is apparent, even from the difficulties that attend it. I have spent more money, and time, and care on this than almost any design I ever had, and still it exercises all the patience I have; but it is worth all the labor."

Yes, and so good a design might well have asked from its benevolent founder a reconsideration of the *principles* on which he had so vainly labored to effect it Every one knows that the management of schools, public or private, is a labor peculiarly encompassed with difficulties; nevertheless they are not absolutely insurmountable; that is to say, when a true knowledge of human nature, and an experienced skill or tact in the treatment of boys, are fairly brought to bear upon the task. Wesley's Kingswood School was, or he would fain have made it, a miniature Methodism; and therefore he failed to render it, in even an ordinary degree, efficient for the common purposes of education. If, in a word, one might give expression to Wesley's leading error, it would be in this way:—at Kingswood he treated children, as if already they were men; in his Society he treated men as if they must always be children.

Note *to Section on Field Preaching*, p. 43.

It was not without extreme reluctance that Wesley followed Whitefield's example, and obeyed his own convictions, in the practice of field-preaching. His opinion, as recorded in his Journal on this subject, has frequently been cited, and such passages need not be repeated here: in a word, he soon became thoroughly convinced that it must be in this mode, if at all, that the Gospel is to be brought to the hearing of the people. "Thousands of hearers, rich and poor, received the Word near the New Square, with the deepest attention. This is the way to shake the trembling gates of Hell. Still I see nothing can do this so effectually as *field-preaching*."—*Journal, August* 21, 1768. Again:—

"Monday, about noon, I preached on the Green at Clare, to an exceeding serious congregation; and in the evening at Tullamore. Tuesday, 27th, I found a little increase to the Society; but there can not be much without more field-preaching. Wherever this is intermitted, the work of God stands still, if it does not go back."—*Journal, June,* 1770.

In the Minutes of Conference for 1744, occur the following answers to queries, relative to the practice of field-preaching:— "*Q*. Have we not used it too sparingly? *A*. It seems we have: 1. Because our call is, to save that which is lost. Now we can not expect such to seek *us;* therefore we should go and seek *them* 2. Because we are particularly called, by going into the highways and hedges (which none else will), to compel them to come in. 3. Because that reason against it is not good: 'The house will hold all that come.' The house may hold all that come to the house, but not all that *would come* to the field."

"In the evening I came to Cork, and at seven was surprised at the unusual largeness of the congregation. I had often been grieved at the smallness of the congregation here; and it could be no other while we cooped ourselves up in the house. But now the alarm is sounded abroad, the people flock from all quarters. So plain it is, that field-preaching is the most effectual way of overturning Satan's kingdom. . . . . At seven in the evening I stood in a vacant place near Blackpool, famous from time immemorial for all manner of wickedness, for riot in particular, and cried aloud, 'Why will ye die, O House of Israel.' Abundance of papists gathered at a distance; but they drew nearer and nearer, till nine parts in ten mingled with the congregation, and were all attention. Surely this is the way to spread religion, to publish it in the face of the sun."—*Journal, June* 18, 1763.

NOTE to page 85.

Many passages occur in the Journals, and in the Minutes of Conference, expressive of Wesley's earnest desire to impart to his system of popular instruction a deeper tone, and to send piety home from the "preaching house" to the families of his people. That there was great and urgent need of reform in this respect, he thoroughly understood, and he very often expresses his sense of it in his usual emphatic style. Wesleyan Methodism did but very imperfectly Christianize Wesleyan *families.* He knew this, and he acknowledged it: so far therefore the allegations, to this effect, which the writer has repeatedly advanced, are borne out. But Wesley labored to bring in a remedy; and perhaps his endeavors were not wholly without effect, although the same sort of complaint meets us to the end.

On this ground, then, the writer would render justice to Wesley, while he is compelled to adhere to the statements he has made; nor must he be blamed, on this ground, seeing that Wesley, at a time when his system had been many years in operation—1766, records his deliberate opinion of its influence upon the domestic habits of his people, in terms such as these:—"Family religion is shamefully wanting, and almost in every branch. And the Methodists in general will be little better till we take quite another course with them. For what avails public *preaching alone,* though we could preach like angels."

This is an acknowledgment conclusively proving that, in Wesley's matured judgment, a society framed for the purpose of making and retaining converts, wants that which is of the highest importance and necessity, in giving full effect to Christianity. "Religion is a very superficial thing among us." Such were his often repeated confessions and complaints. The fact he attributes to causes short of those whence actually it resulted. A ministry itinerating always, and therefore never competent to discharge pastoral functions—a crude theology, adapted indeed to the field preacher's purpose, and to nothing else, and a style of address to the people that tended always more to produce excitement than movement, or than progress:—such surely were the causes of this characteristic of Wesleyan Methodism—its shallowness.

NOTE to page 70.

The following passages from Wesley's Journal, of different dates, might be compared with what occurs so plentifully in the biographies of the Romish saints, and which at a glance would seem to be much of the same quality. The difference, however, is real, and it is such as indicates the very different issue of an ascetic course, in the one case, when the light of scriptural piety was gradually breaking in upon the mind—and in the other, when a thick darkness encompassed the ascetic on every side.

"*October* 20*th*, 1735. Believing the denying ourselves even in the smallest instances, might, by the blessing of God, be helpful to us, we wholly left off the use of flesh and wine, and confined ourselves to vegetable food, chiefly rice and biscuit."

"*December* 7*th*, *Sunday*. Finding nature did not require so frequent supplies as we had been accustomed to, we agreed to leave off suppers, from doing which we have hitherto found no inconvenience."

"*March* 30*th*, 1736. Mr. Ingham, coming from Frederica, brought me letters pressing me to go thither. The next day, Mr. Delamotte and I began to try whether life might not as well be sustained by one sort, as by variety of food. We chose to make the experiment with bread, and were never more vigorous and healthy than while we tasted nothing else. '*Blessed are the pure in heart!*' who, whether they eat or drink, or whatever they do, have no end therein but to please God. To them all things are pure. Every creature is good to them, and nothing to be rejected. But let them, who know and feel that they are not thus pure, use every help and remove every hindrance; always remembering, *He that despiseth little things, shall fall by little and little.*"

June 6th, 1737. I began visiting the prisons, assisting the poor and sick in town, and doing what other good I could, by my presence or my little fortune, to the bodies and souls of all men. To this end I abridged myself of all superfluities, and many that are called necessaries of life. I soon became a *by-word* for so doing, and I rejoiced that *my name was cast out as evil.* The next spring I began observing the Wednesday and Friday fasts, commonly observed in the ancient Church; tasting no food till three in the afternoon. And now I knew not how to go any farther. I diligently strove against all sin. I omitted no sort of self-denial which I thought lawful. I carefully used, both in public and in private, all the means of grace at all opportunities. I omitted no occasion of doing good; I for that reason suffered evil. And all this I knew to be nothing unless it was directed toward inward holiness. Accordingly this, the image of God, was what I aimed at in all, by doing his will, not my own. Yet when after continuing some years in this course, I apprehended myself to be near death, I could not find that all this gave me any comfort, or any assurance of acceptance with God. At this I was then not a little surprised, not imagining I had been all this time building on the sand—nor considering that '*other foundation can no man lay than that which is laid by God, even Christ Jesus*' . . . . .

"1736. On Monday 9th, and the following days, I reflected much on that vain desire, which had pursued me for so many years, of being in solitude, in order to be a Christian. I have now, thought I, solitude enough; but am I, therefore, the nearer being a Christian? Not if Jesus Christ be the model of Christianity. I doubt, indeed, I am much nearer that mystery of Satan which some writers affect to call by that name. So near, that I had probably sunk wholly into it, had not the great mercy of God just now thrown me upon reading St. Cyprian's works: '*Oh my soul, come not thou into their secret, stand thou in the good old paths.*'"

Wesley here refers to that *first principle* of the ascetic life, which renders it a condensed selfishness, or egotism.

NOTES *illustrative of the Four Sections on Wesleyan Methodism*, from p. 188 to p. 268.

To those who stand unconnected with Wesleyan Methodism, but who are conversant with Wesley's Journal, Letters, and Tracts, and with the Minutes of Conference, it must seem superfluous to occupy a page in establishing a fact so conspicuously certain as this—namely, that, in constituting his Society, and in conferring upon a hundred of his preachers an absolute and unmitigated spiritual sovereignty, he did—what a man *may* do with *his own*, as for example with a charity, created by himself, and endowed from his own funds—but what no Christian man could dare attempt who was *knowingly* constituting a Church, and setting on foot a scheme of government, for perpetuity, on principles consonant with those which are obviously deducible from the tenor of the apostolic writings.

From the severe blame that would be involved in the supposition that Wesley contemplated, and that he aimed indirectly to bring about a plan of this comprehensive kind—a blame injurious alike to his reputation for wisdom, and for simplicity of purpose, he stands clearly and wholly exempt, this exculpation resting, as it does, upon the ground of those many passages, scattered through the documents above mentioned, which show what, in fact, were his views, and his intentions, in giving form and consistency to his Society. Of these passages a sample only is now presented to the reader to whom the subject is not familiar. A few sentences, extracted from the Minutes of Conference, will best introduce these extracts. It is well known that Wesley, from the first to the last, shrunk from the idea of separation from the Established Church. In a Conference held five years after the commencement of Methodism, these questions were put and answered.

"*Wednesday, June 27th*, 1744. *Q.* 6. How far is it our duty to obey the bishops? *A.* In all things indifferent; and on this ground of obeying them, we should observe the canons so far as we can with a safe conscience. *Q.* 7. Do we separate from the Church? *A.* We conceive not. We hold communion therewith, for conscience sake, by constantly attending both the Word preached and the sacraments administered therein. *Q.* 9. But do you not weaken the Church? *A.* Do not they who ask this, by *the Church*, mean *themselves?* We do not purposely weaken any man's hands. But accidentally we may thus far; they who come to know the truth by us, will esteem such as deny it less than they did before. *Q.* 10. Do you not entail a schism on the Church? *i.e.* Is it not probable that your hearers, after your death, will be scattered into all sects and parties? or that they will form themselves into a distinct sect? *A.* 1. We are persuaded the body of our hearers will, even after our death, remain in the Church, unless they be thrust out. 2. We believe, notwithstanding, either they will be thrust out, or that they will leaven the whole Church. 3. We do, and will do, all we can, to prevent these consequences, which are supposed likely to happen after our death. 4. But we can not, with a good conscience, neglect the present opportunity of saving souls while we live, for fear of consequences which may possibly or probably happen after we are dead."

While making these professions, in so formal a manner, Wesley could not—consistently with his repute as a simple-minded and ingenuous man—go about so to frame his Society as should at once facilitate, and *suggest,* to his followers, a separation—a schism. Again—

"*Q.* What may we reasonably believe to be God's design, in raising up the preachers called Methodists? *A.* To reform the nation, more particularly the Church; to spread scriptural holiness over the land."

If Wesley thought himself the head of a Church, not the leader of a merely voluntary association, then did he assume an autocratic power over his ministers of the most absolute kind, Among the Rules of a "Helper"—a superior minister in fact, this is one—too nearly resembling, in its tone, Loyola's Noted Letter on Obedience:—"2. Act in all things, not according to your own will, but as a son in the Gospel (*i.e.* Wesley's son); as such, it is your part to employ your time, in the manner which we direct: partly in preaching, and visiting the flock from house to house; partly in reading, meditation and prayer. Above all, if you labor with us in our Lord's vineyard, it is needful that you should do *that part* of the work which we advise, at *those* times and places which we judge most for his glory."

In the Conference of 1749, the phrase "Mother Church," as applied incidentally to the Central Society in London, occurs; but a few lines on, in answer to the question, "How should an assistant be qualified for this charge?" it is answered, " and by loving the Church of England, and resolving not to separate from it." The term "Mother Church" did not, therefore, mean more than a centre of management for the societies scattered over the country. Again, further on, it is asked: "Is there any other advice which you would give the assistants? *A.* Yes. In every place exhort those who were brought up in the Church, constantly to attend its service: and in visiting the classes, ask every one,—Do *you* go to Church as often as you ever did? Set the example yourself, and immediately alter any plan that interferes therewith. Is there not a cause for this? Are not we, unawares, by little and little, tending to a separation from the Church? O remove every tendency thereto with all diligence. 1. Let all our preachers go to Church. 2. Let all our people go constantly. 3. Receive the Sacrament at every opportunity. 4. Warn all against niceness in hearing, a great and prevailing evil. 5. Warn them likewise against despising the prayers of the Church. 6. Against calling our Society *a Church*, or *the Church.* 7. Against calling our Preachers, *Ministers;* our houses, *meeting houses;* (call them plain preaching houses). 8. Do not license them as such. 9. Do not license yourself till you are constrained; and then, not as a *Dissenter*, but a *Methodist* preacher.

In the Conference of 1766, and after the lapse of seventeen years, Wesley again earnestly rejects the imputation of intending to create a separation from the Church, and repudiates the designation *Dissenter*. P. 57.

"Are we not then Dissenters? We are irregular; 1st. By calling sinners to repentance, in *all places* of God's dominion. 2d. By frequently using *extemporary prayer*. Yet we are not *Dissenters*, in the only sense which our law acknowledges:—namely, persons who believe it is sinful to attend the service of the Church: for we do attend it at all opportunities.

"We will not, dare not, separate from the Church, for the reasons given several years ago. We are not *Seceders*, nor do we bear any resemblance to them. We set out upon quite opposite principles. The Seceders laid the very foundation of their work in judging and condemning *others*. We laid the foundation of our work, in judging and condemning ourselves. They begin every where with showing their hearers how fallen *the Church and ministers* are. We begin every where with showing our hearers how fallen they are *themselves.*

"And as we are not dissenters from the Church now, so we

will do nothing willingly, which tends to a separation from it. Therefore let every assistant so order his circuit, that no preacher may be hindered from attending the Church more than two Sundays in the month. Never make light of going to Church, either by word or deed. Remember Mr. Hook, a very eminent and a zealous Papist. When I asked him, 'Sir, what do you for public worship here, where you have no Romish sermon?' He answered: 'Sir, I am so fully convinced it is the duty of every man to worship God in public, that I go to Church every Sunday. If I can not have such worship as I would, I will have such worship as I can.'

"But some may say, 'Our own service is public worship.' Yes, *in a sense:* but not such as supersedes the Church Service. We never designed it should. We have a hundred times professed the contrary. It presupposes public prayer like the sermons at the university. Therefore I have over and over advised: use no *long prayer*, either before or after sermon. Therefore, I myself frequently use only a collect, and never enlarge in prayer, unless at Intercession, or on a Watch-night, or on some extraordinary occasion. If it were designed to be instead of Church Service, it would be essentially defective. For it seldom has the four grand parts of public prayer; deprecation, petition, intercession, and thanksgiving. Neither is it, even on the Lord's Day, concluded with the Lord's Supper. The hour for it on that day, unless where there is some peculiar reason for a variation, should be five in the morning, as well as five in the evening. Why should we make God's day the shortest of the seven? But if the people put ours in the place of the Church Service, we *hurt* them that stay with us, and ruin them that leave us. For then they will go nowhere, but lounge the Sabbath away without any public worship at all.

"I advise, therefore, all the Methodists in England and Ireland, who have been brought up in the Church, constantly to attend the service of the Church, at least every Lord's Day."

Wesley's own account of the origin of his Power, as occurring in the Minutes of 1766, and elsewhere, has so frequently been brought forward that it need not again be cited. It is conclusive to this effect, that the circumstances attending the rise of Methodism threw into his hands such a control over preachers and people as is far too absolute for any uninspired man to pretend to, or lawfully to exercise—*except for some temporary purpose*, and on the ground of some urgent necessity. One paragraph, containing the pith of several, may properly be brought forward.

"Observe, I myself sent for these (preachers) of my own free choice; and I sent for them to *advise*, not *govern* me. Neither did I at any of those times divest myself of any part of that *power* above described, which the providence of God had cast upon me, without any design or choice of mine. What is that power? It is a power of admitting into, and excluding from, the societies under my care: of choosing and removing stewards; of receiving, or not receiving, helpers; of appointing them when, where, and how, to help me; and of desiring any of them to meet me when I see good. And as it was merely in obedience to the providence of God, and for the good of the people, that I at first accepted this power, which I never sought, nay, a hundred times labored to throw off; so it is on the same consideration, not for profit, honor, or pleasure, that I use it at this day. But several gentlemen are much offended at my having *so much power*. My answer to them is this:—I did not seek any part of this power. It came upon me unawares. But when it was come, not daring to bury that talent, I used it to the best of my judgment.

"Yet I never was fond of it; I always did, and do now, bear it as my burden; the burden which God lays upon me, and therefore I dare not yet lay it down. But if you can tell me any one, or any five men, to whom I may transfer this burden, who *can* and *will* do just what I do now, I will heartily thank both them and you."

In this, and much more to the same effect, there is no indication leading to the belief that Wesley ever thought of his *people* as coming into the position of instructed Christian men, to whom might be assigned the functions proper to such, and which unquestionably were undertaken and discharged by the laity of the Apostolic Churches. In answer to the allegation—"this (power which you exercise) is *arbitrary power*, this is no less than making yourself a pope," he says, "If by arbitrary power, you mean a power which I exercise singly, without any colleagues therein, this is certainly true; but I see no hurt in it. *Arbitrary*, in this sense, is a very harmless word. If you mean *unjust, unreasonable*, or *tyrannical*, then it is not true. As to the other branch of the charge, it carries no face of truth. The pope affirms, that every Christian must do all he bids, and believe all he says, under pain of damnation. I never affirmed any thing that bears any, the most distant, resemblance to this. All I affirm is, the preachers who choose to labor with me, choose to serve me as sons in the gospel; and the people who choose to be under my care, choose to be so on the same terms they were at first. Therefore all talk of this kind is highly injurious to *me*, who bear the burden merely for *your* sakes. And it is exceedingly mischievous to the people, tending to confound their understandings, and to fill their hearts with evil surmisings, and unkind tempers toward *me*, to whom they really owe more, for taking all this load upon me, for exercising this very *power*, for shackling myself in this manner, than for all my preaching put together. Because preaching twice or thrice a day is no burden to me at all; but the care of all the preachers, and all the people, is a burden indeed."

In the Conference of 1769, *August 4th*, Wesley read a paper, which he had no doubt carefully prepared, and which shows that, in looking forward to the time when his society should no longer be cemented by means of his personal influence, the measures he propounded to his preachers did not include at that time constitutional changes, intended to bring the body of preachers and the people into any other relationship than that which had hitherto subsisted between them.

"MY DEAR BRETHREN—It has long been my desire that all those *ministers* of our Church, who believe and preach salvation by faith, might cordially agree between themselves, and not hinder, but help one another. After occasionally pressing this in private conversation, wherever I had opportunity, I wrote down my thoughts upon the head, and sent them to each in a letter. Out of fifty or sixty to whom I wrote, only three vouchsafed me an answer. So I gave this up. I can do no more. They are a rope of sand, and such they will continue.

"But it is otherwise with the *Traveling Preachers* in our connection. You are at present one body; you act in concert with each other, and by united counsels. And now is the time to consider what can be done, in order to continue this union. Indeed as long as I live, there will be no great difficulty: I am, under God, a centre of union to all our Traveling, as well as Local Preachers. They all know me and my communication. They all love me for my work's sake; and, therefore, were it only out of regard to me, they will continue connected with each other. But by what means may this connection be preserved, when God removes me from you? I take it for granted it can not be preserved by any means, between those who have not a single eye. Those who aim at any thing but the glory of God, and the salvation of men; who desire or seek any earthly thing, whether honor, profit, or ease, will not continue in the connection: it will not answer their design. Some of them, perhaps a fourth of the whole number, will procure preferment in the Church. Others will turn Independents, and get separate congregations, like John Edwards and Charles Skelton. Lay your accounts with this, and be not surprised if some, you do not suspect, be of this number.

"But what method can be taken to preserve a firm union between those who choose to remain together? Perhaps you might take some such steps as these: On notice of my death, let all the preachers in England and Ireland repair to London within six weeks: Let them seek God by solemn fasting and prayer: Let them draw up articles of agreement, to be signed by those who choose to act in concert: Let those be dismissed who do not choose it, in the most friendly manner possible:

"Let them choose, by votes, a *Committee* of three, five, or seven, each of whom is to be *Moderator* in his turn: Let the Committee do what I do now: propose Preachers to be tried, admitted, or excluded. Fix the place of each Preacher for the ensuing year, and the time of the next Conference.

"Can any thing be done now, in order to lay a foundation for this future union? Would it not be well, for any that are willing, to sign some articles of agreement before God calls me hence? Suppose something like these:

"We whose names are under written, being thoroughly convinced of the necessity of a close union between those whom God is pleased to use as instruments in this glorious work, in order to preserve this union between ourselves, are resolved, God being our helper,

1. *To devote ourselves entirely to God;* denying ourselves, taking up our cross daily, steadily aiming at one thing, to save our own souls, and them that hear us.

2. To preach the *old Methodist doctrines*, and no other, contained in the Minutes of Conference.

3. To observe and enforce the whole *Methodist discipline*, laid down in the said Minutes!

"The Preachers then desired Mr. Wesley to extract the most

material part of the Minutes, and send a copy to each Assistant, which he might communicate to all the Preachers in his Circuit, to be seriously considered.

"Our meeting was then concluded with solemn prayer."

Five years later this engagement was repeated in the same terms.

In the year 1785, Wesley addressed a letter to the preachers constituting the legal body, according to the "Deed of Declaration," which may be regarded as expressing his matured intention as to the constitution of his society, and, therefore, as showing that he entertained no idea of granting to the people any constitutional privilege, or, indeed, that he recognized their existence in any such sense. This letter was brought forward, and was entered upon the minutes, immediately after Wesley's death.

"MANCHESTER; Tuesday, July 26, 1791.

"A copy of a letter from the Rev. John Wesley to the CONFERENCE.

'*To the Methodist Conference.*

Chester, April 7th, 1785.

'MY DEAR BRETHREN,—Some of our traveling preachers have expressed a fear, that, after my decease, you would exclude them either from preaching in connection with you, or from some other privileges which they now enjoy.

'I know no other way to prevent any such inconvenience than to leave these, my last words, with you. I beseech you, by the mercies of God, that you never avail yourselves of the "Deed of Declaration," to assume any superiority over your brethren; but let all things go on, among those itinerants who choose to remain together, exactly in the same manner as when I was with you, so far as circumstances will permit. In particular, I beseech you, if you ever loved me, and if you now love God and your brethren, to have no respect of persons in stationing the preachers, in choosing children for Kingswood School, in disposing of the yearly contribution and the preachers' fund, or any other public money; but do all things with a single eye, as I have done from the beginning. Go on thus, doing all things without prejudice or partiality, and God will be with you even to the end.

'JOHN WESLEY.'

"N.B.—The Conference have unanimously resolved, that all the preachers who are in full connection with them, shall enjoy every privilege that the members of the Conference enjoy, agreeably to the above-written letter of our venerable deceased Father in the Gospel. It may be expected that the Conference make some observations on the death of Mr. Wesley; but they find themselves utterly inadequate to express their ideas and feelings on this awful and affecting event. Their souls do truly mourn for their great loss; and they trust they shall give the most substantial proofs of their veneration for the memory of their most esteemed father and friend, by endeavoring, with great humility and diffidence, to follow and imitate him in doctrine, discipline, and life."

It may seem superfluous to adduce further evidence in proof of what the writer has repeatedly affirmed in the course of this volume, and showing that Wesley abjured the imputation of intending to draw off his people from the Church. This point might be placed beyond all doubt by many extracts from his writings. These same passages would, of themselves, sustain the *inference* that he never entertained the thought of constructing a Church; but we need not rest upon an inference merely, how inevitable soever it may be, for we have his explicit declaration to this effect. In the Tract "against separation from the Church of England" occurs a passage which is most conclusive to this effect. The 8th reason against any such separation is this, that then the Methodistic Society must be framed upon a different model, which would involve a very difficult task—a task to which Wesley modestly thinks neither himself nor his friends competent.

"8. Because to form the plan of a new Church would require infinite time and care (which might be far more profitably bestowed), with much more wisdom and greater depth and extensiveness of thought than any of us are masters of."

But if so—if in Wesley's deliberately expressed opinion, as we find it here and elsewhere, the INSTITUTION of which he was the author, was far from being in his view a Church—and if he solemnly rejected the imputation of having framed it with the reserved design of bringing his people into an independent and separate ecclesiastical condition—if so, we must think that there was an error on the part of those who, when they found that they could not turn aside the course of events which, at length, rendered this separation inevitable—did not, at an early time, set about the work of so reconstructing Wesleyanism as might suffice for introducing into it that rudiment of Church organization which would place the people and their ministers in a true relative position?

In the four sections on Wesleyan Methodism mention has been made, repeatedly, of what is called the Deed of Declaration, which, in fact, is, in a legal sense, the basement-work of the Wesleyan structure, and to which an appeal is always made by the opposed parties, within the Society. This Deed is of considerable length, and the reader who is not a Wesleyan Methodist, and yet who would wish to know something of the purport of so important a document, may be content with an abstract of its clauses, such as shall sufficiently place before him its meaning, viewed as the basis of a legalized corporation.

"To all to whom these presents shall come, John Wesley, late of Lincoln College, Oxford, but now of the City Road, London, Clerk, sendeth greeting.

"Whereas divers buildings, commonly called chapels, with a messuage and dwelling-house, or other appurtenances to each of the same belonging, situate in various parts of Great Britain, have been given and conveyed from time to time, by the said John Wesley, to certain persons, and their heirs, in each of the said gifts and conveyances named, which are enrolled in his Majesty's high court of Chancery, upon the acknowledgment of the said John Wesley, pursuant to the act of Parliament in that case made and provided, UPON TRUST, that the trustees in the said several deeds respectively named, and the survivors of them, and their heirs and assigns, and the trustees for the time being to be elected, as in the said deeds is appointed, should permit and suffer the said John Wesley, and such other person and persons as he should for that purpose from time to time nominate and appoint, at all times during his life, at his will and pleasure, to have and enjoy the free use and benefit of the said premises, that he the said John Wesley, and such person or persons as he should nominate and appoint, might therein preach and expound God's holy Word: And upon further trust, that the said respective trustees, and the survivors of them, and their heirs and assigns, and the trustees for the time being, should permit and suffer Charles Wesley, brother of the said John Wesley, and such other person and persons as the said Charles Wesley should for that purpose, from time to time nominate and appoint, in like manner during his life.—To have, use, and enjoy the said premises, respectively for the like purposes aforesaid; and after the decease of the survivor of them, the said John Wesley, and Charles Wesley, then upon further trust that the said respective trustees, and the survivors of them, and their heirs and assigns, and the trustees for the time being for ever, should permit and suffer such person and persons, and for such time and times as should be appointed at the yearly Conference of the people called Methodists in London, Bristol, or Leeds, and no others, to have and enjoy the said premises for the purposes aforesaid: and whereas divers persons have in like manner, given or conveyed many chapels, with messuages and dwelling-houses, or other appurtenances to the same belonging, situate in various parts of Great Britain, and also in Ireland, to certain trustees in each of the said gifts and conveyances respectively named, upon the like trusts, and for the same uses and purposes as aforesaid, except only that in some of the said gifts and conveyances, no life-estate or other interest is therein or thereby given and reserved to the said Charles Wesley: and whereas for rendering effectual the trusts created by the said several gifts and conveyances, and that no doubt or litigation may arise with respect unto the same, or interpretation and true meaning thereof, it has been thought expedient by the said John Wesley, on behalf of himself as donor of the several chapels, with messuages, dwelling-houses, or appurtenances to the same belonging, given or conveyed to the like uses and trusts, to explain the words, *Yearly Conference of the people called Methodists*, contained in all the said trust deeds, and to declare *what persons* are members of the said Conference, and how the *succession* and *identity* thereof is to be continued: *Now, therefore, these presents witness*, that for accomplishing the aforesaid purposes, the said John Wesley does hereby declare, that the Conference of the people called Methodists, in London, Bristol, or Leeds, ever since there hath been any yearly Conference of the said people called Methodists, in any of the said places, hath always heretofore consisted of the preachers and expounders of God's holy word, commonly called Methodist preachers, in connection with, and under the care of the said John Wesley, whom he hath thought expedient, year after year, to summon to meet him, in one or other of the said places of London, Bristol, or Leeds, to advise with them for the promotion of the Gospel of Christ; to appoint the said persons so summoned, and the other preachers and expounders of

God's holy word, also in connection with, and under the care of the said John Wesley, not summoned to the said yearly Conference, to the use and enjoyment of the said chapels and premises so given and conveyed upon trust to the said John Wesley, and such other person and persons as he shall appoint during his life as aforesaid; and for the expulsion of unworthy, and admission of new persons under his care, and into his connection, to be preachers and expounders as aforesaid; and also of other persons upon trial for the like purposes: the names of all which persons so summoned by the said John Wesley, the persons appointed, with the chapels and premises to which they were so appointed, together with the duration of such appointments, and of those expelled, or admitted into connection, or upon trial, with all other matters transacted and done at the said yearly Conference, have year by year been printed and published under the title of "Minutes of Conference," *and these presents further witness*, and the said John Wesley doth hereby avouch and further declare, that the several persons hereinafter named, to wit, the said John Wesley and Charles Wesley" . . . . .

Then follow the names of those who then constituted the legal Conference, that is to say, one hundred preachers—the two Wesleys inclusive: these being, although some of them are designated "gentlemen"—"Preachers and expounders of God's holy word, under the care and in connection with the said John Wesley;" of whom it is said that they have been, "and now are, and do, on the day of the date hereof, constitute *the members of the said Conference*, according to the true intent and meaning of the said several gifts and conveyances, wherein the words '*Conference of the people called Methodists*' are mentioned and contained. And that the said several persons before named, and their successors for ever, to be chosen as hereinafter mentioned, are and shall for ever be construed, taken and be *the Conference of the people called Methodists*. Nevertheless upon the terms, and subject to the regulations hereinafter prescribed, that is to say:—

Then follow fifteen regulations, or conditions, defining the powers of this body of preachers: an abstract of these conditions will sufficiently inform the reader, as to the true intent and meaning of this "Deed of Declaration."

The first article declares—

That the members of the said Conference, and their successors for the time being for ever, shall assemble once in every year, at London, Bristol, or Leeds (or elsewhere), for the purposes aforesaid; each yearly Conference appointing the time and place of the next.

Second. The act of the majority in number of the Conference so assembled, shall be taken as the act of the whole Conference in all cases.

Third. That the first act of the Conference shall be to fill up all the vacancies that may have been occasioned by death (or absence, under certain conditions).

Fourth. Conference shall not be competent to act with fewer than forty members thereof assembled, unless reduced by death or absence (under circumstances named) since the last Conference, nor until the vacancies have been filled up, so as to make up the number of one hundred. No act of the Conference shall be valid unless forty members have been present at the time of passing the same.

Fifth. Conference shall continue assembled for a time not less than five days, nor more than three weeks. Nothing done at other times than during this yearly assemblage shall stand as an act of Conference.

Sixth. Having filled up all vacancies, the next act of Conference shall be to choose a President and Secretary of their assembly, out of themselves, who shall continue such until the election of another president or secretary, in the next Conference; the said president shall have the privilege and power of two members, in all acts of the Conference.

Seventh. Absence from two successive Conferences shall forfeit membership, that is to say, at the next following Conference.

Eighth. (This article we give verbatim and entire.) "The Conference shall, and may expel and put out from being a member thereof, or from being in connection therewith, or from being upon trial, any person, member of the Conference, admitted into connection or upon trial, for any cause which to the Conference may seem fit or necessary; and every member of the Conference so expelled and put out, shall cease to be a member thereof, to all intents and purposes, as though he was naturally dead. And the Conference, immediately after the expulsion of any member thereof, as aforesaid, shall elect another person to be member of the Conference, in the stead of such member so expelled."

Ninth. The Conference shall have power to admit into connection with tnem, or upon trial, any person or persons whom they shall approve as preachers, under the care and direction of the Conference, such admissions being duly entered in the Minutes of Conference.

Tenth. No person shall be elected as a member of Conference, who has not been one year in connection as a preacher.

Eleventh. The Conference shall not appoint any person to preach in the chapels aforesaid, who is not either a member of the Conference, or has been admitted upon trial as a preacher, nor appoint any person for more than three years successively to the same chapel, except ordained ministers of the Church of England.

Twelfth. The Conference may appoint its meetings elsewhere than in London, Bristol, or Leeds, when expedient so to do.

Thirteenth. The Conference may delegate its powers to any of its members, who shall be appointed to act on its behalf in Ireland, or elsewhere, out of the kingdom of Great Britain, the acts of such delegate or delegates, when duly appointed, being valid as its own.

Fourteenth. All acts of Conference shall be entered in the Minutes of the same, and publicly read, and then subscribed by the President and Secretary thereof, for the time being, during the time such Conference shall be assembled, such entries being received and taken, in all cases, as sufficient evidence of the acts of Conference. No act not so entered and signed shall be of any force.

Lastly. Provision is made on the supposition that, for three successive years, Conference may be reduced to fewer than forty members; or that it may neglect to meet annually for the purposes aforesaid; then, and in that case the Conference of the people called Methodists shall be extinguished, and all its powers and privileges shall cease; and in that event the chapels and premises conveyed by this deed shall vest in the trustees for the time being, and their successors for ever, upon trust that they, and the survivors of them, shall appoint such persons to preach in the said chapels, and in such manner as to them shall seem proper.

Then follows a provision maintaining the life estate of John and Charles Wesley in the chapels of the Society. This deed was signed, sealed, and enrolled in Chancery in 1784. It continues to be binding in law upon the Society.

This declaratory instrument, taken in connection with the trust deeds of Wesleyan Chapels, and other property, exhibits the Wesleyan establishment in the light of a decisive contrast with any church or community wherewith it might be compared. Among the English Dissenters, generally, the Meeting-house or Chapel, with its appurtenances, is vested in local trustees, for the benefit of the society therein usually assembling. The preacher or minister, elected by the society ("Church and Congregation," or the "Church," the congregation informally assenting) is then legally seised of the building, for the purposes of public worship; and he receives the rents or revenues of any property that has been bequeathed to the society, as his fee simple. The control of the people over the minister resolves itself legally into their individual liberty to vacate their pews, and thus to leave him to the enjoyment of the walls, and the endowments. But in fact, the instances are very rare in which things are pushed to this extreme. Effectively there is an understanding between the congregation and the minister, to this effect, that when his services cease to be acceptable to them, or to those among them whose influence is paramount, he retires. It is evident that a relationship of this sort is quite susceptible of being so worked, in practice, as to leave no substantial ground of complaint, either with the people or the minister; all it wants to secure his comfort and independence, is some easily imagined modification of the *congregational* principle.

But the Wesleyan system, as constituted by Wesley, thoroughly and absolutely ignores the people, and it did this as well legally as ecclesiastically; and hence, from the moment almost of his death, to the present time, successive heavings and convulsions —allayed for a time by concessions, palliative rather than rudimental, have made up the history of the Society. Nevertheless such convulsions are so far auspicious, that they indicate an interior vitality, and could never occur in a society that was not powerfully wrought upon by a deep-seated attachment to the system itself. Tumultuous secessions may diminish Wesleyanism for a time, but they will not destroy, or permanently weaken it. What it might more fear would be the occurrence of noiseless defections, from year to year—the falling away of its people who —with reason, or without reason, yet becoming alienated from the Wesleyan organization, should cease to be seen in their places.

Too often such a falling away would be—a relapse into the world; but even if it went to swell the numbers of other churches, it would be thought of with anxiety and grief by many who, though not of the society, cordially desire its continued prosperity.

The reader will not doubt that the writer has given some attention to the controversies that, of late, have agitated the Wesleyan body: a pile of publications, thereto relating, he has thought it incumbent upon him to read; but he is very far from thinking himself called upon to express any opinion whatever upon the points debated in these pamphlets. The several questions, either of Wesleyan constitutional structure, or of discipline, therein discussed, are, unquestionably, of high moment; but they are quite foreign to the purport of this volume, which relates only to METHODISM—now long ago gone from among us, and to Wesley's Wesleyanism, considered *as a part* of the writer's general subject. To form a competent opinion upon the question—How far Wesley's Wesleyanism is the Wesleyanism of the present time, would demand, not merely an extensive reading of polemical Tracts, Minutes of Conference, and Reports of legal proceedings, but much personal conference with leading persons on both sides the pending controversy. To no such scrutiny as this is the writer impelled, either by a sense of duty, or by his tastes: controversy of all kinds he abhors; nor should easily be induced to make himself one in any discussions whatever, that he saw to be moving the passions of the disputants; nevertheless, while thus thinking himself quite free to hold off from strife, and while using this liberty, and intending to use it, the writer anticipates, as probable, encountering a smart rejoinder from some who will say—"You abstain from mingling in the fray; but, in fact, you take a part in it, by expressing opinions concerning Wesley's Institute, of which a factious use will be made by those who now trouble our Israel." It may be so; yet the writer has seen no way of forefending this possible consequence. Never hitherto has he written or printed a line which did not convey his sincere and undisguised belief, and he can not—*at so late a time*—learn the art of dressing his published opinions from motives of fear or favor, The Wesleyan reader he will ask to be content with the assurance that, to witness the *effective* pacification of the Society, and its re-instauration on principles *substantially apostolic*, would be an event giving him the most cordial satisfaction.

The time is not yet come—perhaps it is remote—when any one of the existing (orthodox) communions might, without damage to the community, fail from its place among us. Each of these bodies has its destined function to discharge, during this transition period. The means, the labors, the organization of each are too few, too small; all is too little:—the aggregate of Christian ministrations in this home of Christianity, is a tenth of what it should be.

THE END.

Preparing for Publication, by the Same Author,

THE NONCONFORMISTS OF THE PAST AGE.

www.ingramcontent.com/pod-product-compliance
Lightning Source LLC
LaVergne TN
LVHW020228110826
845151LV00003B/852
9781425534134